CASES IN MODERN FINANCIAL MANAGEMENT
Private and public sector perspectives

The Irwin Series in Finance
Editors **Myron J. Gordon**
University of Toronto

Robert W. Johnson
Purdue University

Cases in modern financial MANAGEMENT

PRIVATE AND PUBLIC SECTOR PERSPECTIVES

RONALD F. WIPPERN
Professor of Finance
School of Organization and Management
Yale University

1980
RICHARD D. IRWIN, INC. Homewood, Illinois 60430
Irwin-Dorsey Limited Georgetown, Ontario L7G 4B3

ISBN 0-256-02363-8
Library of Congress Catalog Card No. 80–80956

Printed in the United States of America

1 2 3 4 5 6 7 8 9 0 K 7 6 5 4 3 2 1 0

For
Chris, Mitch, and Stacy

Preface

Modern financial theory has evolved rapidly in recent years, offering present and potential practitioners a rich and productive array of problem-illuminating insights. It is becoming increasingly clear that the practice of financial management in both the private and the public sectors, and in not-for-profit organizations, can be substantially enhanced through managerial actions based on a firm foundation in financial theory.

It is also clear, however, that effectively converting knowledge of finance theory into a usable working framework is a difficult task. Doing so must involve acquiring both a solid appreciation of the relevance of financial theory and its empirical validation and, for that learning to be truly internalized, a set of experiences which provide opportunities to productively link theory with practice. Focusing on a set of real world managerial decisions which offer opportunities to test, use, and communicate the insights derived from the mainstream of modern finance permits the knowledge-into-action, theory-into-practice loop to be more quickly and effectively closed.

The development of the cases in this book evolved out of my own concepts of course design which, while undoubtedly not unique, should be made explicit. I believe that students should:

1. Be thoroughly familiar with the major elements of modern finance theory.
2. Have an opportunity to develop a solid understanding of the relevance of modern finance theory to the practitioner.
3. Have substantial classroom experience in applying many dimensions of finance theory to real and significant managerial decisions.
4. Acquire experience in communicating clearly and convincingly the results of their analyses.

The cases in this book are designed to provide students with the opportunity both to recognize and to test the relevance of modern financial concepts in the context of real managerial decisions in both

ix

public and private sector organizations and to apply many of those concepts in the process of analyzing the issues presented in the cases. The cases are not fictional situations contrived to permit application of a particular concept. Rather, they are either examples of actual attempts by firms to apply modern concepts to significant problems or they are cases focusing on real and significant decisions in private, public, and not-for-profit organizations where traditional and/or elementary analysis leads to very different conclusions from those derived using modern, empirically validated financial theory.

These cases have been used in financial management courses at Yale's School of Organization and Management and at the Harvard Business School. Some of the cases have also been used in continuing education programs for both managers and consultants. All of the cases are based on either field interviews, internal memoranda, transcripts of regulatory proceedings, or combinations of these.

All of the cases are intended to provide a basis for class discussion, and not to illustrate necessarily correct or incorrect solutions to managerial or regulatory issues. Extensive conceptual and quantitative analysis of each case is both possible and desirable, and the cases permit students to draw heavily on their knowledge of financial concepts. It is rare that analysis alone can provide definitive answers to complex problems in real organizations. What does emerge, however, is that thoughtful analysis based on a solid theoretical foundation can lead to achieving greater precision in problem definitions and a greatly reduced range within which managerial judgment must be exercised.

Acknowledgments

I am grateful to the many executives, consultants, investment bankers, regulators, and faculty colleagues who by sharing their experiences and insights made it possible for me to develop these cases. I am particularly grateful to Colin Carter of Pappas and Carter, Melbourne, Australia, to Professor Richard Bower of the Amos Tuck School and to Professor Sam Hayes of the Harvard Business School, not only for their superb ideas, but for their warm friendship and encouragement as well. Professor Jack McDonald of Stanford's Graduate School of Business was most generous in permitting me to include the Acidex case, the one case in this volume that is not my own.

Many graduate student assistants gave freely of their time, energy, and creativity while helping me to develop these materials. I want to extend my deep appreciation to Fred Bloch, Nina Schapiro, Anne

Glover, Allan Chamberlain, Hap Ellis, Nancy Raybin, Ed McKinley, Pam Bronk, Guillermo Schultz, Larry Wynant, Don Van Deventer, and Doug Breeden. All contributed significantly to these cases.

The Harvard Graduate School of Business, Yale's School of Organization and Management, the Ford Foundation, the Alfred P. Sloan Foundation, and the Henry J. Kaiser Family Foundation provided financial assistance for the development of many of these cases. I very much appreciate their support.

Editorial, typing, and logistic support tasks can often be the most difficult things to cope with on projects like this one. I am grateful to Flo Wilkins at Harvard and to Betty Walker at Yale for getting me through the early stages of this project. Finally, it is no exaggeration to state that the final product would never have appeared without the extraordinary effort, patience, good cheer, and efficiency of Dolly Lawrence. To her, a very special thanks.

February 1980 Ronald F. Wippern

CONTENTS

PART ONE

INVESTMENT DECISIONS

Acidex, Inc.

In December 1971, Thomas Quinn, president of Acidex, Inc., announced at the monthly meeting of the board of directors that members of the treasurer's department were studying a change in the firm's capital budgeting policy. The treasurer, Peter Fellows, had recently attended a seminar on finance sponsored by a large New York City bank. Mr. Fellows had become convinced that Acidex should evaluate capital projects on a discounted cash flow rate of return basis. The company had been using a payback period method for ranking proposed capital expenditures.

Founded in 1949, Acidex, Inc., manufactured a specialized line of industrial acids in its single plant near Huntsville, Ohio. Acidex had borrowed heavily to finance capital expansion in the past ten years. In November 1971, the company's investment banker had told Mr. Quinn that further debt financing would be impracticable at that time owing to the relatively high percentage of debt in the firm's capital structure. Since 1969 the price earnings ratio on the common stock had declined from 20.4 to 14.7. Accordingly, Mr. Quinn felt that an attempt to sell new stock in the present market would not be wise.

Acidex had never paid a dividend. The board of directors had recommended to Acidex officers that internally generated funds be used to finance capital expenditures and to meet needs for increased working capital. The directors felt that it was impracticable to determine the rate of return at which stockholders might reinvest dividends, hence it was wiser to put earnings to use in any "reasonable" project within the company. Further, the directors implied that they would consider declaring a dividend in the future only if it might result in a higher market price for Acidex stock at a time when they planned to sell new equity. With the great difficulty anticipated in raising new debt or equity capital in the near future, Mr. Quinn expected that the 1972 capital budget would be limited to internally generated funds, totaling approximately $1.2 million in 1971.

For the purposes of capital budgeting Acidex was organized into six departments: production I, II, and III; warehousing and intraplant distribution; administration, sales and clerical; research and development. In applying the payback period method of ranking projects, Acidex management had set the following minimum payback requirements, based on estimated useful life of the project as specified by the Internal Revenue Service for the purpose of depreciation:

	Years			
Estimated useful life of project	5	10	15	20
Required payback period	2	3	4	5

These requirements applied to all departments except research and development, which each year had been awarded 15 percent of the approved capital budget. Estimates of gross revenues and costs for proposed projects were collected in each department. In December each department manager submitted to Mr. Fellows a list of proposed projects meeting minimum requirements. Each project was assigned a ratio calculated by dividing its *required* payback period by its *expected* payback period, and the projects were ranked in order of desirability according to this ratio. After allocating 15 percent of available funds to research and development, Mr. Fellows combined the lists of projects submitted by each department and assigned the remaining funds to the projects showing the highest ratios. The resulting capital budget was then referred to Mr. Quinn and the board of directors for final approval.

In August 1971, Mr. Fellows had initiated an auditing program to ascertain actual payback periods for projects completed in the previous 12 years. By comparing actual results with the original estimated of payback period, Mr. Fellows hoped to learn which departments had consistently underestimated or overestimated the profitability of projects. This initial audit disclosed the following information:

	Average ratio of actual payback period to expected payback
Department	period
Production I	.80
Production II	.65
Production III	.75
Administration	1.45
Warehousing	1.15

An accountant in the treasurer's office suggested that the expectation of future audits might encourage more accurate estimates of costs and savings for proposed projects. Mr. Fellows wondered if a postcompletion audit might be more difficult if projects were evaluated on a discounted cash flow rate of return basis.

One of Mr. Fellow's assistants, Richard Crane, a recent business school graduate, suggested that an attempt be made under a new rate of return method to consider differences in risk among possible projects. Mr. Fellows had planned to ask each department for the estimated cash inflow and outflow for each year in the life of the proposed project. Mr. Crane felt that each department should submit a "most optimistic," "best guess," and "most pessimistic" estimate of yearly cash flow for each project. It was Mr. Crane's intention that the estimator assign probabilities to the three outcomes, reflecting both the degree of risk in the project and the increasing uncertainty as estimates were projected further into the future. In explaining this plan to Mr. Fellows, Mr. Crane used the following example:

	1st year of project			10th year of project		
	Pessi-mistic	Best guess	Opti-mistic	Pessi-mistic	Best guess	Opti-mistic
Estimates of net cash inflow	$10	$30	$50	$10	$30	$50
Assigned probabilities	20%	70%	10%	50%	40%	10%
Expected net cash inflow		$28			$22	

Mr. Crane said that the resulting expected net cash inflow would be more certain than a "one-shot" yearly estimate.

Mr. Fellows requested expected yearly inflow and outflow figures for projects submitted by each department for each 1972 capital budget.

In early December 1971, Mr. Fellows received the estimates on eight projects. From these estimates, his staff calculated the following discounted cash flow rates of return (viz, the discount rate for each project at which the present value of the annual cash inflow equaled the present value of the annual cash outflow plus the original investment):

Proposed project	Original investment ($000)	Discounted cash flow rate of return (percent)
A	$105	36%
B	85	35
C	400	31
D	225	28
E	285	27
F	100	15
G	100	15
H	100	10

Since total available funds were limited to $1 million, Mr. Fellows knew that he must choose between projects F and G, each having a ten-year life and rate of return of 15 percent. Mr. Fellows recalled that at the finance seminar which he had attended one speaker had suggested a method for choosing between two mutually exclusive investment alternatives, such as projects F and G: discount to the present the estimated net cash inflow for each year in the life of each project, and select the project with the larger total present value. The schedule of expected cash flow for projects F and G was summarized as follows:

Yearly cash flow ($000)

	1972	1973	1974	1975	1976	1977	1978	1979	1980	1981
Project F:										
Cash inflow	$90	$90	$90	$86	$82	$78	$74	$70	$ 66	$ 62
Cash outflow	70	70	70	66	62	58	54	50	46	42
Project G:										
Cash inflow	50	50	50	50	65	65	95	95	105	107
Cash outflow	45	45	45	45	45	45	45	45	45	45

Mr. Fellows faced the problem of choosing an appropriate discount rate. The seminar had stated that "the theoretically appropriate discount rate is always the rate of return on the marginal investment opportunity available in the period over which one is discounting." He had stressed that the discounting procedure recognized the foregoing of returns on alternative investments, therefore each firm should discount at the rate of return on the best alternative project not allocated funds in the capital budget; i.e., the marginal investment rate. At the marginal investment rate which he derived from the list of projects submitted for the 1972 capital budget, Mr. Fellows said that the present value calculation was no help in choosing between projects F and G.

Because of the difficulty in obtaining new debt or equity financing at that time, Mr. Fellows found it hard to calculate a weighted average cost of capital. While it was difficult to forecast for even two or three years, Mr. Fellows felt that as market conditions improved, Acidex' average cost of capital would be approximately 12 percent over the life of project F or G. Discounting at 12 percent, he observed that project G appeared to be the more profitable of the two projects.

Based on optimistic reports from the research and development department, Mr. Fellows considered it probable that projects available in the next several years would offer generally higher returns than the projects being considered for the 1972 capital budget. If his expectation of a 12 percent average cost of capital were correct, Mr. Fellows anticipated that Acidex would invest in all projects showing an expected return greater than 12 percent. Mr. Crane observed that if Acidex followed this policy the rate of return on the firm's marginal investment opportunity would equal the average cost of capital. However, Mr. Fellows had some doubts about the future willingness of the board of directors to authorize the sale of the new stock. He considered the possibility that Acidex' capital investment funds might be limited in the future as they were in 1971. If more profitable projects were available and if funds remained limited, he felt that the firm's marginal investment rate might be as high as 25 percent in the next several years. Discounting at 25 percent, Mr. Fellows found that project F appeared more desirable than project G.

CASE 1-2

LEVERAGEd LEASE SinkiNG-FuNd ANAlysEs

Tax leveraged leases can, in certain circumstances, provide substantial benefits to lessees through lower financing costs. These transactions can, at the same time, offer equity investors substantial returns through the combination of the tax benefits they receive and the high leverage on their equity.

The basic structure of a tax leveraged lease is that, typically:

1. Lessors invest 15 percent to 30 percent of the asset cost. In return, they receive 100 percent of the tax benefits of ownership of the asset, i.e., the Investment Tax Credit, where applicable, depreciation on the asset and interest on the loan. Legal ownership of the asset is retained by the lessors. Thus, any asset value remaining upon expiration of the lease accrues to the lessor.

2. A lender, or a group of lenders, provide 70 percent to 85 percent of the funds required to purchase the asset. Security for the loan is provided by a mortgage on the asset and a pledge, by the lessor, of the lease payments due from the lessee. Typically, these loans are written without recourse to the lessor, and the amount of the lease payments are very close to the amount of the loan payment. Therefore, it is unusual for a lessor to have cash remaining from the lease payments after deducting principal and interest payments on the loan.

Exhibit 1 shows the details of an illustrative leverage lease transaction with particular emphasis on the lessor's (equity investor's) position.

Since many equity investors are seriously concerned about committing to a transaction which requires negative cash flows in the future (e.g., the flows for years 8 through 15 in Exhibit 1). Investment bankers and

8

Exhibit 1
Investment analysis
(assume no residual value)

Total investment	$1,000,000	Depreciable investment	$1,000,000
Equity investment	$ 300,000	Residual value	None
Years	15	Depreciable life	7
Sinking-fund reinvestment	None	Sum-of-the-years'-digits depreciation	
Borrowed capital	$ 700,000	Investment tax credit	7%
Interest rate (per year)	9.00%	Period taken	1
Number of years	15	Tax rate	48%
Payment	$ 86,841		

(1)	(2)	(3)	(4)	(5)	(6)	(7)	(8)	(9)	(10)
Period	Lease payments	Depreciation	Interest	Principal	Taxes	Book value	Aftertax cash flow	Payment to sinking fund	Sinking-fund balance
0		—	—	—		$1,000,000	−$300,000	—	—
1	$ 96,342	$ 250,000	$ 63,000	$ 23,841	−$173,996	750,000	183,497	0	0
2	96,342	214,286	60,854	25,987	−85,823	535,714	95,324	0	0
3	96,342	178,571	58,515	28,326	−67,558	357,143	77,058	$ 67,773	$ 67,773
4	96,342	142,857	55,966	30,875	−49,191	214,286	58,692	58,692	126,465
5	96,342	107,143	53,187	33,654	−30,714	107,143	40,215	40,215	166,680
6	96,342	71,429	50,159	36,683	−12,118	35,714	21,618	21,618	188,298
7	96,342	35,714	46,857	39,984	6,610	0	2,891	2,891	191,189
8	96,342	0	43,259	43,583	25,480	0	−15,980	−15,980	175,209
9	96,342	0	39,336	47,505	27,363	0	−17,862	−17,862	157,347
10	96,342	0	35,061	51,780	29,415	0	−19,914	−19,914	137,433
11	96,342	0	30,400	56,441	31,652	0	−22,151	−22,151	115,282
12	96,342	0	25,321	61,521	34,090	0	−24,590	−24,590	90,692
13	96,342	0	19,784	67,057	36,748	0	−27,247	−27,247	63,445
14	96,342	0	13,749	73,092	39,645	0	−30,144	−30,144	33,301
15	96,342	0	7,170	79,671	42,802	0	−33,301	−33,301	0
Totals	$1,445,130	$1,000,000	$602,618	$700,000	−$145,595		$ −11,894	$ 0	

Note: The internal rate of return on this lease is −2.85 percent if no residual and a zero reinvestment rate on the sinking fund are used. (The sinking-fund flows are given by subtracting the flows in column [9] from the flows in column [8].) The internal rates of return on the lease without consideration of a sinking fund are 1.2 percent and 17.9 percent.

Exhibit 2
Method 1
Sinking-fund reinvestment rate = 5.0 percent
Internal rate of return = 9.026 percent

Period	Cash flows	Recovery of investment	Return on outstanding investment	Outstanding investment	Contribution to sinking fund	Return on accumulated sinking fund	Sinking fund
0	−300,000	0	0	300,000	0	0	0
1	183,497	156,418	27,078	143,581	0	0	0
2	95,324	82,363	12,960	61,217	0	0	0
3	77,058	61,217	5,525	0	10,314	0	10,314
4	58,692	0	0	0	58,692	515	69,522
5	40,215	0	0	0	40,215	3,476	113,213
6	21,618	0	0	0	21,618	5,660	140,492
7	2,891	0	0	0	2,891	7,024	150,407
8	− 15,980	0	0	0	−15,980	7,520	141,948
9	− 17,862	0	0	0	−17,862	7,097	131,183
10	− 19,914	0	0	0	−19,914	6,559	117,828
11	− 22,151	0	0	0	−22,151	5,891	101,569
12	− 24,590	0	0	0	−24,590	5,078	82,057
13	− 27,247	0	0	0	−27,247	4,102	58,913
14	− 30,144	0	0	0	−30,144	2,945	31,715
15	− 33,301	0	0	0	−33,301	1,585	0

Method 2
Sinking-fund reinvestment rate = 5.0 percent
Internal rate of return = 7.308 percent

Period	Cash flows	Recovery of investment	Return on outstanding investment	Outstanding investment	Contribution to sinking fund	Return on accumulated sinking fund	Sinking fund
0	−300,000	0	0	300,000	0	0	0
1	183,497	49,335	21,925	250,664	112,236	0	112,236
2	95,324	77,004	18,319	173,660	0	5,611	117,848
3	77,058	64,366	12,691	109,293	0	5,892	123,740
4	58,692	50,704	7,987	58,589	0	6,187	129,927
5	40,215	35,933	4,281	22,656	0	6,496	136,424
6	21,618	19,962	1,655	2,694	0	6,821	143,245
7	2,891	2,694	196	0	0	7,162	150,407
8	−15,980	0	0	0	−15,980	7,520	141,948
9	−17,862	0	0	0	−17,862	7,097	131,183
10	−19,914	0	0	0	−19,914	6,559	117,828
11	−22,151	0	0	0	−22,151	5,891	101,569
12	−24,590	0	0	0	−24,590	5,078	82,057
13	−27,247	0	0	0	−27,247	4,102	58,913
14	−30,144	0	0	0	−30,144	2,945	31,715
15	−33,301	0	0	0	−33,301	1,585	0

Exhibit 2 *(continued)*
Method 3
Sinking-fund reinvestment rate = 5.0 percent
Internal rate of return = 8.264 percent

Period	Cash flows	Recovery of investment	Return on outstanding investment	Outstanding investment	Contribution to sinking fund	Return on accumulated sinking fund	Sinking fund
0	−300,000	0	0	300,000	0	0	0
1	183,497	138,049	24,792	161,950	20,654	0	20,654
2	95,324	61,285	13,383	100,664	20,654	1,032	42,342
3	77,058	48,084	8,319	52,580	20,654	2,117	65,114
4	58,692	33,691	4,345	18,888	20,654	3,255	89,024
5	40,215	17,999	1,560	889	20,654	4,451	114,130
6	21,618	889	73	0	20,654	5,706	140,492
7	2,891	0	0	0	2,891	7,024	150,407
8	− 15,980	0	0	0	−15,980	7,520	141,948
9	− 17,862	0	0	0	−17,862	7,097	131,183
10	− 19,914	0	0	0	−19,914	6,559	117,828
11	− 22,151	0	0	0	−22,151	5,891	101,569
12	− 24,590	0	0	0	−24,590	5,078	82,057
13	− 27,247	0	0	0	−27,247	4,102	58,913
14	− 30,144	0	0	0	−30,144	2,945	31,715
15	− 33,301	0	0	0	−33,301	1,585	0

Method 4
Sinking-fund reinvestment rate = 5.0 percent
Internal rate of return = 7.773 percent

Period	Cash flows	Recovery of investment	Return on outstanding investment	Outstanding investment	Contribution to sinking fund	Return on accumulated sinking fund	Sinking fund
0	-300,000	0	0	300,000	0	0	0
1	183,497	114,410	23,318	185,889	46,068	0	46,068
2	95,324	56,943	14,448	128,946	23,931	2,303	72,303
3	77,058	47,689	10,022	81,256	19,345	3,615	95,264
4	58,692	37,641	6,315	43,615	14,735	4,763	114,762
5	40,215	26,728	3,390	16,887	10,096	5,738	130,597
6	21,618	14,878	1,312	2,008	5,427	6,529	142,554
7	2,891	2,008	156	0	725	7,127	150,407
8	- 15,980	0	0	0	-15,980	7,520	141,948
9	- 17,862	0	0	0	-17,862	7,097	131,183
10	- 19,914	0	0	0	-19,914	6,559	117,828
11	- 22,151	0	0	0	-22,151	5,891	101,569
12	- 24,590	0	0	0	-24,590	5,078	82,057
13	- 27,247	0	0	0	-27,247	4,102	58,913
14	- 30,144	0	0	0	-30,144	2,945	31,715
15	- 33,301	0	0	0	-33,301	1,585	0

lease packagers often suggest that equity investors set up a sinking fund, or analyze a lease opportunity as if a sinking fund were to be set up. The sinking fund is established by making deposits from the early years' positive cash flow such that sufficient cash will accumulate to pay the negative cash flows required during the later years of the lease. The timing and pattern of cash flow deposits could, theoretically, vary widely and the total cash deposits required will depend upon the assumed rate of earnings on the sinking fund. The net effect of the sinking fund, if used, is to leave the investor with the normal, positive cash flow stream following the initial outlay. The sinking fund is used to pay the negative cash outflows.

An example of a sinking fund with an assumed zero rate of earnings is shown in columns (9) and (10) on Exhibit 1.

Exhibit 2 shows the same cash flows to the lessor and four different possible patterns of deposits to the sinking funds. In all cases, a 5 percent aftertax sinking-fund earnings rate is assumed. The internal rate of return for each sinking-fund method is computed on the basis of the cash flows remaining after sinking-fund deposits and withdrawals (i.e., Exhibit 2, Cash Flows minus Contributions to Sinking Fund).

Case 1-3

A Gas Conservation Proposal

In May 1977, Diane Hamilton, a financial analyst for the Federal
Energy Administration, was asked to examine and analyze a gas conservation proposal made by William Rosenberg, assistant administrator for
Energy Resource Development at the FEA. Mr. Rosenberg proposed
that public utility companies invest in gas-saving devices for single-family
homes in order to increase the supply of gas by maximizing conservation
efforts. Ms. Hamilton was concerned with the cost effectiveness of
this proposal, and she realized that the analysis would be a complex
one. Costs and benefits needed to be considered from several view-
points; the utility companies, the individual consumers, and society in
general.

THE PROPOSAL

Mr. Rosenberg has expressed his concern with the declining supply
of natural gas and increased costs of new investments for gas exploration.
He noted that substantial energy and cost savings are available to home-
owners who install insulation, automatic thermostat controls, and modifications that improve furnace efficiency. However, even after significant
price increases and awareness of declining gas supplies, only a small
percentage of the nation's homes were properly insulated and equipped.
That observation prompted him to make his proposal. He stated that
his plan and analysis started with the following observations and assumptions:

1. Conservation gas is a new gas supply made available from investment by the utility companies in conservation measures for customer homes.
2. Where the cost of conservation gas is less than the cost of

15

alternative gas supplies, the utility's investment in conservation measures is cost effective.

3. The cost of conservation gas should be included in utility cost of service and rates like other gas supplies purchased or produced.
4. Conservation gas would be sold to curtailed or to new priority customers as determined by a public utility commission.

Mr. Rosenberg went on to describe the proposal in more detail, focusing on the structure to be used by the utility companies to finance the investments and the need to convince state utility commissions of the merits of investment in gas conservation measures.

The conservation program would be implemented by a wholly owned subsidiary of the utility, which would supervise and finance installation of residential conservation measures. The improvements would be owned by the utility companies and carried on their balance sheets for depreciation purposes. Independent contractors who regularly offer conservation measures to the public would undertake the installation under contract with the subsidiary. The utility would make an equity investment in the subsidiary and contract to make regular payments to the subsidiary to cover all of the subsidiary's expenses associated with the conservation activities, including interest and return on equity. The utility would include these payments in its rates. With payment assured by a cost of service contract, the subsidiary could arrange for debt financing.

In advance of program implementation, the state regulatory commission must approve the conservation program, including the conservation investments of the subsidiary, the operating plan of the program, the allowed return on conservation investments, the service contract between the utility and subsidiary, inclusion of the contract payment in the cost of service of the utility, and a method for timely recovery of contract payments through customer rates.

Production and energy conservation are closely interrelated. On the production side, utility ventures currently under way include gas exploration, Alaskan gas transportation, liquefied natural gas imports, and gas manufactured from oil and coal. On the conservation side, many utilities are actively encouraging their customers to use gas more efficiently and are developing energy-conserving end-use devices. Both can increase future access to gas service for customers who lack equally clean and economical fuel alternatives. Further, the economics of production and conservation are interrelated. The higher prices required to make new production investments make investments in more efficient end-use devices more attractive. Finally, both new production and conservation require major capital investments, although the capital investment to produce conservation gas is generally lower than for new production.

The program is not being suggested as an alternative to supplemental gas development and cannot substitute for pricing policies to stimulate development of new natural gas supplies. Residential conservation gas could provide at best less than 5 percent of national gas supplies in 1985. But as supply projects become more expensive and take longer to implement, a conservation investment program would provide a bridge between declining natural gas supplies and the availability of supplemental sources.

Historically, however, the gas utilities and state commissions have not treated production and conservation investments in the same manner. Only the costs of production investments are capitalized by the utility and recovered over their useful life through monthly charges to customers. The proposal is designed to put investments for making gas available through energy conservation on an equal footing with investments in new production. Under the proposal, gas utility investments which increase the efficiency of gas use also would be capitalized and recovered over their life through customer charges.

Financing of the subsidiary is assumed to be a type of project financing that would not be restricted by the provisions of the parent utility's bond indenture. Like other projects to produce supplemental gas currently being proposed by the industry, the proposal assumes a 75 to 25 debt-equity ratio, a debt life of 15 years, a debt rate of 9.5 percent, and an allowed 17 percent aftertax return on equity. This proposal also assumes straight-line asset depreciation and equal annual principal repayment. The higher return on equity has been selected because of the thinness of the equity in the subsidiary and the risk of the new venture. In addition, because of the favorable economics to the customer and the national interest of promoting energy conservation, higher equity returns provide a strong incentive for aggressive utility participation. Properly structured by the state commission, conservation investments can become the most attractive investment available to the company at the same time consumer-heating costs are held down. Of course, each state commission must decide the authorized earnings level on a case-by-case basis.

Mr. Rosenberg believes that if this program were implemented nationally for all residential customers, the following benefits could be realized:

1. By the early 1980s, improved gas use in single-family residences alone could make available a quantity of gas equivalent to 130 percent of the gas deliveries estimated to come from the Alaskan North Slope.
2. Gas bills of existing residential customers could be reduced and additional high-priority customers could gain access to clean fuel at a cost well below the cost of electricity.
3. Investment in energy conservation could provide an attractive business opportunity for the gas utility industry.
4. Demands for capital could be reduced and domestic employment could be increased.

ANALYSIS

In order to illustrate the costs and benefits of his proposal, Mr. Rosenberg analyzed the effects that a residential conservation program would have on the companies and on the customers of gas utility systems in three different parts of the country: Southern California Gas Company (SOCAL), Michigan Consolidated Gas Company (MICH-CON), and Public Service Electric and Gas Company, New Jersey (PSE&G). The three conservation measures studied were ceiling insulation, automatic thermostat controls, and furnace modifications. The analysis was based upon company information and engineering studies and simulations.

Ceiling insulation

Exhibit 1 presents the thermal characteristics estimated for single-family residences in the three service areas and the benefits resulting from insulating up to the federal standards.

Exhibit 1
Gas savings associated with various levels of ceiling insulation
(thousand cubic feet annually)

Level of ceiling insulation	Percent of residential customers	Current consumption (MCFs)	Potential savings* (MCFs)
SOCAL:			
None	43	67	14
Moderate	21	59	6
Currently at federal standards	36	53	—
Weighted average		60†	11‡
MICH-CON:			
None	39	156	66
Moderate	39	101	11
Currently at federal standards	22	90	—
Weighted average		120†	38‡
PSE&G:			
None	24	151	58
Moderate	32	102	9
Currently at federal standards	44	93	—
Weighted average		110†	30‡

* Based on engineering estimates derived by assuming insulation increased to federal standards.
† Weighted by percent of residential customers at each level of ceiling insulation.
‡ Weighted by percent of residential customers with no or moderate ceiling insulation (e.g., SOCAL 43/64(14) + 21/64(6)).

The cost of insulating typical residences in each area has been estimated from data supplied by the individual companies (Exhibit 2).

Using the data shown in Exhibit 2, the cost per MCF (thousand cubic feet) of gas saved was then calculated (Exhibit 3).

Since some residences cannot easily or economically receive ceiling insulation, it is assumed that 75 percent of the residences in the PSE&G service area and 94 percent of the residences in the SOCAL and MICH-

Exhibit 2
Cost of insulation

	SOCAL	MICH–CON	PSE&G
No insulation to federal standards	$218	$266	$299
Moderate insulation to federal standards	186	184	199
Weighted average*	$208	$225	$242

* Weighted by percent of residential customers with no or moderate ceiling insulation from Exhibit 1 (e.g., SOCAL 43/64(218) + 21/64(186)).

Exhibit 3

	Average insula- tion cost for underinsulated homes*	Average investment carrying cost†	Savings‡		Cost per MCF
			(MCF)	Percent	MCF
SOCAL	$208	$35	11	17	$3.08
MICH-CON	225	38	38	30	1.00
PSE&G	242	41	30	24	1.36

* From Exhibit 2.
† To translate the installation cost into an annual cost, the costs to service the investment (9.5 percent interest on debt, 17 percent aftertax return on equity, taxes, and operating costs) were identified and calculated to be 14.75 percent per annum on the original cost over a 15-year life.
‡ From Exhibit 1.

CON service areas which do not have insulation up to federal standards can and will be insulated.

Automatic thermostat control

Automatic thermostat controls are capable of being set to reduce a nighttime household heating requirements and thus to lower total gas consumption. For this analysis a setback of 5° to 7° for an eight-hour nighttime period is assumed. Consumption savings are estimated based upon the load remaining after installation of ceiling insulation up to federal standards where feasible. It is assumed that 100 percent of the residences in the service area would receive these devices and that the following savings would result (Exhibit 4).

Furnace modifications

Furnace modification measures are designed to improve the seasonal efficiency of existing gas furnaces in single-family residences.

It is being assumed that 100 percent of the residences can be retrofit-

Exhibit 4

	Installation cost	Annual investment carrying cost*	Savings		Cost per MCF
			(MCF)	Percent	MCF
SOCAL	$75	$13	7.4	14	$1.71
MICH–CON	75	13	8.1	9	1.56
PSE&G	75	13	9.3	10	1.36

* 15.3 percent factor. (This factor differs from the 14.5 percent factor for ceiling insulation due to differing operating costs.)

ted with devices which will yield a 15 percent savings at a cost of approximately $100. The assumption reduction would apply to the thermal load remaining after (1) the installation of ceiling insulation up to federal standards, and (2) the installation of automatic thermostat controls, and would result in the savings shown in (Exhibit 5).

Exhibit 5

	Installation cost	Annual investment carrying cost*	Savings		Cost per MCF
			(MCF)	Percent	MCF
SOCAL	$100	$17	6.8	15	$2.48
MICH–CON	100	17	12.3	15	1.37
PSE&G	100	17	12.6	15	1.34

* The 14.9 percent factor. (This factor differs from the 14.75 percent factor for ceiling insulation due to differing operating costs.)

Using this analysis, Mr. Rosenberg concluded that in virtually all instances the cost of gas saved through the investment by the utility company in conservation measures is competitive with other new gas supplies (Exhibit 6).

Systemwide effects

To measure the effects on each of the three systems several assumptions were made to specify future supply, demand, and pricing factors for each system.

- Current interstate gas supplies will decline 10 percent annually (where a utility forecast was available, actual forecasts were employed).

Exhibit 6
Conservation gas compared with other alternative supplies

Conservation		Production	
Source	Average dollar per MCF	Source	Average dollar per MCF
SOCAL:			
Thermostat	$1.74	Current gas*	$0.76
Furnace	2.48	New interstate gas (L-48)	1.90
Insulation	3.08	No. 2 oil (MCF-equivalent)	2.75
		LNG imports	2.75
		Alaskan Gas	3.00
		Gas from Western Coal	3.65
		Electric (MCF-equivalent)	6.10
MICH–CON:			
Insulation	$1.00	Current gas*	$0.85
Furnace	1.37	New interstate gas (L-48)	1.80
Thermostat	1.56	Canadian Gas	2.10
		No. 2 oil (MCF-equivalent)	2.70
		Alaskan Gas	3.10
		Gas from Western Coal	—
		Electric (MCF-equivalent)	6.05
PSE&G:			
Insulation	$1.34	Current gas*	$1.05
Furnace	1.36	New interstate gas (L-48)	2.00
Thermostat	1.36	No. 2 oil (MCF-equivalent)	2.75
		LNG imports	2.80
		Alaskan Gas	—
		SNG	4.00†
		Gas from Eastern Coal	5.15
		Electric (MCF-equivalent)	7.00

* Excluding peaking supplementals; costs at city gate, 1976 dollars.
† Assumes base-load operation.

- New lower 48 interstate supplies will be sufficient to produce a net decline in interstate pipeline supplies of 6.7 percent annually. (The weighted average price of new supplies will be $1.42 per year, growth $0.04 per year in current dollars.)
- Other new gas sources will be priced in current dollar terms, their average costs will increase at one half the inflation rate, or 2.5 percent annually.
- The costs of conservation measures will inflate at 5 percent annually and the service component of residential gas changes will inflate at 2.5 percent annually.
- New residential hookups will be permitted as forecast by each system; these systems can accommodate substantial residential customer growth without major additional distribution capacity.

Additionally it was assumed that the program would be implemented fully over a seven-year period beginning in 1978, that the cost is recovered over all customers in the system and that conservation gas is allocated to new residential hookups.

Mr. Rosenberg noted that when the conservation case was compared with a 1976 reference case (Exhibit 7), the average space heating bill declines for virtually every class of residential consumer.

Exhibit 7

	1976 Refer- ence	1985		
		Refer- ence	Conser- vation	Percent change
SOCAL:				
Gas made available (BCF per year)		—	61	—
Added residences served (000)		—	656	—
Average annual use per home (MCF)	60	60	39	(35)
Average charge per MCF (dollars)	$1.16	$3.01	$3.25	8
Annual charge per category (dollars):*				
No insulation (43 percent)	77	202	127	(37)
Inadequate insulation (21 percent)	68	178	127	(29)
Adequate insulation (36 percent)	60	157	127	(19)
New customer	60	157	127	(19)
Average	$ 69	$ 181	$ 127	(30)
MICH-CON:				
Gas made available (BCF per year)			42	—
Added residences served (000)			300	
Average annual use per home (MCF)	120	120	70	(42)
Average charge per MCF (dollars)	$1.65	$3.00	$ 313	4
Annual charge per category (dollars):*				
No insulation (39 percent)	257	468	219	(53)
Inadequate insulation (39 percent)	167	303	219	(28)
Adequate insulation (22 percent)	148	270	219	(19)
New customer	148	270	219	(19)
Average	$ 198	$ 360	$ 219	(39)
PSE&G				
Gas made available (BCF per year)			17.5	—
Added residences served (000)			122	—
Average annual use per home (MCF)	110	110	71	(35)
Average charge per MCF (dollars)	$2.54	$3.86	$3.99	3
Annual charge per category (dollars):*				
No insulation (24 percent)	384	583	283	(51)
Inadequate insulation (32 percent)	259	394	283	(28)
Adequate insulation (44 percent)	236	359	283	(21)
New customer	236	359	283	(21)
Average	$ 279	$ 425	$ 283	(33)

* Annual cost per home per year for the purchase of gas.

National effects

Mr. Rosenberg believed that, if fully implemented, the conservation proposal would have a major national impact on gas utility systems, including the conservation of gas, reduction in consumption and heating bills, mobilization of capital and increased employment. He explained that:

Assuming full national implementation by 1984 of the three conservation measures to the extent physically feasible, and assuming a 100 percent penetration by all gas utilities for all residential heating customers, I estimate that natural gas savings in 1985 would amount to 1.2 trillion cubic feet per year. This amount would be the energy equivalent to:

- 130 percent of the annual deliveries estimated to come from the North Slope of Alaska.
- 13 high-Btu coal gasification plants (250 million MCF per day).
- 39 major electric power plants (1,000 megawatts).
- 575,000 barrels per day of imported oil.

As would be expected, the greatest energy savings would occur in the Middle Atlantic, East North Central, and West Central states, since these areas have the greatest degree-day heating loads, large populations, and relatively high use of gas for space heating.

Using the three systems in the analysis as representative of what might be expected in a national program, substantial savings could be realized by residential customers. By 1985 consumer savings would be significant due to lower consumption levels which more than offset the increased rates necessary to cover the costs of the conservation measures. These maximum consumer savings are derived from what would otherwise be the cost of gas service in the absence of any other conservation program and are shown in Exhibit 8 for cases (1) where "saved" gas adds new consumers and (2) where "saved" gas backs out the highest priced incremental gas.

Based upon a 100 percent implementation nationwide, the conservation measures

Exhibit 8
Increased gas availability and consumer savings, 1985

Region	Billion cubic feet per year available	Annual consumer savings ($ millions)	
		(1)	(2)
New England	42	$ 96	$ 36
Middle Atlantic	170	464	171
East North Central	363	1,018	523
West North Central	122	391	202
South Atlantic	92	122	70
East South Central	60	77	44
West South Central	103	185	106
Mountain	69	245	126
Pacific	191	261	148
Total	1,212	$2,859	$1,426

would require a capital investment of $8.3 billion by the utility systems which would compare favorably with other sources of energy (Exhibit 9).

Unlike the other supplemental gas projects the conservation gas would have little cost other than that of the initial capital investment. There would be no "fuel" cost for coal, liquefied natural gas, or synthetic gas, and there would be minimal operating costs. In addition, there are significant environmental benefits from producing conservation gas.

Finally, I estimate that the manufacture and installation of the conservation measures contained in the proposal would result in 506,000 man-years of employment over the seven-year implementation period, or 72,200 jobs per year.

Exhibit 9
Amount of capital to produce equivalent energy

	Billions
Alaskan North Slope gas (.9 TCF per year)	$ 7–10
13 high-Btu coal gasification plants (250 million MCF per day)	$11–13
39 Electric power plants (1,000 megawatts)*	$17–20

* Adjusted for higher distribution losses and higher end-use efficiency for heat.

Diane was intrigued with Mr. Rosenberg's concept. She was, however, uncertain about whether this particular plan was, indeed, cost effective. She thought she should look in more detail at the costs and benefits involved and consider alternative ways to finance these conservation measures, before she could comment to the FEA on Mr. Rosenberg's proposal.

PART TWO

Capital structure and financing choices

Case 2-1

Leverage and the Value of American Luggage Works Common Stock

INTRODUCTION

Following are excerpts of an expert witness' report on the valuation of the closely held common and preferred shares of American Luggage Works, Inc. (ALW), manufacturers of American Tourister Luggage. The report was prepared as testimony filed with the U.S. Tax Court. The issue for the court was to determine the value of the shares for gift tax purposes.

In his multifaceted approach to valuation of ALW, the expert witness had earlier in the testimony appraised such factors internal to the firm as its earning power, dividend paying capacity, book value and financial and competitive position. This excerpt begins with the witness' appraisal of the *market value* of ALW.

Because ALW stock is not publicly traded, the approach of the witness is to use the market price of a similar company's stock to derive the value of ALW. The only publicly traded luggage manufacturer in the United States at the time was Samsonite Luggage. He thus starts with the market price of Samsonite in his appraisal of value for ALW.

DETERMINING A MARKET VALUE FOR SAMSONITE

We have studied the investing public's market appraisal of Samsonite's outstanding securities as of June 30, 1971. By "market appraisal" we mean the relationship between the total market value of all outstanding long-term debt, preferred stocks, and common stocks and: (1) total adjusted earnings and (2) adjusted total invested capital.

It will be evident that we are measuring the market appraisal of companies' entire capital structures rather than the market appraisal of their common stocks only. This approach compensates for differences in the degree of "leverage" inherent in various common stocks resulting from individual variations in capital structure. The market value represents the sum total of the values of the securities of Samsonite.

In our computation of the total market value we have included the deferred federal income tax at two thirds its par value. This is done to reflect the fact that this is a noninterest bearing form of long-term debt and its payback is relatively long (related to the life of the fixed assets subject to fast depreciation for tax purposes).

All of Samsonite's long-term debt is privately held and has been included in these computations at its par value.

There are 5,000 shares of preferred stock which have been included at the call price of $110 per share.

Finally, Samsonite had 5,009,315 shares of common stock outstanding and on the valuation date it was quoted at $13⅝ bid, $14 asked. We have taken the midpoint of this quotation and multiplied it by the number of shares, deriving the total market value of the company's entire common issue of $69,191,000. The sum of these four components of the total market value of Samsonite is $81,679,000.

Samsonite on June 30, 1971 had a book value of its invested capital of $59,165,000.[1] Therefore its market value is 138 percent of its total invested capital ($81,697,000 as a percent of $59,165,000). Using this ratio as an indicator of the value of the stock of American Luggage Works results in an indicated value, based only upon the size of American's capital of $15,590,000 (138 percent of American's capital of $11,-297,000[2]).

We have also related Samsonite's total market value of $81,679,000 to its earnings. In deriving this relationship, we have used a weighted average of earnings[3] for the five years preceding the date of this valuation. We have followed this procedure because we want to derive a reasonable measure of the indicated earning power of American Luggage relative to Samsonite and American's trend of income had been decidedly better than that of Samsonite. Some reflection should be given to this better trend and in order to do this we have used a *weighted* average of earnings. (This places a weight of 1 on the earnings of 1967 and a weight of 2 on the earnings of 1968, on up to a weight of 5 to the earnings of 1971). Samsonite's price-earnings ratio computed on this basis is 19.4 times. We have computed American's 1967–71 weighted average earnings[3] to be $2,025,000. The use of the 19.4 price-earnings ratio (with this earning figure) results in an indicated value for American Luggage, based solely upon the factor of earnings of $39,285,000.

The witness went on to further refine these two estimates of common stock value to come up with a market value for ALW common and preferred stock: He compared other companies which had "investment

---

[1] Long-term debt	$11,000,000
Deferred taxes...................	1,165,000
Preferred stock	550,000
Common stock and surplus	46,450,000
	$59,165,000
[2] Preferred stock	$ 2,500,000
Common stock and surplus	8,797,000
	11,297,000

[3] "Earnings" are defined as income after tax but before preferred and common dividends.

characteristics and growth patterns" similar to ALW. Using both these additional data and the valuation based on Samsonite, he derived a figure of $26 million.

This figure of $26 million represents the total combined value of the preferred and common stock equity before allowing for the fact that the company had a substantial amount of cash.

As of June 30, 1971, we eliminated $4,236,000 of cash from the company's balance sheet as a nonoperating asset. It is now necessary to make some judgment as to the premium which an investor would pay for the common stock of American Luggage Works for his participation in the ownership of this cash asset. We do believe that an investor could not reasonably be expected to pay 100 cents on the dollar for his share in the equity of this asset. There are two reasons for this.

First, an investor in American Luggage Works is buying indirect ownership in this cash. If we were to value this cash at 100 cents on the dollar, we would be involved in the assumption that an investor regarded a dollar of cash in the corporation as having equal value to a dollar in cash owned directly. Such an assumption is not reasonable. In our judgment, a discount of 10 percent is reasonable.

There is, however, a second factor which should be given consideration. In mid-1971, the Internal Revenue Service had claimed the company owed an additional $1.9 million of taxes under Section 531 of the Internal Revenue Code. In a previous audit a nominal tax under this section had been paid. An investor in the company in June 1971 would be concerned that the earlier payment of the nominal tax had established the company's susceptibility to that tax, and the intervening years of substantial earnings and no dividends had simply compounded the exposure. An investor in the company in June 1971 could reasonably expect the company to pay some additional Section 531 tax, but he would have no way of gauging how much might ultimately be paid under Section 531.

We have valued the nonoperating cash ($4,236,000) at $3 million. This makes an allowance of about 10 percent for indirect ownership and reduces that figure by roughly $800,000 to reflect a potential Section 531 liability. The latter figure is roughly half of the government's initial position. The addition of the $3 million results in a total preliminary valuation of the preferred and common stock equity of $29 million.

It is now necessary to allocate the total valuation of $29 million between preferred and common stock.

There are 6,250 shares of preferred stock with a par value of $1,000 per share. This stock is redeemable at $1,000 and is entitled to $1,000 upon liquidation. It is entitled to one vote per share.

We consider this preferred stock to be of good quality. Its total asset coverage (total assets divided by the sum of total liabilities and preferred stock) is 2.33. That is, the company has $2.33 of assets (at book value) per dollar of liabilities and preferred. The current asset coverage (current assets divided by total liabilities plus the preferred) is 1.92 times.

Earnings coverage (earnings divided by the preferred stock dividend requirement) was 8.4 times in fiscal 1971. The five-year weighted average was 6.7 times.

The excess cash which the company had on June 30, 1971 covered the preferred stock dividend requirement for 13½ years.

This is a good quality preferred stock, so that it is appropriate to use as a guideline in its valuation, the prices of good quality preferred stocks at the end of June 1971. At the end of June 1971, high-grade preferred stocks had an average yield of 6.8 percent and medium-grade preferred stocks had an average yield of 7.0 percent. We think that this preferred stock should be valued to yield approximately 7 percent which represents a valuation of $714 per share at the end of June 1971, except that some reflection should be given to the fact that this preferred is entitled to one vote per share. Those publicly held preferred stocks which were yielding about 7 percent at the end of June 1971, were nonvoting.

Unfortunately it is not possible to determine the premium which should be attributed to the voting power of the preferred stock. There are, to our knowledge, no publicly held preferred stocks which would be useful as a guideline or benchmark, in this respect. It is important to point out that we are dealing with minority interest blocks of preferred and common stock which, taken together, still represent a minority interest. The voting power of a minority interest theoretically has some value because it at least theoretically enables the holder to exert some influence upon the affairs of the corporation. However, in this case the preferred stockholder has a relatively secure preferred and some marginal influence that he might have upon corporate policy would have no more than a marginal influence upon the safety of that preferred stock. Nevertheless, some premium should be attributed to the preferred stock for its voting power.

In making an allocation for the voting power of the preferred stock, we have assumed that the value of voting power in minority interest blocks has a value of 5 percent of the total value of all outstanding preferred and common stock equity (on a minority interest basis). In this case, that would amount to $1,450,000 (5 percent of $29 million). The preferred stock has 42 percent of the voting power (6,230 votes out of a total of 14,980 votes) and taking 42 percent of $1,450,000 results in an allocation attributable to the voting power of $609,000 which is equal to $98 per share.

We have concluded that the preferred stock has a value of approximately $800 per share before allowance is made for its lack of marketability. It has a value of approximately $700 as a straight preferred and we have added an increment of $100 for its voting power, resulting in this total valuation of $800 per share.

The deduction of the issue of preferred stock at $4,984,000 (6,230 shares at $800 per share) leaves a value for the common stock of $24,016,000, or let us say $24 million. We have then simply divided by the number of common shares outstanding (8,750) and this results in a total valuation of the common stock of $2,743. We conclude that if the common stock of American Luggage Works, Inc., were publicly held and actively traded on June 30, 1971, it would have traded at a price of approximately $2,743.

CASE 2-2

INTER CITY HEALTH CARE, INC.

INTRODUCTION

Frank Parker had worked in hospital administration since his graduation in 1962. Thirteen years and several career moves later, he had finally achieved one of his more coveted goals: he had been appointed president and chief executive officer of a major hospital group. What's more, 1975 was a particularly exciting time for Inter City Health Care (ICHC). It was about to embark on a $75 million expansion in its hospital facilities, and needed $30 million in financing immediately.

Frank's only trouble was that it had also been 13 years since he had studied finance. Admittedly, ICHC's controller knew the organization inside out, but like Frank, he had never been involved in arranging external financing.

Feeling somewhat at the mercy of the financial institutions, Frank had asked an investment bank to prepare some alternative financing suggestions. They were now before him on the table (Exhibit 1).

Trends within the health care industry

Hospital chains are relatively new to the health care industry. Increasing awareness of the need for health care, rising costs for such care, and an increasing need for centralized planning in health care delivery have given rise to these which can be found in either for-profit ("proprietary") or not-for-profit form. In both cases chains have emphasized getting established in good locations and increasing their revenue base, rather than concentrating on construction. Acquisitions have become fashionable, causing severe competition and inflated prices. This has encouraged the flood of ailing local hospitals clamoring to join a major group.

31

Exhibit 1
Alternative financing methods available to hospitals

I. *Publicly offered tax-exempt bonds*
   Advantages:
   1. Tax-exempt financing provides the lowest cost of borrowed money of all financing alternatives available to hospitals. Twenty-seven year AA-rated hospital obligations are currently being offered at approximately 8.5–9 percent. Taxable hospital obligations generally sell at 1.5–2 percent higher. Thus, the interest cost savings over taxable financing on every $10 million borrowed through tax-exempt financing is $150–$200,000 per year, or $3–$4 million over the course of a 27-year bond issue having an average maturity of 20 years.
   2. Tax-exempt financing provides the greatest flexibility in structuring repayment terms of a loan. Repayment schedules of up to 30 years are common in this type of financing. (The larger the period over which a loan is amortized, the smaller is the annual debt service payment that must be made.) Furthermore, the bond issue can be sold as serial bonds (which have shorter maturities and, therefore, lower interest rates) and term bonds, giving the issuer the benefit of lower interest rates in the earlier years of the loan.
   3. A broad public market exists for tax-exempt hospital revenue bonds. A $30 million offering of bonds for ICHC would be marketed through a national syndicate of securities firms, providing maximum competition among potential buyers.
   4. Under state law, title to the facilities being financed may be held by the hospital.

   Disadvantages:
   1. Because the investment banker serves as underwriter of the bonds, financing fees are generally higher than for the taxable private placement alternative. In order to earn all the underwriting fees, a bond discount of 2–3 percent of the total bond issue is normally required.
   2. A successful sale of tax-exempt bonds requires the cooperation of the city or county that would serve as issuer. Generally such municipalities are cooperative, but in some cases (e.g., Denver or Milwaukee) they are not.

Tax-exempt revenue bond
8.75 percent interest rate
27-year maturity
25-year amortization
(all figures $000)

Summary of terms:

Amount of bond issue	$36,750
Level annual debt payments	$ 3,666
Average interest cost	8.75%
Expected rating	Aa/AA
Repayment schedule (*)	Annual principal
(See Table A)	Semiannual interest

Exhibit 1 *(continued)*

Table A

	Principal		Interest	
Year	December 31	June 30		December 31
1978	$ 450	$ 1,608		$ 1,608
1979	490	1,588		1,588
1980	532	1,567		1,567
1981	580	1,543		1,543
1982	630	1,518		1,518
1983	684	1,491		1,491
1984	744	1,461		1,461
1985	810	1,428		1,428
1986	880	1,393		1,393
1987	958	1,354		1,354
1988	1,042	1,312		1,312
1989	1,132	1,267		1,267
1990	1,232	1,217		1,217
1991	1,340	1,163		1,163
1992	1,456	1,105		1,105
1993	1,584	1,041		1,041
1994	1,724	971		971
1995	1,874	896		896
1996	2,038	814		814
1997	2,216	725		725
1998	2,410	628		628
1999	2,622	522		522
2000	2,850	408		408
2001	3,100	283		283
2002	3,372†	147†		147†
	$36,750	$27,450		$27,450

Total debt service = $91,650

* Payments begin upon completion of construction. This is presently estimated to be December 31,1977.

† Final annual payment made from debt service reserve—see cost breakdown.

Cost breakdown:

Construction costs $26,645
Net capitalized interest,*
    fees and other expenses   5,520
Debt service reserve requirement†
    (1 year's maximum annual debt service)   3,666
Bond discount (2.5 percent)   919
                                                                                        $36,750

* During construction, interest will be capitalized on the amount of the bond issue which is used.

† Interest on the debt service reserve requirement can be used to offset the annual debt payments. Assuming an earnings rate of 8 percent, each annual payment could be reduced by $293. The reserve itself is then used to pay off the final year's installment.

Exhibit 1 *(continued)*

II. *Taxable bonds privately placed*

Advantages:

1. Disclosure of information on the hospital's operations and financial conditions need not be made to the general public.
2. If, after the financing has been arranged, it becomes necessary or desirable to modify a financial convenant or any of the terms of the financing, it is easier to get the permission of bondholders to do so when the outstanding obligations are held by a limited number of professional investors.
3. For certain hospitals, generally those of the highest credit ratings, it may not be necessary to have prepared an independent feasibility study. In such a case the financing may be structured and a commitment made by lenders in a shorter period of time than would be required to structure and market a tax-exempt issue.
4. Financing costs for a taxable bond issue are less than those for a tax-exempt issue. The principal difference is that the investment banker in a private placement does not underwrite the bond issue, but acts only as the hospital's placement agent thus earning only a placement fee. A charge of 1 percent of the total bond issue is normally sufficient to cover the placement cost.

Disadvantages:

1. Interest rates on taxable hospital bond issues privately placed are generally 1.5–2.0 percent higher than rates on comparably rated tax-exempt obligations. Currently a 20-year AA-rated taxable hospital bond privately placed would command an interest rate of 10–10.5 percent.
2. A private placement, which is a distribution of securities to a limited number of institutional investors, eliminates individual investors as potential buyers of the securities. Individual investors are by far the largest investor sector for hospital obligations.
3. There is a relatively limited number of institutional investors with interests in purchasing hospital credits. If some of the major lenders are not interested in the hospital as a credit, interest rates might have to rise considerably to attract additional institutional investors needed to complete this financing.
4. Institutional lenders will not generally lend beyond 20 years. If market conditions are good at the time of the hospital's financing, however, it may be possible to arrange a 25-year obligation. Of course, shorter amortization periods mean higher annual debt service payments, thus diminishing the hospital's annual cash flow. Furthermore, repaying an obligation issued to finance a project whose useful life is longer than the repayment period, means that users of the facility after the obligation is repaid are not properly being charged for its use.
5. Because the investment banker acts, not as an underwriter of the bonds, but only as the hospital's placement agent, it is not uncommon to find that after lenders have been located and commitments made to purchase the obligations, the lenders will change the terms of the financing, including asking for more security. This is especially the case for hospitals because of the relatively limited number of institutional lenders interested in hospital obligations.
6. Generally, security provisions are more stringent than for tax-exempt financings. Private placement lenders will not infrequently require a first mortgage on the hospital buildings, while mortgages securing tax-exempt financings are rare.

Exhibit 1 *(continued)*

Taxable private placement
10.25 percent interest rate
22-year maturity
20-year amortization
(all figures in $000)

Summary of terms:

Amount of placement	$30,300
Level annual payment	$ 3,620
Average interest cost	10.25%
Expected rating	Aa/AA
Repayment schedule*	Annual principal
(See Table B)	Semiannual interest

Table B

	Principal	Interest	
Year	December 31	June 30	December 31
1978	$ 514	$ 1,553	$ 1,553
1979	566	1,521	1,521
1980	626	1,497	1,497
1981	690	1,465	1,465
1982	760	1,430	1,430
1983	838	1,391	1,391
1984	924	1,348	1,348
1985	1,018	1,301	1,301
1986	1,122	1,249	1,249
1987	1,238	1,191	1,191
1988	1,364	1,128	1,128
1989	1,504	1,058	1,058
1990	1,658	981	981
1991	1,828	896	896
1992	2,016	802	802
1993	2,222	699	699
1994	2,450	585	585
1995	2,702	459	459
1996	2,978	321	321
1997	3,282	168	168
	$30,300	$21,043	$21,043

Total debt service = $72,386

* Payments begin upon completion of construction. This is estimated to be December 31, 1977.

Cost breakdown:

Construction costs	$26,645
Capitalized interest* and legal fees	3,352
Placement fee (1%)	303
Amount of placement	$30,300

* Interest is capitalized during the 24-month construction period, but only on those funds which have been drawn down. In addition, ICHC is required to pay one half of 1 percent as a stand-by fee on the funds which have not been drawn down. This is equivalent to a lump-sum payment of $131.5 on December 31, 1977.

Exhibit 1 *(continued)*

III. *FHA-insured mortgage loans*

Advantages:

1. Because the loan is insured by the Federal Housing Administration (FHA), a U.S. government-sponsored corporation, the loan assumes a credit-worthiness nearly equivalent to obligations of agencies of the federal government.

   FHA-insured mortgage loans for hospitals are generally structured as 25-year loans with amortization through equal annual payments of principal and interest. Because of their similarity to GNMA projects, the FHA-insured loans are generally marketed against GNMA pass-throughs. Customarily rates on FHA-insured mortgage loans are 25–30 basis points higher than GNMA projects, primarily because the FHA-insured loans are not as liquid.

   Currently rates for FHA-insured mortgage loans are approximately 9.00 percent.

2. Because of their "government-guaranteed" credit quality, a broad market for such securities exists.

   Investment bankers' fees are generally 1–2 percent of the principal amount of the loan, often less than for a tax-exempt bond issue.

Disadvantages:

1. Requires a first mortgage on the facility being financed.
2. Such loans are limited in size to 90 percent of the estimated "replacement cost" of the mortgaged facility as defined by FHA. This provision usually means that the hospital must provide up to 10 percent of the cost of the project in cash.
3. Maturity of loans for hospital projects is limited to 25 years.
4. The hospital must agree to certain federal government conditions respecting nondiscrimination.
5. The hospital may not employ a contractor who pays wages lower than the prevailing construction wages as determined by the secretary of labor.
6. Because of red tape, considerable uncertainty exists as to when a loan will be ready for marketing. Delays of up to one year have occurred.
7. The hospital must pay to FHA one-time front-end fees of 0.8 percent as application and commitment fees.
8. A fee of 0.05 percent of the mortgage amount is paid to FHA annually as an insurance premium for its insurance on the loan.

FHA mortgage/GNMA mortgage-backed securities
9 percent FHA interest rate plus 0.05 percent insurance premium
8.75 percent GNMA reoffered to yield 9.25 percent
27-year maturity
25-year amortization
(all figures $000)

Summary of terms:

Mortgage amount	$31,820
Level annual debt payments	3,372
Proposed interest rate	9.5%
Repayment schedule*	Annual principal
(See Table C)	Semiannual interest

Exhibit 1 *(concluded)*

Table C

	Principal		Interest	
Year	December 31		June 30	December 31
1978	$ 350		$ 1,511	$ 1,511
1979	382		1,495	1,495
1980	418		1,477	1,477
1981	458		1,457	1,457
1982	502		1,435	1,435
1983	550		1,411	1,411
1984	602		1,385	1,385
1985	658		1,357	1,357
1986	722		1,325	1,325
1987	790		1,291	1,291
1988	866		1,253	1,253
1989	948		1,212	1,212
1990	1,038		1,167	1,167
1991	1,136		1,118	1,118
1992	1,244		1,064	1,064
1993	1,362		1,005	1,005
1994	1,492		940	940
1995	1,634		869	869
1996	1,788		792	792
1997	1,958		707	707
1998	2,144		614	614
1999	2,348		512	512
2000	2,570		401	401
2001	2,814		279	279
2002	3,046		145	145
	$31,820		$26,222	$26,222

Total debt service = $84,264

* Payments begin upon completion of construction. This is presently estimated to be December 31, 1977.

Cost breakdown:

Construction costs (Cottonwood and Valley City hospitals)	$26,645
Capitalized interest*, FHA/HEW and underwriting fees	3,902
Equity in existing facilities†	4,808
Replacement cost as determined by FHA	$35,355

The equity portion is determined as follows:	
Replacement cost	$35,355
Less: Minimum equity required (10%)	3,535
Maximum mortgage amount	$31,820
Less: Market discount to produce 9.25% yield	1,273
Net proceeds to ICHC	$30,547
Total equity required†	$ 4,808
	$35,355

* Assumes a construction period of 24 months. During this time interest will accrue only on those funds which have been drawn down.
† The equity required is more than covered by ICHC's existing facilities.

At the same time, the purchaser of medical services has become institutionalized. Rather than the individual or his private insurer paying for health care, organizations such as Blue Cross or Blue Shield have assumed much of the responsibility for expense reimbursement. These organizations have become powerful enough to question rising costs, as well as to question the inclusion of certain expenses and capital charges as legitimate costs of health care (e.g., the return on the "good-will" portion of equity). Although it is claimed that hospitals have thus become more accountable and efficient, in fact these cost reimbursement schemes have contorted many of the normal hospital purchasing activities. Expensive equipment is leased rather than funds being invested in such nonreimbursable items as teaching or research. Specialized but essential services suffer, even if only for the benefit of general medical care. The hospital's revenues from other sources have been curtailed, and thus their discretion has been limited. What discretionary cash flow hospitals may receive is no longer supplemented by philanthropic contributions.

As a consequence, hospital boards have turned increasingly to outside bond financing, even though it brings greater regulation of their institutions. The accompanying scrutiny of the securities industry has alerted them to the need for better financial management, and has forced them to continually assess their revenue potential.

Under these conditions, Inter City's area has become a very attractive region for hospital expansion, as the area's population is growing at three times the national rate. Many hospital groups are therefore attempting to gain footholds in the region, but are facing well-established competition from Inter City Health Care. The largest group in the region, ICHC, presently controls 45 percent of the beds and 51 percent of all admissions. Recognizing the challenge to its market share from new entrants, ICHC has planned to develop several new clinic sites, in addition to expanding their existing facilities. Only the largest of entering groups can hope to penetrate this defensive strategy, indicating that, indeed, the era of independent hospital management may already have passed.

Inter City Health Care, Inc.

Inter City Health Care, Inc. (ICHC) is a nonprofit corporation which was organized in 1970 under the name of Health Services Corporation to own or operate the hospitals formerly owned or leased by a major religious group (the "Church"). Commencing in the early 20th century, the Church constructed or acquired hospital facilities in a three-state region to provide health care in areas where it was not available. Prior to 1970 each of the 15 hospitals within the Church's system functioned on an autonomous basis, with relatively little coordination or centralized management. In 1970 all the hospitals in the Church system were consolidated into a single nonprofit corporation, Health Services Corporation, which, in addition to operating the Church hospitals, was also responsible for the development of the worldwide health program of the Church.

The Church authorities determined in 1974 that the operation of hospitals was not central to the Church's mission, and initiated action to divest its hospitals from Church control by transferring the management and direction of Health Services Corporation to a group of independent trustees, changing the name of Health Services Corporation to Inter City Health Care, Inc. This reorganization was accomplished as of April 1, 1975.

There are 17 ICHC hospitals, all of which provide inpatient and outpatient services, in addition to standard emergency facilities. Although the scope of services offered by each hospital varies with the size of the facility and the needs of the community, most are general acute care hospitals. Two, however, are specialized referral centers for the region: Primary Children's Medical Center—pediatrics; and OPC—open-heart surgery, pulmonary medicine, and coronary care.

Of the 17, 8 are owned, 4 are leased, and 5 are managed. Managed hospitals are small isolated hospitals which had been losing money under local community management. ICHC's management contract offers them centralized services, but assumes no financial risk.

By contrast, the leased hospitals are for all intents and purposes owned. They are generally leased for $1 and then carried on ICHC's books. These two categories together provide less than 3 percent of ICHC's operating income. (Forecasted statements of income and balance sheets are laid out in Exhibit 2).

ICHC's latest strategy is to build small clinics in key locations around the region, only transforming them into full-size hospitals when demand has been established. More pressing, however, are the expansions at existing hospitals, some of which are operating at 96 percent occupancy. (Within the health care industry, 85 percent is considered full occupancy.) The two most urgent projects consist of a 92-bed expansion at Cottonwood Hospital and a 120-bed expansion at Valley City Hospital. Together these projects require $30 million in financing.

Exhibit 2
Inter City Health Care, Inc.
Forecasted statements of revenues and expenses
($000)

	Years Ending December 31			
	1976	*1977*	*1978*	*1979*
Statistics				
Beds available	1,996	2,038	2,211	2,211
Patient days	555,800	572,900	613,100	636,700
Occupancy percent	76%	77%	76%	79%
Patient service revenue				
Daily hospital services	$ 46,658	$ 51,006	$ 56,048	$ 60,764
Ancillary services	63,825	71,646	79,217	87,422
Gross Patient Service Revenue .	$110,483	$122,652	$135,265	$148,186
Deductions from revenue				
Medicare contractual adjustment	4,496	4,925	4,270	4,644
Provision for uncollectibles and				
other allowances	2,406	2,688	2,998	3,291
	$ 6,902	$ 7,613	$ 7,268	$ 7,935
Net Patient Service Revenue ...	$103,581	$115,039	$127,997	$140,251
Other operating revenue	3,709	3,967	4,540	4,653
Total Operating Revenues	$107,290	$119,006	$132,537	$144,904
Operating expenses				
Nursing services	32,725	36,349	41,413	47,763
Other professional services..........	26,348	29,330	33,495	37,044
General services	13,903	15,484	17,692	19,571
Fiscal and administrative services	17,547	19,473	22,179	24,512
Provision for depreciation	3,824	4,124	5,668	5,750
Interest*	1,372	1,283	3,658	3,621
Amortization	13	40	40	40
Total Operating Expenses	$ 95,732	$106,083	$124,145	$136,301
Operating Income	$ 11,558	$ 12,923	$ 8,392	$ 8,603
Nonoperating income				
Unrestricted gifts and bequests	677	677	677	677
Unrestricted interest income	1,486	1,861	2,534	3,117
Income on funds held by trustee	0	0	168	168
Other nonoperating income	33	37	40	45
Total Nonoperating Income	$ 2,196	$ 2,575	$ 3,419	$ 4,007
Excess of Revenues over Expenses..	$ 13,754	$ 15,498	$ 11,811	$ 12,610

* Interest costs are includable along with other operating expenses as reimbursable items under the provisions of Medicare and Medicaid. Normally, 85 percent of these expenses are reimbursed under the Medicare-Medicaid plans.

Exhibit 2 *(continued)*

INTER CITY HEALTH CARE, INC.
Forecasted Balance Sheets
($000)

			Years Ending December 31	
Assets	1976	1977	1978	1979
Unrestricted Funds:				
Current Assets:				
Cash	$ 721	$ 1,977	$ 3,951	$ 7,256
Investment in time certificates				
of deposit	9,310	19,704	25,939	31,551
Patient accounts receivable	19,887	22,077	24,338	26,658
Less allowance for doubtful accounts	(2,386)	(2,649)	(2,921)	(3,199)
	$ 17,501	$ 19,428	$ 21,417	$ 23,459
Other receivables	2,210	2,453	2,704	2,962
Inventories	2,831	3,144	3,558	3,933
Prepaid expenses	196	217	254	279
Total Current Assets	$ 32,769	$ 46,923	$ 57,823	$ 69,440
Board Designated Assets:				
Investment in time certificates				
of deposit	16,487	19,393	24,383	29,425
Investment in securities	5,309	5,309	5,309	5,309
Total Board Designated Assets	$ 21,796	$ 24,702	$ 29,692	$ 34,734
Property, Plant and Equipment:				
Land	3,375	4,051	4,051	4,051
Land improvements	879	1,064	1,064	1,064
Buildings	53,377	72,285	72,285	72,285
Equipment	23,303	33,810	33,810	33,810
Renewals and replacements	4,302	6,884	9,134	11,679
	$ 85,236	$118,094	$120,344	$122,889
Less allowance for depreciation	(34,481)	(38,605)	(44,273)	(50,023)
	$ 50,755	$ 79,489	$ 76,071	$ 72,866
Construction in progress	16,060	1,007	1,007	1,007
Total Property, Plant and				
Equipment	$ 66,815	$ 80,496	$ 77,078	$ 73,873
Deferred charges	1,198	1,158	1,118	1,078
Funds held by trustee:				
Bond fund		704	704	
Debt service reserve fund*	4,800	2,718	2,718	2,718
Loan fund*	13,527			
Total Funds Held by Trustee	$ 18,327	$ 3,422	$ 3,422	$ 2,718
	$140,905	156,701	169,133	181,843

Exhibit 2 *(concluded)*

	Years Ending December 31			
Liabilities and Fund Balances	*1976*	*1977*	*1978*	*1979*
Unrestricted Funds:				
Current Liabilities:				
Accounts payable	$ 3,592	3,989	4,564	5,601
Accrued salaries, wages and related				
liabilities	2,319	2,566	2,913	3,215
Other accrued expenses	1,453	1,508	1,628	1,685
Current portion of long-term debt	401	421	756·	700
Total Current Liabilities	7,765	8,484	9,861	10,661
Long-term debt—Less portion due				
within one year†	51,382	50,961	50,205	49,505
Fund Balances:				
Retained for general purposes	59,962	72,554	79,375	86,943
Board designated funds	21,796	24,702	29,692	34,734
	81,758	97,256	109,067	121,677
Total Liabilities and				
Fund Balances	$140,905	$156,701	$169,133	$181,843

* This assumes that a 30-year tax-exempt issue has been used to finance the construction.
† This includes $30 million tax-exempt bond issue used to finance construction during 1976 and 1977.

THE FINANCING ALTERNATIVES

Parker felt that each of the financing alternatives had its problems, but that none of those problems seemed insurmountable. Both hospitals were profitable and were located within well-established communities. They could therefore anticipate healthy bond ratings, which, depending on the instrument, would result in either a low bond discount or an easy placement. Neither the feasibility study required for the revenue bonds nor the equity interest in the FHA mortgage presented a problem.

There was some question, however, about the validity of using revenue bond financing for hospitals. Despite feeling confident that each of the local communities would approve a tax-exempt issue if it was at all possible, Parker still wondered whether he could get similar approval from this board. At least one of its members felt that accepting government dollars was tantamount to accepting government control.

Whatever his choice, Frank knew that he would need some concrete analysis to back up his presentation to the board.

THE WICKES CORPORATION

On May 30, 1974, the Wickes Corporation, a large and rapidly growing supplier of building and shelter materials, announced a public exchange offer of new convertible debentures for an outstanding $40 million convertible debenture issue. Terms of the new offer called for an exchange of $675 principal of 9 percent convertible subordinated debentures due in 1999, for each $1,000 principal amount of the existing 5⅛ percent convertible subordinated debentures maturing in 1994.

COMPANY BACKGROUND

The Wickes Corporation started in 1854 as a small machine shop building gangsaws for Michigan sawmills. In 1951 Wickes opened its first building supply center and by 1974 the company was the largest retailer of lumber, plywood, and related building materials in the United States.

Over the past two decades the corporation had diversified into a number of other new activities. In 1974, Wickes classified its operations into three major groups: Shelter, Industrial and Agricultural, and Financial Services.

Shelter products

Shelter-related activities accounted for approximately 85 percent of total company sales revenues in 1974, with retail lumber representing roughly 50 percent of total divisional sales. In April 1974 the lumber division operated 263 building and home supply stores in 36 states and three foreign countries, offering a wide range of building materials, hardware items, and appliances to contractors and do-it-yourself householders. In addition the company whole-saled lumber and mill products such as sawdust, shavings, and wood scrap, throughout the United States.

Other shelter-related operations included retail furniture sales; manufacture and marketing of mobile homes and recreational vehicles, and the design and construction of commercial, industrial, and farm buildings. According to Wickes' president, the company had experienced problems in recreational vehicles and manufactured housing, and some of these operations were being shut down or transformed into more profitable ventures. The furniture divisions had also run into high start-up costs and initial market-entry problems, but the company's efforts in these areas began to show satisfactory results by mid-1973.

Industrial and agricultural

The industrial and agricultural divisions manufactured machine tools, agricultural equipment, and precision parts from powder metals, as well as processing and distributing agricultural products. Recently, the company had established a number of grain elevators and a network of farm supply stores. These operations, along with sales of farm building materials, contributed almost $200 million to company sales during 1972.

Financial services

Through the newly formed Financial Services Group, Wickes hoped to provide a number of financial services such as consumer installment contracts, dealer credit arrangements, leasing services, and insurance operations. Wickes aimed these efforts at a market comprised of 30,000 contractors, 10 million retail consumers, and 10,000–12,000 dealers. Operations would not, however, be restricted to these consumers of Wickes' traditional product lines. These companies are unconsolidated subsidiaries of the parent corporation.

Wickes achieved its diversified base of operations and leadership in the retail lumber industry through rapid growth in both sales and assets. From 1964 to 1974, total assets grew by 360 percent to $502 million, while consolidated sales increased 250 percent to $1,118 million. (Wickes' balance sheets and income statements for fiscal years 1970–74 are shown in Exhibits 1 and 2.)[1]

Exhibit 1

THE WICKES CORPORATION
Consolidated Balance Sheet—January 26, 1974
($000)

Assets		Liabilities and Equity	
Cash	$ 15,036	Notes payable—banks	$ 15,407
Notes and accounts receivable, net	92,102	Commercial paper	44,525
Advances to unconsolidated subsidiaries	7,729	Current portion—long-term debt	2,456
Inventories (lower of cost or market)	219,130	Accounts payable	58,640
Prepaid expenses	10,458	Dividends payable	2,423
		Income taxes payable	10,312
Total Current Assets	$344,455	Accrued expenses	36,456
		Total Current Liabilities	$170,219
Property, plant and equipment, at cost	$201,335	Long-term debt*	$120,827
Less: Reserves for depreciation	65,670	Deferred income taxes	16,286
Net property, plant & equipment	$135,665	Common stock:	
		Authorized: 25,000,000 shares	
Investments in unconsolidated subsidiaries	$ 9,695	Outstanding: 9,692,484 shares	24,231
		Other paid-in capital	60,361
Investments, deferred charges and other	12,411	Retained earnings	110,302
Total Assets	$502,226		
		Total Liabilities and Equity	$502,226

* Breakdown of long-term debt:

7⅞ percent sinking-fund debentures due May 1998	$ 59,841
6 percent debentures due June 1974 and subsequently	12,752
5¼ percent convertible subordinated debentures due May 1994	40,000
Notes payable to banks and other (various rates to 12.6%)	10,690
Total, including current portion	$123,283

Various covenants relating to debt agreements restrict cash dividends and prohibit the repurchase of common stock. A current ratio of not less than 2 to 1 and earnings before interest, income taxes and rents equal to not less than 2.1 times total rents and interest is required. In addition, the company had to maintain consolidated net tangible assets (total assets minus current liabilities and intangibles) greater than 250 percent of senior funded debt and 200 percent of total funded debt.

Wickes had tapped several sources of funds to finance increasing capital requirements during the past five years, including convertible and straight debentures as well as common stock. The company had also used sale and leaseback transactions to finance most of its new retail furniture facilities and some of its lumber supply centers. (Exhibit 3.)

---

[1] The company's fiscal year ends on the last Saturday in January.

Exhibit 2

THE WICKES CORPORATION
Consolidated Statements of Income*
(fiscal year ends last Saturday of January)

	1974	1973	1972	1971	1970
			($ millions)		
Net sales	$1,118.1	$884.1	$718.2	$587.0	$559.9
Cost of Sales	885.5	704.6	579.6	474.7	450.2
Gross Profit	$ 232.6	$179.5	$138.6	$112.3	$109.7
Selling and administration	$ 169.0	$134.2	$103.8	$ 90.2	$ 79.8
Rent expense	14.5	7.8	4.4		
Interest and debt expense	9.7	5.8	6.3	5.9	4.6
Income before Income Taxes	$ 39.4	$ 31.7	$ 24.1	$ 16.1	$ 25.3
Provision for income taxes	$ 19.1	$ 14.4	$ 11.3	$ 8.4	$ 13.6
Income before equity in net income of unconsolidated subsidiaries	$ 20.3	$ 17.3	$ 12.8	$ 7.7	$ 11.7
Equity in net income of un- consolidated subsidiaries	1.1	2.1	0.6	0.1	0.4
Net income	$ 21.4	$ 19.4	$ 13.4	$ 7.8	$ 12.1
Per common share data:					
Earnings	$2.20	$2.03	$1.62	$1.01	$1.62
Dividends	1.00	1.00	1.00	1.00	1.00

*Net sales and income originally reported for fiscal 1973 and prior years have been restated to reflect poolings of interest for companies acquired.

Exhibit 3
Consolidated statements of changes in financial position

	1974	1973	1972	1971	1970
Sources of Funds:					
Net income and deferred taxes	$ 25.5	$23.4	$ 15.2	$ 8.6	$12.0
Depreciation	14.6	11.5	8.9	7.5	6.2
Total from Operations	$ 40.1	$34.9	$ 24.1	$ 16.1	$18.2
Sale of 5⅛ percent convertible debentures	—	—	—	—	40.0
Sale of 7⅞ debentures	59.9	—	—	—	—
Stock issued for acquisitions	—	3.6	—	.2	5.1
Sale of common stock	—	—	55.7	—	—
Sale and leaseback	—	30.3	20.0	—	—
Sales of assets and other	5.1	3.0	3.6	3.8	1.9
	$105.1	$71.8	$103.4	$ 20.1	$65.2
Disposition of funds:					
Reduction in long-term debt	$ 1.5	—	$ 2.4	$ .8	$ 8.8
Dividends	11.0	$ 8.6	7.9	7.4	6.6
Property, plant and equipment	40.7	50.9	40.3	22.7	23.5
Other	4.1	10.4	3.0	1.5	3.0
	$ 57.3	$69.9	$ 53.6	$ 32.3	$41.9
Increase (decrease) in working capital	$ 47.8	$ 1.9	$ 49.8	$(12.3)	$23.4

FUTURE PLANNING

Management's expressed policy was one of continued strong growth. In a June 1973 address to the New York Society of Security Analysts, Wickes' president said:

> We plan to continue to maintain this posture about the growth of our company, and be very aggressive in that area . . . we're committed to a $2 billion sales goal, and earnings of $60 million after taxes, five years from now.

Such rapid growth, particularly in the retail lumber and furniture divisions had required a heavy commitment of funds to property, equipment, and working capital. Wickes had added 32 new lumber and furniture stores during fiscal 1974 alone, and planned to open 16 new stores during the coming year. The company had budgeted a total of $51 million for capital expenditures in fiscal 1975: $19 million for new outlets and approximately $32 million for construction and modernization of its distribution and manufacturing facilities.

Management anticipated that they would finance roughly $20 million of budgeted capital expenditures for 1975 through sale and leaseback arrangements. They expected to finance the balance of capital expenditures, as well as working capital needs, through internally generated funds, bank borrowings, the sale of senior debt securities, and a private placement of $20 million of preferred stock. A portion of the preferred stock and senior debt issues would be used to reduce short-term indebtedness.

THE HOUSING MARKET IN 1974

In 1973 Wickes' management had expressed little public concern over the condition of the housing market and they emphasized that any problems should be short-term. The executive vice president had stated that consumer spending for housing and durables had remained strong despite the negative nature of several economic indicators. In remarks to the New York Society of Security Analysts, he said, "All in all, we see a healthy level of activity for both 1973 and 1974. . . . We expect the short-term rates to peak late this year, and to ease in 1974 with little or no interruption of funds made available to housing markets."

By mid-1974, however, many manufacturers of housing materials faced problems due to the softness and uncertainty in the shelter market. The following excerpt from a *Standard & Poor's Industry Survey* summarizes the general outlook for the housing market.

The housing industry, which appeared poised for a rebound of significant proportions by mid-1974, now stands at a crossroads, with the possibility of continued slump on one hand and a much anticipated rebound on the other. The main determinant of the path the industry follows will be the degree and/or duration of restraint or ease followed by the federal monetary authorities.

Even before the recent monetary restraint, home building was under pressure from a number of factors, including high interest rates, reduced consumer confidence, lesser availability of mortgage credit, ramifications of the energy shortage, and an above-average inventory of unsold homes. Housing starts were at an average seasonally adjusted rate of 1,603,000 units in the first third of 1974 . . . off some 30 percent from the rate prevailing in the year-earlier period.[2]

WICKES' POSITION IN 1974

To date, Wickes had been reasonably successful in maintaining sales and profitability. Easily hurt by declining housing starts, the lumber division had switched its emphasis from contractor sales to consumer sales. While sales to the do-it-yourself homeowner had taken up some of the slack during the first quarter of fiscal 1975, there were definite signs of softening in this market. Results of operations for the first 13 weeks of fiscal 1975 indicated a decline in net income of 16 percent over the corresponding period for 1974. The company recorded lower aggregate sales and operating income in retail and wholesale lumber, forest products, and mobile homes and recreational vehicles. First quarter earnings were particularly hurt by soaring interest rates.

Because of the company's heavy reliance on the shelter market, Wickes' common stock price closely followed the market performance of building materials suppliers; the recent market price for Wickes' common was at its lowest price in ten years. The price had declined dramatically from its May 1969 level of approximately $47 to a closing price of $12⅛ on May 29, 1974.

The outstanding 5⅛ percent convertible debentures had been issued in May 1969 at par and were presently convertible into common stock, after adjustments for recent stock issues, at $53.06 per share or 18.85 shares per $1,000 principal amount. These debentures held a Ba rating from Moody's and had closed on the New York Stock Exchange at a price of $54¾ on May 29, 1974. The new debentures would initially be traded in the over-the-counter market. The company stated its intention to apply for listing of the new debentures on the New York and Pacific Stock Exchanges. Exhibit 4 provides past market price data for

---

[2] "Building—Current Analysis," *Standard & Poor's Industry Survey,* May 23, 1974.

Exhibit 4

Calendar periods	Market price data				
	Standard and Poor's closing price and yield indexes			Wickes Corporation	
	425 Industrials	Building materials composite	BBB corporate bonds*	5⅛ percent convertible debentures*	Common stock
1970	$100.9	$67.55	8.80%	5.75%	$36.00
1971	112.7	71.27	8.01	4.87	54.75
1972	131.9	61.79	7.92	7.25	26.25
1973:					
1st quarter	125.2	48.26	7.99	8.33	18.875
2d quarter	116.0	42.18	8.05	8.87	17.00
3d quarter	122.2	50.51	8.64	9.07	15.375
4th quarter	107.1	36.45	8.52	10.63	12.125
1974:					
1st quarter	105.1	45.16	8.66	9.27	15.75
2d quarter .... (to May 29)	98.1	37.77	8.82	10.84	12.125

* Yields to maturity based on closing sale or bid prices.

Wickes' common stock, their debentures, and for selected *Standard & Poor's* stock and bond price indexes.

THE EXCHANGE OFFER

In April 1974, Wickes filed a preliminary prospectus with the Securities and Exchange Commission for an exchange of straight debentures for the outstanding convertibles. However, this prospectus was with-

Exhibit 5

	Outstanding issue	Proposed offer
Coupon	5⅛%	9%
Maturity	May 1994	May 1999
Conversion price	$53.06	$25.00
Exchange ratio	—	$675 per $1,000
Market price (per $1,000 principal of outstanding issue)	$547.50	$580.50*
Yield to maturity	10.5%*	10.5%*
Call provision	103.75 percent of principal in 1974 and declining to maturity	109 percent of principal in 1974 and declining to maturity
Sinking-fund provision	$2 million annually, commencing in 1979 to retire 75 percent of the issue prior to maturity	6 percent of total principal annually, commencing in 1985 to retire 84 percent of the issue prior to maturity

* Based upon an estimate by *Standard & Poor's* of 86 bid for the new convertibles when issued.

drawn and the final public offering proposed a new convertible debenture, convertible into common at $25 per share, as the exchange vehicle. The terms of the exchange offering and the major features of the two convertible issues are described in Exhibit 5.

Wickes stated that the major purposes of the exchange offer were to decrease the company's outstanding indebtedness and to increase the possibility of conversion of long-term debt into equity, by offering a lower conversion price on the new convertibles. The company's projections of the effects of the exchange offer are shown in Exhibit 6.

Exhibit 6
Pro forma effects of the exchange offer
($000 except per share data)

	Actual January 26, 1974	Pro forma 50% exchange	Pro forma 100% exchange
Total long-term debt (less current maturities)*	$120,827	$111,897	$102,967
Reduction in book value of indebtedness		8,930	17,860
Interest and amortization of debt:			
Discount and expense†	9,683	10,009	10,320
Net gain on exchange offer‡	—	4,109	8,218
Per common share:			
Net gain on exchange offer	—	.42	.85
Effect of increased interest and amortization of debt discount and expense	—	(.01)	(.03)
Earnings	2.20	2.61	3.02

   * Assumes fair market value of new debentures to be 82 percent of their face value when issued; therefore, net book value would be the face value less the estimated discount.
   † Issue expenses are estimated to include $265,000 for printing, legal services, etc., and $8 per $1,000 principal of old debentures exchanged to the investment bankers.
   ‡ Reflects the gain recognized on the exchange offer and the increase in interest and amortization of debt discount and expense, less applicable income taxes.

The terms of similar exchange offers completed by selected other major firms are shown in Exhibit 7.

Exhibit 7
Exchange offers of new convertible subordinated debentures for outstanding convertible subordinated debentures

Effective date	Company/acquired issue	Exchange offer	Principal amount outstanding ($000)	Exchange data* Percent premium over market value of old debentures	Percent conversion premium	Results ($000)
August 8, 1973	Fibreboard Corporation 4¾ percent convertible subordinated debentures due 1993 ($31.25 conversion price).	Offers $750 principal amount of a 6¾ percent convertible subordinated debenture due 1998 (conversion price $17.25) for each $1,000 principal amount of old debentures.	$19,466	14	8	$15,960 (82%) received. Offer extended to March 1, 1974.
November 30, 1973 .	McCulloch Oil Corporation 5 percent convertible subordinated debentures due 1997 ($31.67 conversion price).	Offers $550 principal amount of a 10½ percent convertible subordinated debenture due 1999 (conversion price $10.00) for each $1,000 principal amount of old debentures.	$30,000	7	95	$20,500 (68%) as of January 6, 1974. Offer extended to January 22, 1974.
December 7, 1973 ...	Dillingham Corporation 5½ percent convertible subordinated debentures due 1994 ($32.00 conversion price).	Offers $625 principal amount of its 9¾ percent convertible subordinated debentures due 1999 (conversion price $13.00) for each $1,000 principal amount of old debentures.	$50,000	6	96	$30,000 (60%) as of January 18, 1974. Offer extended to January 28, 1974.

* Assuming new debentures trade at their face value.

Case 2-4

Moore McCormack Resources, Inc.

In June 1974, the management of Moore McCormack Resources, Inc. (Mooremack), received a stock repurchase proposal from City Investing Company (City). City owned 633,600 shares of Mooremack stock, a 27 percent interest, and was proposing that Mooremack repurchase this block at $25.50 per share. The shares were trading on the NYSE at $19.75.

Repurchase of shares was not an uncommon practice among U.S. companies. The currently depressed stock market had, in fact, sparked a dramatic increase in repurchase activity, with most of these repurchases being implemented through tender offers or previously announced open-market purchases. Nonetheless, management considered this stock repurchase a complex and important decision. Despite heavy pressure to accept the City repurchase proposal, management wanted fully to evaluate the implications before making recommendations to the board and to the shareholders for approval.

CITY'S DECISION TO SELL

The decision to sell the Mooremack block resulted from City's increasing emphasis on internal growth. During the 1967–69 period, City had grown dramatically through the acquisition process, and its investment in Mooremack stemmed from a merger agreement reached during that period but never implemented. During the 1970–73 period, City shifted emphasis to internal growth. City was currently reevaluating its operating units, and the decision was made to seek full ownership of those operations that strongly related to its long-term growth.

Although City's growth record had been impressive, earnings had come under increasing pressure and were expected to be, at best, flat for 1974. High interest rates and a depressed real estate industry resulted in deteriorating earnings in major segments of City's business. City's debt to capitalization ratio had reached an historic high—48.6 percent, up from 44.5 percent in 1972 and 39.0 percent in 1971—and money was very expensive. City's shares reflected these problems. The shares were at their lowest level in years, selling at only four times earnings. (See Exhibit 8 at end of case.)

THE GROWTH AND DEVELOPMENT OF MOOREMACK

Mooremack was incorporated in 1927 under the name of Moore-McCormack Lines, Inc. (Lines). Its principal business was cargo liner services, with routes to South America, South and East Africa, and the North Atlantic.

In 1965, under the leadership of William T. Moore, the company began a program of diversification into nonshipping areas through a series of acquisitions. To facilitate the diversification program, the company was recapitalized and Moore McCormack Co. was organized as a holding company with Lines its principal subsidiary. The name was later changed to Moore McCormack Resources to reflect the widening scope of the company's operations.

In 1966, Mooremack made its first acquisition, Wood Flong Corp., one of the three leading manufacturers of stereotype mats used in the newspaper industry. In 1967, in a second diversification move, the company formed a joint venture with Bolt, Beranek & Newman to research and explore opportunities in the promising field of oceanography.

1967 was a difficult year for Mooremack. Competition in the shipping business was intense, especially on the North Atlantic routes, resulting in a loss from operations. The company also had to make adjustments for having overallowed revenue subsidy accruals during past years. An unusual supplementary call by the company's insurance association also burdened the operations. The result was a loss from operations of $3.5 million before taxes compared with a $5.7 million profit before taxes in 1966.

Early in 1968, Mooremack was being sought by City and Texstar, two active conglomerates. City, with sales and earnings growing dramatically through the acquisition process, reached a merger agreement with Mooremack. Each share of Mooremack stock was to be exchanged for $24 of 5 percent convertible, subordinated debentures and $8 of City common stock. At that time, City cited the belief that Mooremack was becoming a new company by virtue of its commitment to containerization[1] as the keystone to new intermodal transportation systems.

Mr. Moore hailed the merger agreement as a constructive move in the Mooremack diversification plan and felt that the merger would provide the management and capital for the company to proceed with its fleet modernization program and oceanography venture. City acquired 400,000 shares of Mooremack at $30 a share prior to implementing the merger plan. This represented about 17 percent of the outstanding stock and gave City effective control of the company.[2]

Mooremack's financial performance during 1968 was even worse than its 1967 results. Further adjustments in revenue subsidy accruals were necessary. A prolonged longshoremen's strike, foreign port congestion, depressed rate structures, and an unprofitable venture into passenger liners resulted in a loss from operations of $7.8 million. Working capital became tight, and the dividend was slashed to 50 cents from $1 and eliminated in 1969. By November 1968, the stock price declined to the low $20s.

In January 1969, City withdrew from the merger plans. The reason given for the withdrawal was that City's outside accountants said Mooremack's financial condition at that time had run into a "material adverse change." In view of these circumstances and the size of their holdings, City could dispose of the stock only by incurring large losses that would materially affect City's reported earnings as well as reflect adversely on City's management and potentially impede their acquisition growth plans. (City carried the Mooremack investment at cost.)

Within a month after calling off the merger, City's top two executives, George T. Scharffenberger and A. Lightfoot Walker, joined the Mooremack board. Shortly thereafter, James Barker was called in as a consultant to help restore profitability to Mooremack and to redirect the company into growth areas.

---

[1] Containerization is the packing of all components into a giant, reusable box successively transportable by ship, truck, or train with the contents intact. Unitization is the combining of small components of a load into a single larger unit, usually by strapping on a platform. Both methods are designed to facilitate mechanized handling, thereby reducing costs and turnaround time.

[2] In November 1970 and August 1971, City increased its holdings by 227,400 and 6,200 shares, respectively, for an aggregate purchase price of $3,022,735, resulting in total holdings of 633,600 shares at an average price of $23.71 per share.

THE TURNAROUND PROGRAM

The two primary objectives recommended by Barker during the initial phases of the turnaround were consolidation of the fleet into a profitable operating base and restoration of the company's financial strength to allow expansion into areas offering new profit opportunities.

The first phase was essentially defensive. Operating losses had to be stopped. Operations were drastically reduced. Conversion to fully containerized vessels by both American and foreign liners serving the North Atlantic had increased capacity beyond demand and had sparked a vicious rate war. In response, Mooremack sold its four new roll on/ roll off containerized vessels and withdrew from the North Atlantic routes. Overage vessels were sold, the fleet of cargo ships was reduced from 37 to 18, and the number of sailings was reduced. Personnel reductions and other cost-cutting measures reduced overhead by 25 percent. Improved productivity of the fleet was achieved through unitization, a less costly, more basic system than containerization to simplify cargo handling. Important new foreign trade and ocean transport agreements among the U.S., Brazilian, and Argentine governments improved the company's competitive position, helping to establish market share and favorable rates. Management was also reorganized, and strong financial management talent was recruited to implement improved cost analysis and control systems. The Wood Flong Corp., and the oceanography venture were both sold at a modest profit.

As a result of these actions, Mooremack "took its bath" in 1970, reporting the largest deficit in its history—$12.4 million in operating losses and $4.7 million in extraordinary losses.

The second phase of the turnaround program focused on financial resources. Negotiation of new agreement with the Maritime Administration allowed the company to transfer $26 million from restricted funds to general funds. The two passenger liners that had been in layup were sold, converting $14 million to income-producing assets and eliminating a costly burden.

Mr. Barker, who had been elected to the Mooremack board in February 1971, became chairman, president and chief executive officer in April of that same year. In 1971 and 1972, he was able to report substantial progress on the turnaround program. Earnings from operations had made a swing from the heavy losses to $6.5 million in profits before taxes in 1972. More importantly, Mooremack was now ready to move into the third phase of the turnaround plan—growth into new areas. By the end of 1972, approximately $65 million in company funds

Exhibit 1

MOORE McCORMACK RESOURCES, INC.

Statements of Income, 1969–1973
($000 except per share data)

	1973	1972	1971	1970	1969
Results of Continuing Operations:					
Sales and revenue, net of subsidies*	$141,545	$56,933	$56,386	$63,874	$66,979
Costs and expenses	108,837	43,466	47,615	58,966	54,786
	$ 32,708	$13,467	$ 8,771	$ 4,908	$12,193
Loss from discontinued operations				5,405	125
	$ 32,708	$13,467	$ 8,771	$ (497)	$12,068
Administrative, general and selling expenses	17,741	9,088	8,233	11,702	11,329
Interest expense and preferred dividends	5,145	1,061	1,283	1,897	1,098
Interest income	5,414	3,219	2,769	1,187	780
Income (loss) before federal income taxes and extraordinary items	$ 15,736	$ 6,537	$ 2,024	($12,409)	$ 421
Federal income tax (provision) credit	(5,677)	(2,838)	300	—	—
Income (loss) before extraordinary items	$ 10,059	$ 3,699	$ 2,324	($12,409)	$ 421
Extraordinary Items	$ 834	$ 2,757	($210)	($4,685)	$ 594
Net Income (loss)	$ 10,893	$ 6,456	$ 2,114	$17,094	$ 1,015
Per Share Data:					
Income (loss) before extraordinary items	$ 4.21	$ 1.55	$ 0.97	($5.19)	$ 0.18
Extraordinary Items	0.35	1.15	(0.09)	(1.96)	0.25
Net Income (loss)	$ 4.56	$ 2.70	$ 0.88	$ 7.15	$ 0.43

* Under the provisions of the Merchant Marine Act, Mooremack receives federal revenue subsidies. The amount of these subsidies, after estimated recapture, for the last five years are, in $ millions:

1969	1970	1971	1972	1973
$12.58	$14.63	$9.36	$8.53	$11.15

These subsidies are not reported as revenues but are used to offset operating expenses. The company must make a determination each year of the expected subsidy for accrual purposes by comparing costs against estimated costs of the company's principal foreign flag competitors. The company must then await a final determination of subsidy from the Marine Subsidy Board. Without these final rates, subsidies can only be collected on an estimated basis.

were available for expansion purposes. (Exhibits 1, 2, and 3 contain financial data on Mooremack.)

INTERNAL LONG-RANGE GROWTH PROGRAMS

In 1972, Mooremack established Moore-McCormack Bulk Transport to create a significant role in this fast growing area of shipping. The

Exhibit 2
Historical earnings, stock price behavior

Year	Revenues	Net before taxes	Net income	EPS	Divs.	Price range	P/E ratio
1974					$0.20	20¾–12⅜	
1973	$141.5	$15.74	$10.06	$4.21	—	18⅜–10½	4–2
1972	56.9	6.54	3.70	1.55	—	19¾–12¼	13–8
1971	56.4	2.02	2.32	0.97	—	17⅜–12¼	18–13
1970	63.9	(12.41)	(12.41)	(5.19)	—	17½–6⅝	
1969	70.0	0.42	0.42	0.18	—	24⅛–12¼	134–68
1968	106.5	(7.78)	(3.97)	(1.66)	0.50	29⅞–20⅜	—
1967	96.8	(3.55)	(1.65)	(.69)	1.00	26¾–16⅛	
1966	105.4	5.69	3.77	1.58	0.90	31¼–15⅝	20–10
1965	81.3	0.73	0.83	0.35	0.60	18⅜–12½	53–36
1964	88.5	6.24	4.04	1.74	0.85	19–10¼	11–6

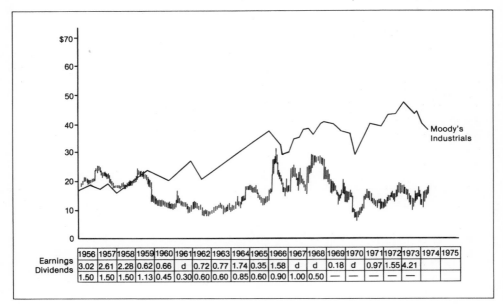

	1956	1957	1958	1959	1960	1961	1962	1963	1964	1965	1966	1967	1968	1969	1970	1971	1972	1973	1974	1975
Earnings	3.02	2.61	2.28	0.62	0.66	d	0.72	0.77	1.74	0.35	1.58	d	d	0.18	d	0.97	1.55	4.21		
Dividends	1.50	1.50	1.50	1.13	0.45	0.30	0.60	0.60	0.85	0.60	0.90	1.00	0.50	—	—	—	—	—		

company contracted to purchase three tankers at a net cost of approximately $45 million, a move generally consistent with the company's long-term program of expanding the use of its transportation capabilities into energy-related activities. Each of these vessels was chartered for a seven-year period to Shell Oil Co., upon delivery in 1975, 1976, and 1977.

Also in 1972, Mooremack organized Moore McCormack Energy to seek opportunities to utilize its transportation and logistic capabilities

Exhibit 3

MOORE McCORMACK RESOURCES, INC.

Consolidated Balance Sheets
December 31, 1973 and 1972
($000)

Assets	1973	1972
Current Assets:		
Cash	$ 5,241	$ 1,904
Preferred stock redemption fund	10,000	—
Mortgage notes receivable	—	4,748
Marketable securities	31,183	23,125
Trade receivables	22,963	7,758
Operating-differential subsidy receivable	5,842	5,104
Inventories	4,748	—
Other current assets	2,066	549
	$ 82,043	$ 43,188
Less: Estimated deposits to Capital Construction Fund	$ 6,619	5,768
	$ 75,424	$ 37,420
Capital Construction Fund:		
Cash, U.S. Government Security Mortgage Notes	$ 16,813	16,927
Estimated deposits to be made	6,619	5,768
	$ 23,432	$ 22,695

Liabilities and Stockholders' Equity	1973	1972
Current Liabilities:		
Current maturity of long-term debt	$ 287	$ 287
Preferred stock redemption current portion	$ 10,000	—
Accounts payable—trade	16,991	1,093
Accrued liabilities	13,232	9,552
Federal income taxes payable	3,535	1,118
	$ 44,045	$ 12,050
Net Unterminated Voyage Revenue	$ 5,652	$ 2,770
Long-term debt	$ 574	$ 860
Payable from Capital Construction Fund:		
8½ percent secured note, due in 1974†	$ 30,000	—
5.75 percent U.S. government-insured bonds	16,518	$ 17,728
	$ 46,518	$ 17,728
Deferred federal income taxes	$ 3,281	$ 1,247
Reserves for claims, etc.	$ 12,527	$ 11,996
Preferred stock of subsidiary	$ 20,000	

Capital Assets:

	1973	1972
Vessels, less accumulated depreciation of $30,656 in 1973 and $26,254 in 1972	88,260	54,912
Other property and equipment	4,603	778
Mineral and other lands	2,878	—
	$ 95,741	$ 55,690
Investments:		
Investments in subsidiaries and corporate joint ventures	7,853	$ 1,218
Preferred Stock Redemption Fund*	$ 25,308	
Mortgage Notes Receivable	—	$ 20,646
Other Assets	$ 7,932	$ 1,191
	$235,690	$138,860

Stockholders' Equity:

	1973	1972
Common stock, par $5.00	$ 12,166	$ 12,166
Capital surplus	22,165	22,165
Retained earnings	69,500	58,607
	$103,831	$ 92,938
Less: Treasury stock at cost		
41,800 shares	738	738
	$103,093	$ 92,200
	$235,690	$138,860

* The senior preferred shares issued in the PM acquisition are callable in three equal installments January 1974, 1975, and 1976. To provide for the retirement of these preferred shares, the company established a redemption fund with $10 million cash and $15.3 million mortgage notes receivable on vessels sold.
† This note was repaid in 1974, by withdrawing $10 million from the CCF and borrowing $20 million repayable from CCF over eight years with interest at 0.75 percent above the prime.

in developing projects aimed at meeting the long-range energy requirements of major consumers. Although still in the process of growing
into a fully operational subsidiary, managment felt the potential was
good. Given the strategic importance of energy and, in particular, of
liquid hydrocarbon, Moore McCormack Energy planned to undertake
the responsibility for analyzing and conducting a companywide energy
acquisition program. In each project, the objective was to retain some
participation in the equity of the nonshipping portion while at the same
time contributing a significant portion of the transportation required.

PICKANDS MATHER (PM) ACQUISITION

During the period 1966 to 1968, Mr. Barker had worked as a planning
executive with Pickands Mather, a major natural resource logistics company. At the initiative of Mr. Barker, Mooremack acquired PM in April
1973. The terms included $6 million cash, $30 million in notes, and
$30 million senior preferred shares. PM's principal activities were the
management of iron ore and coal properties and related transportation
and the manufacture and sale of foundry coke, limestone and quarry
products. The company supervised the mining of the iron ore and coal
and managed the construction and operation of concentration and pelletizing plants to produce high-grade iron ore pellets (Exhibit 4). Compen-
sation was primarily in the form of commissions based on the number
of tons shipped.

The company had a number of promising projects in the development
stage, including a new pelletizing complex in Minnesota, mineral exploration programs in North America and overseas, and three new underground coal mines in Kentucky.

Exhibit 5 gives a breakdown of the sales and operating earnings of
the major segments of PM's business and of their relative importance
in Mooremack's business mix.

TURNAROUND ACCOMPLISHED

By mid-1974, management could conclude that their turnaround program had been successful. The shipping operations had been streamlined
and were profitable. Through the PM acquisition, the company had
achieved a good stake in natural resources and energy, areas with attractive potential. The management team had been strengthened, and the
financial position of the company had been improved. Revenues had
doubled since 1970, and profits were $10.9 million in 1973, contrasted

Exhibit 4
Pickands Mather—Iron and coal properties

Managed iron ore properties

	Owners	PM owner-ship interest (percent)	Estimated life, years*	Annual pellet production capacity in tons† (000s)
Erie Mining Company, Minnesota	Bethlehem Steel Corporation; Youngstown Sheet and Tube Company; Interlake, Inc.; The Steel Company of Canada, Limited.	—	44	10,300
Wabush Mines, Newfoundland and Quebec, Canada	The Steel Company of Canada, Limited; Dominion Foundries and Steel, Limited; Youngstown Sheet and Tube Company; Inland Steel Company; Interlake, Inc.; Wheeling-Pittsburgh Steel Corporation; Finsider (Italy); Pickands Mather & Co.	5.2%	64	6,000
Savage River Mines, Tasmania, Australia	Mitsubishi Corporation; Pickands Mather & Co. International; Sumitomo Shoji Kaisha, Ltd.; Cerro Corporation; Chemical International Finance, Ltd.; seven Australian firms	24	13	2,500
The Hilton Mines, Quebec, Canada	The Steel Company of Canada, Limited; Jones & Laughlin Steel Corporation; Pickands Mather & Co.	25	2	900
The Griffith Mine, Ontario, Canada	The Steel Company of Canada, Limited	—	30	1,500

* Based on the production capacities listed and upon known reserves.
† Dry long tons (2,240 pounds).

Managed coal properties

	Owners	PM owner-ship interest	Estimated life, years*	Annual production capacity in net tons (000s)
Chisholm Mine, Kentucky	The Steel Company of Canada, Limited	—	34	1,000
Madison Mine, West Virginia	The Steel Company of Canada, Limited	—	19	750
Beckley Mine, West Virginia	Jones & Laughlin Steel Corporation; Hoogovens IJmuiden B. V.; The Steel Company of Canada, Limited; Pickands Mather & Co.	12½%	27	1,500

* Based on the production capacities listed and known reserves.

Exhibit 5
Sales and income by major lines of business—1973

		Amount	Percentage
Sales and revenues:			
Cargo liner services		$ 69,668,000	49.2%
Management of properties and related transportation:			
Bulk transportation	$22,873,000		
Management of properties	7,984,000	30,857,000	21.8
Sales of products:			
Coal	$16,928,000		
Coke	9,341,000		
Iron ore	7,816,000		
Limestone	6,935,000	41,020,000	29.0
		$141,545,000	100.0%
Income before federal income tax and extraordinary items:			
Cargo liner services		$ 6,442,000	39.5%
Management of properties and related transportation		6,912,000	42.4
Sales of products		2,941,000	18.1
		$ 16,295,000	100.0%
Less: Corporate administrative expenses, net interest income, etc.		(559,000)	
		$ 15,736,000	

with a $17.1 million loss in 1970. For the 12 months ended June 30, 1974, profits had further improved to $16.4 million, or $6.88 per share.

Although the short-term outlook was characterized by uncertainty brought about by the energy crisis and inflation, the long-term future appeared bright. The demand for shipping was holding firm with reasonably good prospects. The market conditions for PM's business were also favorable. More importantly, Mooremack management was only now starting to implement the third phase of the turnaround program— growth into profitable areas, particularly natural resources and energy.

CAPITAL REQUIREMENTS FOR FIVE-YEAR GROWTH PLAN

Management estimated that over the next four- to five-year period, Mooremack would require $200 million new capital for its investment and growth plans. Only about 5 percent would go into the cargo liner vessels, 40 percent into the mining and manufacturing activities, and 55 percent into the bulk transport business.

Cargo liners. Mooremack had streamlined its liner fleet and now had it on a relatively profitable basis. The short-term outlook was favorable. However, the long-term outlook for unitized and containerized shipping held prospects of very small growth, perhaps in the 2–3 percent range. Bulk shipping was the more rapid growth area of the shipping business. Accordingly, major capital expenditures in the cargo liner area were not contemplated in the intermediate term.

Bulk transport. Mooremack had made a definite commitment to this area of the transportation industry. It purchased three 38,000 ton tankers for a total of $45 million for delivery in 1975, 1976, and 1977. Under certain federal programs, a company could receive government guaranteed loans for up to 75–85 percent of the cost of these vessels. Management, however, hoped to completely eliminate equity requirements by financing these tankers through leveraged leases.

Mooremack also had contracted to purchase two bulk vessels for use on the Great Lakes. The first was scheduled for delivery in 1976 with a maximum cost of $35.4 million. The second was scheduled for delivery in 1977 with a maximum cost of $37.1 million.

Mining, manufacturing and energy. Capital requirements in these areas were more difficult to estimate precisely. This was particularly true of the energy area, an activity still in its formative stage. Mooremack had adopted a policy of seeking an equity interest in future iron ore, coal, and energy projects, in addition to its traditional management role. This policy was likely to require substantial capital investment by the company.

As a participant in the new iron ore mining and pelletizing complex under construction in Minnesota, PM was committed to furnish approximately $30 million for construction and development costs. PM had other commitments to pay its ownership share of operating and financing costs in connection with its investments in major Australian and Canadian iron ore mining ventures and a domestic coal mining venture.

The long-term outlook for this segment of the business was good. World steel production was expected to grow at 4 percent per year through 1980. In the United States, this meant the required addition of some 25 million net tons of capacity over the next six years, and a proportionate increase in the need for ore and coal. Likewise, the coal industry was undergoing a rejuvenation. In the wake of the Arab oil embargo, coal had suddenly come back in demand, and Washington had given coal a starring role in lessening what energy czar William Simon called the U.S. vulnerability to "economic and political blackmail." The gas and oil industries were eyeing the country's huge coal deposits as feedstocks for making synthetic fuel. Utilities were beginning to burn more coal. It was generally proclaimed that during the next ten years the United States would need to double or triple coal production. Given the size of the energy gap and the local opposition and tough reclamation laws that apply to strip mining, underground coal mining, PM's specialty, seemed destined to be an essential and growing part of American economic life.

CAPITALIZATION POLICY AND GOALS

Mooremack management contemplated that from 80 to 85 percent of the $200 million needed through 1978 (excluding funds required for stock repurchase) would be financed by debt or its equivalent. Management expected that most of the projects would be based on medium- to long-term contractual obligations of major companies, creating a predictable revenue base that could support a high level of debt. In their 1973 Annual Report, management stated performance objectives and capitalization goals as follows: "On the total aggregate $200 million investment, Mooremack has an aftertax target rate of return, before financing charges, of approximately 10 percent. The incremental aftertax cost of the new capital is estimated at 6 percent. This would result in an aftertax return on total new capital employed of approximately 4 percent, with the return considerably higher on stockholders' equity alone. Realization of these objectives over the next several years would, therefore, result in a substantial increase to the annual earnings base of Mooremack. Such an achievement would serve as ample justification for a change in the company's debt-to-capitalization ratio, moving from a current 39 percent (1973) to the range of approximately 50–55 percent. Although the company has not yet defined an ideal target mix of debt and equity in its capital structure, management feels that continued involvement in projects of the quality under current development, requiring heavy capital investment, warrants a prospective debt ratio of 50 percent or more."

EARNINGS OUTLOOK

Although Mooremack's earnings had experienced dramatic upward shifts over the 1970–73 period, the outlook for future earnings indicated a changing pattern. In their 1973 Annual Report, management made the following statement regarding the earnings outlook:

At the outset, it is clear that the dramatic rate of increase in earnings will not be sustained as the special circumstances which produced the dramatic 1970–73 turn-around are not likely to occur in the next few years. Likewise, it is clear that anticipation of an earnings growth rate of 15 to 20 percent every year would be unrealistic. Hence, the earnings pattern now must be viewed as being more closely influenced by the course of the economy and by the particular variable factors which directly affect the demand for Mooremack services. Certainly a major variable in the 1974 outlook is the current energy crisis. During 1975, the company's earnings will begin to evolve into a different pattern which will become more evident in 1976 and the years ahead. As each of the capital projects previously discussed comes on stream, it will generate a new package of earnings that will overlay profits which will continue to be generated by the company's present basic activities. Earnings from the new projects will cushion effects of inevitable periodic fluctuations in basic Mooremack activities and will gradually help raise the annual earning power of the company. Consequently, Mooremack can look for an overall growth rate of 15 percent over a five-year period.

This changing pattern of earnings, however, would necessarily be influenced substantially by the basically cyclical nature of the company's activities—activities that were heavily influenced by the general level of national and world economic activity. In addition, especially in the shipping area, the company was exposed to the periodic imbalances between demand and capacity brought about by fluctuating levels of investment. Periods of overcapacity were not uncommon. At the current time, for example, most shipping industry observers believed that there were too many supertankers on order to accommodate demand for the next few years, although they disagreed over the severity of this oversupply. The same pattern applies to the other areas of shipping and impacts both on profitable utilization of capacity and on the level of longer term charter rates.

Currently, the company was enjoying very strong market conditions in all of its major segments of business. At the same time, the course of the United States and world economy for the period ahead was a major concern. It did appear, however, that earnings would continue strong for at least another year due to the current momentum of the company's business.

CAPITAL CONSTRUCTION FUND (CCF) AND TAXATION

Under the 1970 Merchant Marine Act, operators of U.S. flag vessels engaged in domestic or foreign commerce may deposit, tax free, an amount of cash equal to vessel operating earnings into a CCF. Such funds may later be withdrawn without immediate tax liability if they are committed to the acquisition of vessels to be used in the Great Lakes or foreign trade, or to the retirement of debt incurred in acquiring

Exhibit 6
Sources and uses of funds: 1971–73 actual; 1974–78 estimated ($000)

	1971	1972	1973	Pro forma‡				
				1974	1975	1976	1977	1978
Funds Provided:*								
Income†	$ 2,324	$ 3,699	$10,059	$14,000	$15,100	$16,300	$17,600	$19,300
Add: Depreciation and amortization	2,164	2,225	5,206	5,000	6,200	8,200	10,200	11,500
Increase in deferred taxes	—	2,020	2,868	2,000	2,000	2,000	2,000	2,000
Net increase in reserve for claims	2,624	1,758	531	1,000	—	—	—	—
Equity in undistributed earnings	—	—	(409)	(1,600)	(1,730)	(1,870)	(2,000)	(2,180)
Total from Operations	$ 7,112	$ 9,702	$18,255	$20,400	$21,570	$24,630	$27,800	$30,620
Borrowings	—	—	30,000	480	22,990	45,230	46,460	—
Preferred stock of subsidiary, less current portion $10,000	(2,303)	—	20,000	—	—	—	—	—
Other	—	1,760	4,824	—	—	—	—	—
Total from Operations	$ 4,809	11,462	73,079	20,880	44,560	69,860	74,260	30,620
Funds Used:								
Additions to capital assets	—	216	1,533	14,500	34,500	70,000	67,000	15,000
Purchase of PM, less current assets of 10,754	—	—	57,196	—	—	—	—	—
Increase (average) preferred stock redemption fund	—	—	6,108	(10,000)	(10,000)	(5,300)	—	—
Redemption of preferred stock	—	—	—	10,000	10,000	—	—	—
Reduce long-term debt	2,768	10,114	1,496	3,320	3,400	3,500	3,600	4,960
Net increase (decrease) CCF	(10,033)	(13,499)	737	(2,800)	1,400	(4,100)	(2,600)	4,100
Increase (decrease) working capital	12,074	14,631	6,009	4,900	4,300	4,800	5,300	5,600
Dividends	—	—	—	960	960	960	960	960
Total Used	$ 4,809	$11,462	$73,079	$20,880	$44,560	$69,860	$74,260	$30,620

* Funds flow statement based on operations before repurchase on stock.
† Assume 40 percent growth in 1974, average 15 percent compound over five-year period. Effective tax rate all years of 30 percent.
‡ Casewriter's estimates.

such ships. This tax benefit reflects a national policy to encourage construction and operation of U.S. flag vessels, including bulk carriers of natural resources. Mooremack must deposit annually in the CCF *(a)* earnings from the investment and reinvestment of amounts held in the CCF and *(b)* unless exempted by the secretary of commerce, net proceeds from the sale or other disposition of any vessel subject to the agreement. The company may also deposit additional amounts in the CCF, but not in excess of the sum of *(a)* 100 percent of the taxable income of vessels or 100 percent of consolidated income, whichever is less, and *(b)* the depreciation allowable for federal income tax purposes. The depreciable cost basis of any vessels acquired with CCF funds must, however, be lowered by the amount of such funds used.

The company deposited in the CCF taxable income of $7.9 million in 1973, of which $1.1 million was a mandatory deposit of earnings from investments. Management estimated that the company's utilization of the CCF would result in an effective tax rate of approximately 30 percent for at least 1974 and 1975.

Exhibit 6 consolidates these data on projected capital requirements, earnings outlook, capitalization policy, and tax savings through use of the CCF into a five-year pro forma sources and uses of funds statement.

FINANCING THE STOCK REPURCHASE

If Mooremack repurchased the City block, it would pay $8 million of the purchase price from the proceeds of a bank loan and the balance from current cash. The company had obtained a commitment from the Chase Manhattan Bank for an unsecured loan of $8 million to be repaid ratably over a five-year period at an interest rate of three fourths of 1 percent over prime and which required maintenance of 20 percent compensating balances. The current prime rate was 12 percent, and the effective interest cost would be 15.93 percent. Additionally, the loan would restrict cash dividends to the remaining stockholders to $956,000 a year without consent of the bank. This would restrict any increase in the cash dividend from the present rate of $0.40 per year to $0.54 per year.

IMPACT ON EARNINGS PER SHARE

Management's analysis showed that earnings per share would be increased significantly if the City block were repurchased, and this was an important point to include in any proxy statement to the remaining

Exhibit 7
Capitalization data and debt service ratios*

				Pro forma				
	1971	1972	1973	1974	1975	1976	1977	1978
Debt as percent of capitalization:								
Assuming nonrepurchase	26	17	39	36	39	46	51	48
Assuming repurchase	26	17	39	45	48	53	57	54
Debt service ($ millions):								
Assuming nonrepurchase	4.0	4.1	8.1	9.9	10.8	14.0	18.3	21.6
Assuming repurchase	4.0	4.1	8.1	10.7	13.6	16.8	21.3	24.7
Debt coverage ratios:								
Cash flow before taxes and debt service/debt service:								
Assuming nonrepurchase	2.2	2.8	3.2	3.1	3.1	2.9	2.6	2.5
Assuming repurchase	2.2	2.8	3.2	2.9	2.4	2.4	2.2	2.2
Cash flow after current taxes, before debt service/debt service:								
Assuming nonrepurchase	2.1	2.6	2.9	2.7	2.7	2.5	2.3	2.2
Assuming repurchase	2.1	2.6	2.9	2.5	2.2	2.1	2.0	1.9

* Based on the funds flow statement in Exhibit 6. It is assumed that the company proceeds with its regular investment program and in addition borrows $16.2 million to repurchase the shares, at an aftertax cost of 6 percent, or $1 million, which amount is deducted from the earnings each year and added to the net new debt. Interest costs are assumed to be 10 percent of average debt outstanding.

shareholders. Assuming the block had been purchased as of June 30, 1973, plus the capitalized cost of the purchase, estimated at $600,000, using funds having an effective cost to the company of 7 percent (13.5 percent, net of 48 percent tax benefit), the earnings per share would have improved 26 percent for the 12-month period ending June 30, 1974.

	12 months ended June 30, 1974	
	Historical	Pro forma
	($000)	
Income before extraordinary items	$15,893	$14,720
Extraordinary items	555	555
Net income:	$16,448	$15,275
Income before extraordinary items	$ 6.65	$ 8.37
Extraordinary items	0.23	0.32
Net income	$ 6.88	$ 8.69
Number of shares outstanding	2,391,354	1,757,755

This improvement in earnings per share would be a potentially favorable influence on share value. Mooremack stock, based on the latest 12

Exhibit 8
City Investing Company—Historical earnings and stock price data

Year Dec. 31	Income from				Net operating earnings	Per share*	Dividend per share	Price range	Price earnings ratio	
	Housing and manufacturing	Insurance and finance	Equity in affiliates	Total					High	Low
1974	—	—	—	—	—	—	.31½†	14–8½	7	4
1973	70.97	79.06	9.89	159.9	68.2	2.28	.57	16–8¼	11	7
1972	43.81	75.31	15.63	134.8	62.2	1.98	.52	22⅝–13½	15	9
1971	36.98	59.03	12.35	108.4	48.7	1.98	.50	25⅜–14⅝	20	7
1970	32.18	—	76.47	75.8	47.2	1.44	.45	28¼–10½	27	16
1969	34.42	—	68.34	74.1	44.8	2.35	.29	35⅜–21⅛	38	18
1968	53.03	—	42.97	80.9	30.4	1.97	.14½	39¼–18	48	18
1967	14.47	—	6.30	14.5	5.2	1.07	.12½	27⅞–10¼	18	9
1966	13.90	—	—	11.7	6.7	.59	.11½	12¼–6	18	9
1965	5.81	—	—	4.2	2.4	.19	.11	7⅜–2⅜	29	19
1964	2.49	—	—	1.4	1.0	.17	10½	5⅝–4⅛	36	26

* Includes capital gains and net operating earnings.
† Six months.

months' earnings, was selling at about three times earnings. At the same time, general stock market indexes were also depressed, reflecting the prevailing economic gloom, persistent high rates of interest and inflation, and the uncertainty of the duration of these serious investment factors. Exhibit 2 charts Mooremack stock price movements.

STOCK OWNERSHIP FACTORS

City's 633,600 share position was, by a substantial margin, the largest block of stock controlled by one shareholder. Institutional ownership was estimated at only 198,400 shares held by seven institutions, and Mooremack had almost 4,000 stockholders. Stock ownership by management was not substantial, the top officers owning only 57,099 shares as a group. However, Mooremack had a Share Unit Plan under which units were granted to certain key management personnel. Under this plan, a participant becomes entitled to payment of vested units in cash or stock equal to the excess of the market price of the Mooremack stock on the valuation date or upon termination of employment, whichever is earlier, over the market price on the date of grant. One fifth of such units become vested in each year over the five-year period following the date of grant.

BOARD OF DIRECTORS MEETING

It was against this background that management had to evaluate the wide range of factors raised by the City offer. Management faced the decision of what recommendations to make at the specially called Mooremack board meeting and, subsequently, the recommendation to be made to its stockholders.

Case 2-5

American Airlines (A)

In January 1977, Thomas G. Plaskett, senior vice president of finance, was considering what proposal he would make to the board of directors for American Airlines' financing program in the late 70s and early 80s. American had projected their capital investment requirements for aircraft, related equipment and modifications, and ground properties to be over $800 million between 1976 and 1982. $492.5 million had been authorized for 1977 and 1978 of which $200–$250 million would have to come from external sources. Although the immediate decision was focused on 1977–78 financing needs, Mr. Plaskett knew that the impact of this decision on future financing opportunities had to be considered.

Mr. Plaskett had received a variety of financing proposals from several investment bankers. He had narrowed it down to the issuance of a combination of either convertible debentures or preferred stock with warrants and equipment trust certificates (see American Airlines (B), Case 2–6). Mr. Plaskett believed that the equipment trust certificates could be issued with a 16-year maturity at an 8.5–9 percent rate. However, he had also been intrigued by a 16-year lease proposal by one investment banking group (see Exhibit 1) and wanted first to determine if leases were more attractive than the equipment trust certificates, as the investment bankers appeared to believe. If so, he would then want to include leasing as an option in his evaluation of the proposals for financing American Airlines' full funds requirement for 1977–78.

THE COMPANY

American is one of the largest U.S. airlines, serving 49 cities in 24 states and the District of Columbia, as well as points in Canada, Mexico,

---

EQUIPMENT LEASING, INC.
Rockefeller Plaza
New York, New York

October 29, 1976

LEASE PROPOSAL AND ANALYSIS

LESSEE: American Airlines, Inc.
EQUIPMENT: Five Boeing 727/200 Transport Aircraft

The following is a comparative analysis prepared for American Airlines, Inc. ("American") of purchasing versus leasing five (5) Boeing 727/200 transport aircraft costing approximately $50 million manufactured by the Boeing Aircraft Company ("Boeing") for operation by American. The analysis is based on a delivery of these aircraft during the first six months of 1977.

This lease versus purchase analysis is based on an estimated aftertax cost of capital for American. It does not attempt to determine this cost of capital, but rather to indicate what cost of capital would make the lease proposal financially attractive to American. The method utilized in determining this break-even cost of capital is based on the present value of the aftertax cash flow of the direct purchase as compared with that of the lease proposal.

The following are the basic assumptions used in analyzing the direct purchase and lease proposal:

Direct purchase assumptions

The direct purchase assumes that the aircraft will be purchased on delivery for cash either borrowed or generated internally by American. The purchase price, at the option of American, may include any interest expenses related to financing the progress payments required under the purchase contract; the cost of customer furnished equipment, and any other direct expenses which normally would be allocated to the aircraft in determining its depreciation basis. In order to make the purchase comparable to the lease, it has been assumed that the aircraft will be sold at the end of 16 years (the term of the lease) for 25 percent of its original cost. It is also assumed that these aircraft are eligible for depreciation under the old ADR Asset Guideline Class 00.21 over a seven-year period to a zero net salvage value. It has further been assumed that the half-year convention will be elected for 1977 which provides for six months of depreciation during that year and that the initial depreciation will be double-declining balance switching to sum-of-the-years'-digits in 1979. The analysis is made on essentially two assumptions regarding American's ability to utilize the tax attributes of the transaction.

The first assumption is that all depreciation deductions are recognized currently (Schedule I, pages 1 and 2) and the second assumption is that depreciation deductions for the tax years ending December 31, 1977 and 1978 are deferred until 1979 and the remaining years of depreciation are recognized on a current basis. The reason for

Exhibit 1 *(continued)*

the two depreciation schedules is the fact that we have been advised that perhaps American may not be able to utilize fully for tax purposes the depreciation produced by these aircraft on a current basis.

We have also been advised that American may not be able to utilize the Investment Tax Credit (ITC) until the taxable year ending December 31, 1983 despite the liberalized provision of the Tax Reform Act of 1976. Both analyses reflect this deferral of the ITC.

Finally, inasmuch as American will not own the aircraft at the end of the lease period but will have only an option to continue to lease it at the then independently appraised fair rental value, both analyses include in the purchase assumptions the realization by American of 25 percent of the original cost from the sale of the aircraft at the end of 16 years. In 1977, the basic 727/200 aircraft will be in the 10th year of its production by Boeing and although many modifications and improvements have been made, it would appear that 25 percent is a reasonable residual expectation in 1993 when the basic aircraft will have been 26 years in production. In fact, to obtain the Advance Ruling from the Internal Revenue Service, which will be required in the case of the lease, it may be somewhat difficult to obtain an independent estimate to substantiate this 25 percent residual value.

On the other hand, since future technology is always difficult to forecast, we have included in the comparative analysis theoretical residual values up to 50 percent of original cost.

Lease assumptions

The lease rental payments are equivalent to 2.3192 percent of total original cost payable quarterly in arrears and are equivalent to a simple interest rate which repays the original cost of the aircraft at 5.25 percent per annum. The rents are not expensed for tax purposes in the analysis based on the deferral of the depreciation for the same reason that depreciation is not claimed for tax purposes under the comparable direct purchase.

Break-even rate

The first step in the analysis is to establish a break-even cost of capital as between a direct purchase and lease of the aircraft using both depreciation assumptions. This break-even rate is calculated by discounting the difference between the aftertax cash flow of a direct purchase and of the lease proposal in order to determine the rate at which this difference, when discounted, will equal zero.

Pages 2 and 3 of Schedule I show the aftertax cash flows of the direct purchase, the lease proposal and the difference between the two based on the two depreciation assumptions. The break-even cost of capital, thus, determined for current depreciation, is 6.52 percent. The break-even cost of capital determined for deferred depreciation is 6.35 percent.

Therefore, if the aircraft are indeed worth 25 percent of their original cost at the end of the 16-year lease period, then the aftertax cost of capital to American must

Exhibit 1 *(continued)*

be less than 6.52 percent based on current depreciation and 6.35 percent based on deferred depreciation if the direct purchase is to be less expensive than the lease.

Summary

Page 1 of Schedule I summarizes the break-even cost of capital based on residual sale proceeds from zero to 50 percent. It is, of course, reasonable to assume that the aircraft might be worth some amount other than 25 percent used in the analyses. For the residual values for the aircraft as shown on page 1 of Schedule I, the break-even cost of capital varies accordingly. It is impossible for any outsider to come up with a specific cost of capital for American without access to substantially more information than we have at our disposal. Therefore, the following is an effort to show the relative savings in terms of dollars for leasing these aircraft as opposed to purchasing them, assuming that American's cost of capital is somewhere between the break-even cost and the 10 percent estimate shown in the following table. It is difficult, however, to see how this can be determined as anything but an ultraconservative estimate in the case of American, and even on that basis, the savings would be significant.

Comparative savings
(purchase versus lease;
5 Boeing 727/200 aircraft;
total cost $50 million)

	Aftertax cost of capital (000s)			
	Current depreciation		*Deferred depreciation*	
Residual value	6.52%*	10%	6.35%*	10%
15	$275	$4,387	$275	$4,733
20	137	4,246	137	4,591
25	—	4,104	—	4,450
50	—	3,397	—	3,742

* Break-even cost of capital using an estimated residual value equal to 25 percent of cost.

Conclusion

In view of the fact that American has indicated that it cannot utilize the ITC even under the liberalized provision of the Tax Reform Act of 1976 until 1983 and may indeed have to defer some of the benefits of depreciation generated by the purchase of these five aircraft, the savings of the lease transaction are substantial even based on ultraconservative cost of capital and could easily be as much as $5 million for the five aircraft. The results of this study clearly demonstrate that the lease alternative to purchase should be considered seriously by American.

Exhibit 1 *(continued)*

EQUIPMENT LEASING, INC.
Purchase versus lease analysis
Boeing 727/200 transport aircraft

Break-even cost of capital

Sale proceeds	Recognition of depreciation currently	Two-year deferral of depreciation
0	5.54	5.38
5	5.75	5.59
10	5.96	5.80
15	6.15	5.99
20	6.34	6.17
25	6.52	6.35
30	6.69	6.52
35	6.86	6.67
40	7.02	6.85
45	7.18	7.00
50	7.33	7.15

Note: Based on 48 percent marginal tax rate for each tax year.

Exhibit 1 (*continued*)

EQUIPMENT LEASING, INC.
Purchase versus lease analysis
Boeing 727/200 Transport Aircraft

Break-even cost of capital
(all amounts stated as percentage of cost)

(1)	(2)	(3)	(4) Purchase	(5)	(6)	(7)	(8) Lease	(9)	(10)
Tax year ending December 31	Purchase/ sale proceeds	Depreci- ation	Tax savings/ (payments) at 48%	Investment credit	Net cash flow (2 + 4 + 5)	Lease payments	Tax savings at 48% tax rate	Net cash flow (7 + 8)	Advantage of purchase over lease (6 − 9)
1977	(100.0000)	14.2857	6.8571	—	(93.1429)	(4.6384)	2.2262	(2.4122)	(90.7307)
1978	—	24.4898	11.7551	—	11.7551	(9.2768)	4.4529	(4.8239)	16.5790
1979	—	18.7075	8.9796	—	8.9796	(9.2768)	4.4529	(4.8239)	13.8035
1980	—	15.3061	7.3469	—	7.3469	(9.2768)	4.4529	(4.8239)	12.1708
1981	—	11.9048	5.7143	—	5.7143	(9.2768)	4.4529	(4.8239)	10.5382
1982	—	8.5034	4.0816	—	4.0816	(9.2768)	4.4529	(4.8239)	8.9055
1983	—	5.1020	2.4490	10.0000	12.4490	(9.2768)	4.4529	(4.8239)	17.2729
1984	—	1.7007	0.8164	—	0.8164	(9.2768)	4.4529	(4.8239)	5.6403
1985	—	—	—	—	—	(9.2768)	4.4529	(4.8239)	4.8239
1986	—	—	—	—	—	(9.2768)	4.4529	(4.8239)	4.8239
1987	—	—	—	—	—	(9.2768)	4.4529	(4.8239)	4.8239
1988	—	—	—	—	—	(9.2768)	4.4529	(4.8239)	4.8239
1989	—	—	—	—	—	(9.2768)	4.4529	(4.8239)	4.8239
1990	—	—	—	—	—	(9.2768)	4.4529	(4.8239)	4.8239
1991	—	—	—	—	—	(9.2768)	4.4529	(4.8239)	4.8239
1992	—	—	—	—	—	(9.2768)	4.4529	(4.8239)	4.8239
1993	25.0000	—	(12.0000)	—	13.0000	(4.6384)	2.2261	(2.4123)	15.4123
					(29.0000)			(77.1830)	48.1830

Note: 1. AAL is an accrual basis taxpayer and recognizes tax credits from equipment acquisitions of 1977 in tax year ending 12/31/83 in four equal installments as a reduction of estimated tax payments for 1983.

2. The aircraft are delivered on July 1, 1977 and depreciated over seven years using the ADR method to a net salvage of 0 percent of original cost. The half-year convention is elected for 1977 and the initial depreciation is double-declining balance switching to sum-of-years'-digits in 1979. *All* depreciation deductions are recognized currently.

3. The lease is for 16 years with rents payable quarterly in arrears at an effective rate of 5.25 percent per annum.

4. The aircraft are sold and proceeds are recognized at the end of 16 years in the amount noted above.

Exhibit 1 *(concluded)*

EQUIPMENT LEASING, INC.
Purchase vs. lease analysis
Boeing 727/200 Transport Aircraft
Break-even cost of capital
(all amounts staged as percentage of cost)

(Deferred Depreciation)

(1) Tax year ending December 31	(2) Purchase/ sale proceeds	(3) Depreciation	(4) Purchase Tax savings/ (payments) at 48%	(5) Investment credit	(6) Net cash flow (2 + 4 + 5)	(7) Lease payments	(8) Lease Tax savings at 48% tax rate	(9) Net cash flow (7 + 8)	(10) Advantage of purchase over lease (6 − 9)
1977	(100.0000)	—	—	—	(100.0000)	(4.6384)	—	(4.6384)	(95.3616)
1978		—				(9.2768)	—	(9.2768)	9.2768
1979		57.4830	27.5918		27.5918	(9.2768)	11.1320	1.8552	25.7366
1980		15.3061	7.3469		7.3469	(9.2768)	4.4529	(4.8239)	12.1708
1981		11.9048	5.7143		5.7143	(9.2768)	4.4529	(4.8239)	10.5382
1982		8.5034	4.0816		4.0816	(9.2768)	4.4529	(4.8239)	8.9055
1983		5.1020	2.4490	10.0000	12.4490	(9.2768)	4.4529	(4.8239)	17.2729
1984		1.7007	0.8164		0.8164	(9.2768)	4.4529	(4.8239)	5.6403
1985		—			—	(9.2768)	4.4529	(4.8239)	4.8239
1986		—			—	(9.2768)	4.4529	(4.8239)	4.8239
1987		—			—	(9.2768)	4.4529	(4.8239)	4.8239
1988		—			—	(9.2768)	4.4529	(4.8239)	4.8239
1989		—			—	(9.2768)	4.4529	(4.8239)	4.8239
1990		—			—	(9.2768)	4.4529	(4.8239)	4.8239
1991		—			—	(9.2768)	4.4529	(4.8239)	4.8239
1992		—			—	(9.2768)	4.4529	(4.8239)	4.8239
1993	25.0000	—	(12.0000)		13.0000	(4.6384)	2.2261	(2.4123)	15.4123
					(29.0000)			(77.1830)	48.1830

Note: 1. AAL is an accrual basis taxpayer and recognizes tax credits from equipment acquisitions of 1977 in tax year ending 12/31/83 in four equal installments as a reduction of estimated tax payments for 1983.
2. The aircraft are delivered on July 1, 1977 and depreciated over seven years using the ADR method to a net salvage of 0 percent of original cost. The half-year convention is elected for 1977 and the initial depreciation is double-declining balance switching to sum-of-years'-digits in 1979. Depreciation deductions for tax years ending 12/31/77 and 12/31/78 are deferred until 1979 and the remaining years are recognized on a current basis.
3. The lease is for 16 years with rents payable quarterly in arrears at an effective rate of 5.25 percent per annum.
4. The aircraft are sold and proceeds are recognized at the end of 16 years in the amount noted above.

and the Caribbean. During the year ending December 31, 1976 American's scheduled commercial flights averaged over 780,000 airplane miles daily. In 1976, American's scheduled passenger service accounted for approximately 87.2 percent of its revenues, freight operations 7.9 percent, and charter services 2.7 percent. American's domestic and Canadian operations accounted for 88.4 percent of total scheduled passenger revenues, and Caribbean and Mexican operations 11.6 percent.

Flagship International, Incorporated, a wholly owned, unconsolidated subsidiary of American, is engaged in: (1) furnishing food and other services to the air transportation industry through in-flight catering and the operation of airport restaurants by its Sky Chef Division; and (2) operating or participating in the operation of 20 hotels by Americana Hotels, Inc., a wholly owned subsidiary of Flagship. All but two of these hotels are in American's route system.

INDUSTRY ENVIRONMENT

Mr. Plaskett was acutely aware of the unique combination of factors that exerted enormous influence on patterns of financial requirements, sources of capital available, and the airline's ability to attract the capital it needed. These factors included the economics of airline operations, regulatory environment, tax laws, and capital market changes.

Capital requirements and aircraft financing

Capital requirements for the air transportation industry have increased dramatically over the last 30 years and it is estimated that another $65 billion will be needed between now and 1989.[1] A combination of these increasing capital requirements and erratic profitability patterns caused a variety of investment vehicles to evolve for use in aircraft financing. In a speech to company management, Mr. Plaskett traced this historical pattern of funds sources.

Turning now to the history of airline financing, there are five phases or periods we can examine. The first phase we have called the equity period, spanning the time from the birth of the industry until 1954. During this period the airline industry was blossoming; it was a growth business and people were anxious to invest their money in what looked to be a sound, profitable industry with a good future. Common stock

---

[1] Theodore Shen, *Domestic Trunk Airlines: A Shortage Industry in the Making* (New York: Donaldson, Lufkin and Jenrette, June 1976).

could be easily sold at prices well above book value. In terms of raising capital, the equity period built a solid base under the industry and our company.

In the period 1954–59, referred to as the insurance company period, the industry required $2.2 billion of additional capital. However, the airlines were still very strong and we were able to fund 55 percent of our requirements internally, with 90 percent of the remainder coming from unsecured 25–30-year debt issued to insurance companies at interest rates of 4 percent to 5 percent. Needless to say, insurance companies are not interested in making loans that stretch out that far today. In the period 1960–65, the industry required an additional $4.2 billion of capital and we were able to finance 71 percent of this through internal growth. Generally, this period was very stable. We were favored with major technological improvements and with substantial productivity increases as we completed the transition from piston to jet aircraft.

Then the 1966–71 period came along—the "get it where you can" phase. This was the time when our industry required about $11.9 billion in additional capital, wide bodies were coming on line, fleets were expanding, traffic was increasing at double-digit rates, and the sky was the limit. But we had great difficulties in financing during this period. Inflation was becoming a dangerous factor in the economy and in our financing as interest rates started rising. Because of a long list of problems, we had erratic earnings. Investors and lenders began to get nervous. They saw we were not able to continue to grow at double-digit growth rates, nor were we able to demonstrate that we could earn them a reasonable return on their investment. The dark clouds on the horizon, large forecast losses with the introduction of wide bodies, and cost problems attributable to their introduction, simply made lenders and investors look elsewhere to invest their money.

In order to pay for airplanes soon to be delivered, new and more expensive financing instruments were developed. During this period the industry sold about $1 billion worth of subordinated convertible debentures, again primarily to insurance companies. The insurance companies were back investing in the business and began hoping for the possibility of a big equity conversion as earnings returned to normal, further strengthening the company. However, converts became much less attractive as the bottom fell out of airline stock prices in the 1967–68 recession. Also, we turned to banks during this period to establish a revolving credit agreement whereby they approved a line of credit. With fluctuating interest rates, it was very expensive financing, but it was essential financing to get us through some difficult times. This time period also saw the investment tax credit lease enter as a major financing vehicle. Estimates of the uncapitalized leases in the industry range from $3 to $5 billion.

The 1972–76 period was one of curtailed expansion while the industry was plagued with problems. The most significant of these problems was dramatically lower levels of traffic growth—no more double-digit traffic passenger-mile annual growth rates. Also, earnings were inconsistent and in some years nonexistent. The result was little equipment expansion during that period.

What is American Airlines going to do for the future? New common equity does not seem prudent. And it is far from certain that we could attract enough investors at our present stock price to generate the amount of money we need. Long-term unsecured debt similar to that which we have with our senior lenders is not possible and we all know the drawbacks of government guaranteed loans and grants. Convertible debentures present some of the same problems as selling common stock. We could use investment tax credit leases or equipment trust certificates. The question is which ones and how much of each.[2]

Regulation

The air transportation industry is subject to extensive federal regulation. Under the Federal Aviation Act and the Department of Transportation Act, the Civil Aeronautics Board (CAB) and the Federal Aviation Administration (FAA) exercise regulatory authority over air carriers.

CAB. The CAB has jurisdiction over:

1. The issuance of Certificates of Public Convenience and Necessity, containing route authorization and operating restrictions under which airline services are furnished. (Since profitability in the industry is partially dependent on route structure American and other airlines continually seek adjustments and additions to their route authority that will improve their competitive position.)
2. The consolidation, merger and acquisition of control of air carriers.
3. Tariffs with respect to transportation rates, fares and charges. (Although the CAB has allowed certain fare increases in recent years, American's management believed that these increases have not fully compensated for increased expenses over that period, particularly the increased cost of jet fuel.)

FAA. The FAA regulates flying operations generally, including personnel, aircraft, maintenance, security, and other technical matters.

Deregulation proposals. During 1976, several bills were introduced in Congress to revise the Federal Aviation Act. These bills proposed significant changes in the regulation of the airline industry which would increase competition and ease entry into the industry for new carriers. The proposed bills would reduce the authority of the CAB over routes, fares and charges and eliminate or modify certain antitrust exemptions for air carriers. Although the final form of any deregulation legislation cannot be predicted, the enactment of such legislation could have an adverse impact on individual carriers, including American.

---

[2] Thomas Plaskett, "Financing the Business under Uncertainty" (Speech before company's management).

Environmental regulation. Regulations with respect to aircraft noise were adopted by the FAA in January 1977. The regulations require modification or replacement of aircraft that do not meet present FAA noise control standards for new aircraft, with compliance required over a four-year period beginning in 1981. American estimates that it will cost approximately $20 million to modify its 727, 747, and DC-10 aircraft. The cost of modifying or replacing its 62 owned or leased 707 aircraft would be substantial and could have an adverse financial effect on American. Legislation has been proposed to permit financing of a portion of the cost of compliance with these regulations from special ticket-tax revenues presently allocated to airport development.

Tax Reform Act of 1976

The Tax Reform Act of 1976 continued the 10 percent investment tax credit through December 31, 1980. Additionally, the utilization of investment tax credits was enhanced by increasing the investment tax credit allowable for air carriers from 50 percent of any tax liability in excess of $25,000 to 100 percent of any tax liability in excess of $25,000 for taxable years ending in 1977 and 1978. The 100 percent limitation is then reduced 10 percent per year until it returns to 50 percent of the tax liability in excess of $25,000 for taxable years ending after 1982. The act also provides that investment tax credit may be used on a "first-in, first-out" basis for 1976 and later years.

AMERICAN AIRLINES FINANCIAL POSITION

Capitalization

At December 31, 1976, the long-term debt:equity ratio (excluding noncapitalized leases) was .68:1. Long-term debt included a combination of promissory notes and convertible debentures with varying maturities. Mr. Plaskett had made substantial progress in restructuring some of this debt by renegotiating with lenders and eliminating restrictive covenants that had severely limited American's financial flexibility. Exhibit 2 shows American's balance sheet as of December 31, 1976.

At December 31, 1976, American Airlines owned or leased a total of 236 aircraft. (See Table A.)

Exhibit 2

AMERICAN AIRLINES, INC. AND CONSOLIDATED SUBSIDIARY
Consolidated Balance Sheet
December 31, 1976 ($000)

Assets

Current Assets:

Cash and short-term investments	$ 307,246
Receivables, less allowances for uncollectible accounts ($10,067)	304,819
Inventories, less allowances for obsolescence ($15,626)	75,863
Prepayments and other current assets	7,660
Total Current Assets	$ 695,588

Equipment and Property:

Flight equipment, at cost	1,459,069
Less: Allowances for depreciation	781,759
	$ 677,310
Purchase deposits with manufacturer of flight equipment	40,019
	$ 717,329
Land, buildings and other equipment, at cost	314,654
Less: Allowances for depreciation	155,770
	$ 158,884
Total Equipment and Property—Net	$ 876,213

Investments and Other Assets:

Investment in and advances to Flagship International, Inc.	61,523
Noncurrent receivables, less allowances and deferred income ($12,392)	28,704
Route acquisition costs	43,700
Other assets and deferred charges	9,501
Total Investments and Other Assets	$ 143,428
TOTAL ASSETS	$1,715,229

Liabilities and Stockholders' Equity

Current Liabilities:

Accounts payable	$ 157,859
Accrued salaries and wages	75,035
Other accrued liabilities	89,934
Air traffic liability and customers' deposits	157,990
Current maturities of long-term debt	20,210
Total Current Liabilities	$ 501,028

Long-term Debt, less current maturities:*

Senior debt	243,885
Subordinated convertible debentures	172,370
Total Long-Term Debt	$ 416,255

Other Liabilities:

Deferred federal income tax	176,194
Other liabilities and deferred credits	11,678
Total Other Liabilities	$ 187,872

Exhibit 2 *(continued)*

Stockholders' Equity:
Preferred stock—no par value
 5,000,000 shares authorized; none issued
Common stock—$1 par value
 60,000,000 shares authorized;
 28,608,000 shares issued and outstanding .... | 28,608
Additional paid-in capital .... | 317,592
Retained earnings .... | 263,874

  Total Stockholders' Equity .... | $ 610,074

  Total Liabilities and Stockholders' Equity .... | $1,715,229

* American's debt (excluding amounts maturing within one year) consisted of the following ($000):

Senior debt: *December 31, 1976*
 4¼ percent promissory notes due 1978–1996 .... | $ 66,500
 4.55 percent promissory notes due 1978–1996 .... | 19,000
 5 percent promissory notes due 1978–1996 .... | 19,000
 5⅛ percent promissory notes due 1978–1991 .... | 77,000
 5¾ percent promissory notes due 1978–1996 .... | 53,833
 5 percent equipment obligations due 1978 and 1979 .... | 8,552

                                                                       $243,885

Subordinated convertible debt:
 4¼ percent subordinated (convertible to 1980) debentures
  due 1992 .... | $167,335
 6 percent subordinated (convertible to 1982) debentures
  due 1982 .... | 1,602
 6⅞ percent subordinated (convertible to 1984) debentures
  due 1984 .... | 3,433
                                                                       $172,370

Maturities of long-term debt (including sinking-fund requirements) for the next five years are: 1977—$20,-210,000; 1978—$20,339,000; 1979—$16,357,000; 1980—$21,293,000; 1981—$21,293,000.

Table A

		Number of Aircraft		
Aircraft type	*Number of seats*	*Owned*	*Leased*	*Total*
McDonnell Douglas DC-10	240	19	6	25
Boeing 747	340–424	1	7	8
Boeing 747 (air freighter)	—	3	—	3
Boeing 707	138	43	13	56
Boeing 707 (convertible)	147–173	11	9	20
Boeing 707 (air freighter)	—	8	1	9
Boeing 727 (extended version)	127	10	48	58
Boeing 727	100	56	1	57
		151	85	236

Rental expense for the leases during the five years ended December 31, 1976 is shown in Table B.

Table B

	Year ended December 31				
	1972	*1973*	*1974*	*1975*	*1976*
Noncapitalized financing leases, less sublease income	$82,700	$ 86,000	$ 87,100	$ 89,900	$ 99,900
Other leases, less sub-lease income	15,900	16,600	20,600	21,400	22,200
	$98,600	$102,600	$107,700	$111,300	$122,100

Future minimum rental commitments under all noncancellable leases for aircraft, airport and office facilities, and other assets as estimated in Table C.

Table C

	Aircraft	Airport facilities*	Office facilities and other*	Net amount	Portion of net amount applicable to noncapitalized financing leases
1977	$ 70,000	$24,700	$18,800	$113,500	$105,400
1978	70,000	23,900	8,300	102,200	95,800
1979	68,200	21,700	6,600	96,500	90,900
1980	67,200	19,900	5,600	92,700	88,000
1981	66,700	19,000	4,600	90,300	86,400
1982–86	278,400	84,200	17,500	380,100	364,100
1987–91	121,200	76,300	8,900	206,400	199,700
1992–96	—	71,400	8,300	79,700	76,000
1997 and subsequent	—	74,900	4,800	79,700	76,800

* Certain of these leases are renewable for varying periods of time.

The present value of minimum lease commitments (less subleases) for all noncapitalized financing leases in effect at December 31, 1976 is as stated in Table D.

Table D

	(000s)
Aircraft	$542,400
Airport facilities	197,100
Office facilities and other	38,500
Total	$778,000*

* See Exhibit 3, note §.

American has also guaranteed payment under noncapitalized lease financing for hotels and other properties operated by Flagship having a present value of approximately $123.3 million.[3]

For substantially all the aircraft leased by American, the lease contains an option to purchase or a right of first refusal to purcahse or re-lease the aircraft. For tax reasons, however, this price or renewal rental must be based on the market value of the aircraft at the end of the term of lease. Table E lists the expiration dates for the leased aircraft American operates.

Table E

Number and type of aircraft	Leases expire in
3 Boeing 707	1979
1 Boeing 727	1980
1 Boeing 727 (extended version)	1982
10 Boeing 707 (9 convertible and 1 air freighter)	1983
10 Boeing 707 and	
2 Boeing 727 (extended version)	1984
2 Boeing 727 (extended version)	1985
22 Boeing 727 (extended version)	1986
5 Boeing 727 (extended version)	1987
7 Boeing 747	1988
2 McDonnell Douglas DC-10	1989
16 Boeing 727 (extended version)	
4 McDonnell Douglas DC-10	1991

For financial reporting purposes, provisions for depreciation of operating equipment and property is computed by the straight-line method. The estimated useful lives and residual values for the principal asset classifications are as shown in Table F.

Operating results

Although American's revenues have grown at a compound rate of 10.4 percent over the period 1972–76, earnings have been erratic, with substantial losses in both 1973 and 1975. Because of earnings uncertainty, American has not paid a dividend on its common shares since 1971. Exhibit 3 shows a five-year summary of operating results. An adverse economic climate causing a slowdown in traffic growth, the effects of inflation and increased fuel costs on operating expenses,

---

[3] See Exhibit 3, note §.

Table F

	Estimated useful life	Residual value
Boeing 747 and DC-10 aircraft and engines	14 years	15%
Boeing 707 aircraft and engines:		
Acquired 1959 to 1961	*	$100,000
Acquired 1963 to 1968	15 years	$100,000
Boeing 727 aircrafts and engines†	16 years	10%
Major rotable parts, avionics, and assemblies	Life of equipment to which applicable	None to 15%
Improvements to leased flight equipment	Term of lease	None
Buildings and improvements (principally on leased land)	10 to 20 years or term of lease whichever is shorter	None
Ground and other equipment	4 to 10 years	None

* Common retirement date of December 31, 1977.
† The estimated useful life of the 21 Boeing 727/200 aircraft on order is 20 years.

and aircraft fleet commitments based on unrealized growth projection have all contributed to American's earnings instability. Fare increases, granted by the CAB of 10 percent in 1974, 3 percent in 1975, and 7 percent in 1976, have helped offset some of these adverse effects.

CURRENT INVESTMENT COMMITMENTS

The specific aircraft acquisitions listed in the board of directors $492.5 million authorization for 1977–78 included 21 727/200 passenger aircraft on order from Boeing, 12 of which were scheduled for delivery during 1977 and 9 during 1978, 1 Boeing 747 freighter to be purchased from another airline, and 3 McDonnell Douglas DC–10 passenger aircraft for delivery during 1978. $40 million in advance payments had been made to Boeing. Future payments for the 25 aircraft and related equipment are as forecasted in Table G.

Table G

	3 McDonnell Douglas DC–10	21 Boeing 727	1 Boeing 747	Total
1977	$36,700	$111,500	$25,300	$173,500
1978	57,500	64,800	—	122,300
	$94,200	$176,300	$25,300	$295,800

Additionally, as of December, 1976, America's board of directors had authorized expenditures for spare parts and modifications to presently owned or leased aircraft amounting to approximately $80.3 million and for ground properties amounting to approximately $76.4 million. American estimates that approximately $114.1 million will be expended during 1977.

Mr. Plaskett's first task was to review carefully the investment banker's lease proposal to determine if and how it might fit into a total financing program for presentation to the board of directors.

Exhibit 3
Consolidated statement of operations

			Year ended December 31 ($000)		
	1972	1973	1974	1975	1976
Revenues:					
Passenger	$1,215,251	$1,334,797	$1,480,170	$1,540,906	$1,801,968
Freight	109,682	123,362	126,390	135,271	159,757
Mail	21,100	26,174	24,339	26,067	29,663
Other	7,775	(2,346)	10,408	7,761	16,495
Total operating revenues	$1,353,808	$1,481,987	$1,641,307	$1,710,005	$2,007,883
Expenses:					
Flying operations	$ 368,872	$ 415,499	$ 490,014	$ 574,008	$ 634,047
Maintenance	216,645	268,901	248,193	249,433	275,664
Passenger service	144,040	166,017	164,363	183,210	203,378
Aircraft and traffic servicing	264,738	305,891	327,725	351,137	392,229
Promotion and sales	152,092	168,599	172,437	187,738	229,680
General and administrative	58,173	70,554	71,890	78,450	91,313
Depreciation and obsolescence	114,156	125,797	120,966	105,695	109,813
Total Operating Expenses	$1,318,716	$1,521,258	1,595,588	$1,729,671	$1,936,124
Operating income (loss)	$ 35,092	$ (39,271)	$ 45,719	$ (19,666)	$ 71,759
Other income (deductions)					
Interest on long-term debt	$ (33,848)	$ (35,688)	$ (28,500)	$ (23,815)	$ (21,626)
Interest income	6,204	15,746	11,966	15,130	22,613
Interest capitalized	2,925	83	631	1,183	1,772
Gain on disposal of property	1,509	5,519	2,253	10,723	4,268
Net earnings (loss) of Flagship International, Inc.*	778	(1,822)	477	183	(3,918)
Miscellaneous—net	(6,554)	(8,107)	(4,811)	(12,548)	(653)
	$ (28,986)	$ (24,269)	$ (17,984)	$ (9,144)	2,456

Earnings (loss) before Federal Income Tax	6,106	(63,540)	27,735	(28,810)	74,215
Federal income Tax (Credit)†	979	(13,600)	6,900	(6,400)	17,900
Net Earnings (loss)	$ 5,127	$ (49,940)	$ 20,835	$ (22,410)	$ 56,315
Earnings (loss) per Share of Common Stock:‡					
Primary	$0.18	$(1.75)	$0.73	$(0.79)	$1.97
Fully diluted	$0.18	$ —	$0.73	$ —	$1.90
Ratio of earnings to fixed charges§	1.1	0.4	1.3	0.7	1.8

* Effective November 1, 1976, Flagship acquired from Loews Corporation the land and building occupied by the Americana Hotel of San Juan and Loews' leasehold interest in the Americana Hotel of Bal Harbour. The aggregate purchase price of approximately $14.4 million includes the assumption of a 7.6 million mortgage. As a result of this transaction, the net earnings (loss) of Flagship includes a write-down of approximately $5.9 million (before tax effect), representing the excess of the purchase price over the fair market value of the net assets acquired. This write-down decreased American's 1976 earnings per share by $0.16.

† American has made no payment of federal income tax during the five years ended December 31, 1976. The provision (credit) for federal income tax for each of the five years ended December 31, 1976 represents deferred taxes or the elimination of deferred taxes previously provided. Additionally, American had accumulated $50 million of unused investment tax credits which may be applied as a reduction of future tax provisions.

‡ Primary earnings (loss) per share are based on the average number of shares outstanding during the respective periods: 1972—28,446,000; 1973—28,486,000; 1974—28,520,000; 1975—28,549,000; 1976—28,574,000. Fully diluted EPS assume conversion of the subordinated convertible debentures, if such conversion would have a dilutive effect.

§ Earnings of American and all its subsidiaries represent net earnings (loss) plus the provision (credit) for federal income tax and fixed charges. Fixed charges of American and all its subsidiaries represent interest and amortization of debt expense plus the interest portion of rentals of financing leases. The interest rates implicit in the terms of leases at the time of entering into such leases and also used in discounting net lease commitments vary from 2 percent to 10 percent. The weighted average interest rate was 6.1 percent at December 31, 1972, 6.5 percent at December 31, 1973, 1974, 1975, and 1976. The ratio of earnings to fixed charges of American, exclusive of its unconsolidated subsidiaries was: 1972—1.1; 1973—.3; 1974—1.3; 1975—6; 1976—2.0.

Case 2-6

American Airlines (B)

By late January 1977, Mr. Plaskett was under pressure to finalize the financing program for 1977–78 that he would present to American Airlines board of directors. Although he had considered leasing as an option for part of American's aircraft acquisition requirements (see American Airlines [A], Case 2–5), he felt that the total package should include both debt, and equity or equity-related financing. Realizing that raising an adequate amount of capital through an equity offering would be impossible at the current price of American's common stock (see Exhibit 1). Mr. Plaskett had narrowed his decision down to the following two proposals from American's investment bankers:

1. Convertible subordinated debentures and privately placed equipment trust certificates.
2. Preferred stock with warrants and privately placed equipment trust certificates.

Sherman, Reed Co. suggested that they could place privately approximately $125 million in 8½–9 percent equipment trust certificates with a 15-year maturity. Additionally, they felt that $125 million in 7½ percent, 20-year, convertible subordinated debentures could be marketed (see Exhibit 2). They believed the debentures could be issued without provision for a sinking fund, but could not be callable for at least three years.

Bateman, Shields, Weber & Co., Inc., felt that a $125 million package of 8¾ percent cumulative preferred stock with warrants (see Exhibit 3) would be an excellent way to raise capital while, at the same time, increasing American's equity position and strengthening its balance sheet. They felt that the warrants were a significant element for the preferred stock offer. Without them, the rate on the preferreds would be in the 9–9¼ percent range. Although not mentioned in the proposal, the total package included privately placed equipment trust certificates in the same amount and with the same terms as the Sherman, Reed proposal.

Mr. Plaskett, eager to make a decision, but wanting more input, asked several younger members of the finance department to analyze the proposals and make recommendations to him.

Exhibit 1 sets forth the high and low sales prices for American's common stock for the years 1972 through 1976 and January 1977.

Exhibit 1
Price range of common stock

	High	Low
1972:		
1st quarter	48⅝	39⅜
2d quarter	49⅞	34⅝
3d quarter	39	23½
4th quarter	30½	22½
1973:		
1st quarter	25⅜	17⅛
2d quarter	21⅞	10⅛
3d quarter	13⅛	9¼
4th quarter	14	8
1974:		
1st quarter	13⅜	7⅝
2d quarter	12⅛	8¼
3d quarter	9¼	5⅝
4th quarter	8⅞	4⅞
1975:		
1st quarter	10⅛	5⅛
2d quarter	9¾	7
3d quarter	9⅝	7
4th quarter	9¼	6¾
1976:		
1st quarter	12⅜	8⅝
2d quarter	14½	9¼
3d quarter	16⅜	12¾
4th quarter	14¼	11⅛
1977:		
January	14¾	13⅛

Exhibit 2

November 8, 1976

Mr. Thomas C. Plaskett
Senior Vice President—Finance
American Airlines, Inc.
633 Third Avenue
New York, N.Y. 10017

Dear Tom:

This letter sets forth our recommendations for American Airlines regarding financing 21 Boeing 727/200s, costing approximately $250 million, to be delivered in 1977 and 1978.

Any financing undertaken by American in 1977 and 1978 must assist the company in improving its future financing flexibility in view of its very large continuing financing needs through 1980 and beyond. Second, American's near-term financings must be designed to maintain American's Baa/BBB debt ratings. A reduction in these ratings would close off many financing alternatives to American and sharply reduce its ability to raise capital. In order to maintain its financing flexibility and its debt ratings, we believe that American should continue to retain large amounts of cash, keep the average life of its debt maturities as long as possible and sell equity or an equity-related security during 1977. Our specific recommendations for raising approximately $250 million during the next year are as follows: first, American should sell privately in the current market as much equipment trust certificates as can be sold, which we believe is in the $125 million area. American should follow this private sale with approximately a $125 million offering of convertible subordinated debentures. In order to accomplish this ambitious financing program, you should start working with your investment bankers as soon as possible.

Private equipment trust financing

As we have said previously, the private debt markets today are very attractive both in terms of cost and availability. We believe it would be impossible to arrange a financing of significant size on an unsecured basis for American. Even on a secured basis, we believe it would be extremely difficult (and costly) to arrange a financing of the $200 million magnitude. That would be possible only if one of the four major insurance companies committed for a significant portion.

We believe that a more appropriate size for a private secured debt offering today would be about $100–$125 million. We believe that a transaction of this size could be arranged for a term of up to 15 years at a cost of 8½–9 percent.

We would go out into the market with a private placement as soon as the company has received positive indications from its existing lenders that they will allow an increase in secured debt. Work should be started on writing the private placement memorandum

Exhibit 2 *(continued)*

now. If we went into the market on about December 1, we should be able to have indications of interest prior to Christmas and firm commitments by mid- to late January.

Public issue of convertible subordinated debentures

We believe that it would be highly desirable for American to strengthen its balance sheet with an equity-related offering. Although a substantial straight common stock offering would be difficult to sell today because of the lack of a dividend, a substantial issue of convertible debentures (such as $125 million) would be very salable under current market conditions. The pricing of a convertible debenture issue today would include a coupon in the area of 7½ percent, a 20-year maturity, and a conversion premium of about 14 percent above the then-market price of the common stock. We believe that the rating services would probably raise the question of an equity-related financing even if American does not, and we recommend a strong offense with the rating services of stating your intention to sell an equity-related security in the near future.

We are pleased to submit these financing recommendations to you and hope that we may assist you in implementing them.

Very truly yours,

Sherman, Reed & Co.

Exhibit 3

American Airlines, Inc.

Proposed Public Offering of Preferred Stock with Warrants

Bateman, Shields, Weber, & Co.

December 20, 1976

$125,000,000

AMERICAN AIRLINES, INC.
5,000,000 units
5,000,000 shares of 8¾% cumulative preferred stock with warrants to purchase 5,000,000 common shares

SUMMARY OF PROPOSED TERMS

Authorized:	5 million shares authorized issuable in series (the "preferred stock").
This series:	5 million shares, 8¾ percent cumulative preferred stock, $25 par value, liquidating value $25 per share.
Dividend rate:	8¾ percent per annum, payable quarterly.
Offering price:	$25.00 per unit.
Dividend rights:	The holders of the preferred stock are entitled to receive, when, as and if declared by American's board of directors, cumulative dividends from the date of issuance at the annual dividend rate of $2.1875. No dividends may be paid, or funds set apart for payment, on the common stock of American until all dividends accrued on the preferred stock have been paid for the current and all prior dividend periods and funds for required sinking-fund payments on the preferred stock are paid or set apart for payment.
Redemption provisions:	The preferred stock may be redeemed in whole or in part at any time after the fifth year on at least 30 days' notice at a redemption price equal to the liquidating value plus the annual dividend rate and declining annually in equal amounts to the liquidating value after the 20th year, in each case, plus accrued dividends to the date of redemption.
Sinking fund:	As a sinking fund to retire all of the preferred stock by the end of the 30th year (25th year of the sinking fund), American will redeem 150,000 preferred shares annually from 1983 through 1992 and 250,000 shares annually thereafter until all shares have been retired at a sinking-fund redemption price of $25 plus accrued dividends. The sinking-fund redemptions are cumulative. The shares of preferred stock required to be redeemed for the sinking fund may be reduced, at American's option, by application of preferred stock previously acquired (other than through the sinking fund).
Voting rights:	The preferred stock is nonvoting, except that while dividends are in arrears in an amount equal to at least six quarterly dividends, the holders of the preferred stock, voting separately

Exhibit 3 *(continued)*

	as a class, may elect two additional members of the board of directors.
	Without the affirmative vote of two thirds of the outstanding preferred stock, American may not *(a)* modify or affect adversely the voting rights, rights or preferences of the preferred stock or *(b)* authorize or create any class of stock ranking prior to the preferred stock with respect to dividends or to the distribution of assets in liquidation.
	Authorization by the holders of a majority of the outstanding preferred stock is required for *(a)* the issuance of additional preferred stock unless the net earnings of American available for dividends for a period of 12 consecutive calendar months out of the immediately preceding 18 months shall amount to more than three times the annual pro forma dividend requirements on all preferred stock to be outstanding and *(b)* any consolidation or merger, unless American is to be the surviving corporation and would be able to satisfy the provision of *(a)* of this paragraph.
Liquidation rights:	Holders of the preferred stock are entitled to receive, in the event of any voluntary liquidation, the then applicable optional redemption price and, in the event of any involuntary liquidation, $25 per share, plus, in either case, all dividends accrued and unpaid.

Description of warrants to purchase common shares

Number of warrants:	5,000,000 (one warrant per unit).
Form:	Registered form issued under and governed by a warrant agreement.
Warrant agent:	To be determined.
Listing:	New York Stock Exchange
Exercise price:	$14.00. Each warrant will entitle the holder to purchase one share of common stock of American. Once the warrants are separately transferable (a date not later than 60 days following the offer), they may be exercised up to the expiration date.
Expiration Date:	Seven years after the date of sale of the warrants.

Exhibit 3 ***(continued)***

Comparison of terms of recent preferred stock issues:

	The B.F. Goodrich Company	*Pennzoil Company*	*Boston Edison Company*	*Occidental Petroleum Corporation**	*The Quaker Oats Company*	*Michigan Wisconsin Pipe Line Company*	*The Detroit Edison Company*	*City Home Corporation*	*Reliance Insurance Company*	*The Western Union Telegraph Company*
Offering date	8/9/72	5/10/73	3/19/75	4/23/75	5/21/75	9/23/75	12/4/75	12/9/75	8/17/76	6/29/76
Aggregate amount of offering	$25,000,000	$65,000,000	$50,000,000	$75,000,000	$50,000,000	$50,000,000	$50,000,000	$50,000,000	$50,000,000	$50,000,000
Number of shares	250,000	650,000	5,000,000	3,000,000	500,000	2,000,000	2,000,000	5,000,000	2,000,000	2,000,000
Offering price per share	$100	$100	$10	$25*	$100	$25	$25	$10	$25	$25
Dividend	$7.85	$8.00	$1.175	$2.50	$9.56	$2.675	$2.75	$1.10	$2.68	$2.5625
Yield	7.85%	8.00%	11.75%	10%	9.56%	10.7%	11.00%	11.00%	10.72%	10.25%
Gross spread per share	$2.00	$1.75	$0.67	$1.40	$1.75	$1.00	$1.15	$0.56	$1.40	$1.00
Gross spread as a percent of offering price	2.00%	1.75%	6.70%	5.60%	1.75%	4.00%	4.60%	5.60%	5.60%	4.00%
Is a prior stock outstanding?	No	No	Yes	No	Yes	No	Yes	No	No	No
Are dividend rights cumulative?	Yes	Yes	Yes	Yes	Yes	Yes	Yes	Yes	Yes	Yes
Voting rights:										
To elect directors after quarterly dividends arrears	2–6	2–6	2–6	2–4	2–6	2–4	2–4	2–6	††	2–6
Approval of holders requirements for adverse changes	⅔	⅔	No	⅔	⅔	⅔	⅔	⅔	⅔	⅔
Approval of holders requirements to issue a prior preferred	‡	§	No	⅔	⅔	⅔	⅔	⅔	⅔	⅔
Approval of holders requirements for merger	⅔	½	No	⅔†	No	½	½	½	5	½
On general corporate matters votes per share	None	None	None	1	1	None	None	None	‖	¼
Redemption provisions:										
Years nonredeemable	0	0	5	5½	0	0	0	0	0	5
Years nonrefundable	10	10	5	5½	5	5	5	5	5	5
Initial redemption premium (IRP)	$7.85	$8.00	$1.175	$2.50	$9.56	$2.675	$2.75	$1.10	$2.68	$2.5625
IRP as a percent of dividend	100%	100%	100%	100%	100%	100%	100%	100%	100%	100%
Year-end in which IRP first declines	1	1	10	6½	10	1	5	1	1	6
RP reaches 0 after years	20	20	15	20½	25	20	#	20	20	25
Rate of decline in redemption premium	level	level	level	leven	5 yr. steps	level	5 yr. steps	level	level	level
Minimum maximum notice for redemption	30,—	30,60	30,60 ‖	30,—	30,90	30,60	30,—	30,60	30,60	30,—

Sinking-fund provisions:									
Year before first payment	7	6	5	6½	6	5	11	11	5
Annual payment	5%	5%	4%	5%	4%	5%	5%	6.67%	2%
Cumulative	Yes	Yes	No	Yes	Yes	Yes	Yes	Yes	Yes
Credit for purchases and redemptions preferred	Yes	Yes	Yes	Yes	Yes	Yes	Yes	Yes	Yes
Optional double-up	Yes	Yes	n.a.	Yes	Yes	Yes	Yes	Yes	Yes
Liquidation rights (RP if = redemption price)									
Voluntary	RP	RP	RP	$25	RP	RP	$10	RP	RP
Involuntary (plus accrued dividends)	$100	$100	$10	$25	$25	$10	$10	$25	$25
Dividend restrictions on junior stock when dividends or sinking fund on preferred in arrears	Yes	Yes	Yes	Yes	Yes	Yes	Yes	Yes	Yes
Issuance test for additional preferred	†	§	No	No	¶	No	**	§§	††
Pro forma ratio of earnings to fixed charges and preferred dividend requirements	2.00	2.00	1.42	3.30	2.19	1.55	3.92	4.01	1.98
Ratings									
Senior debt	A/BBB	Baa/BBB	Baa/BBB	Baa/BBB	A/A+	Baa/BBB	–/–	–/–	Baa/BBB
This issue	/BB	/BB	/BB	/B	+/A	ba/BB	baa/BBB	–/BBB	ba/BB

n.a. not available.

* Offered as units consisting of one share of $2.50 cumulative preferred stock (liquidating value of $25 per share) and one warrant to purchase one common share at $16.25 until April 22, 1980.

† Voting as a class with other series of preferred.

‡ Two-thirds approval required if earnings are less than two times pro forma preferred dividend requirements for 12 consecutive months during latest 18 months.

§ Two-thirds approval required for issuance of a prior preferred if earnings are less than three times actual preferred dividends for 12 consecutive months during latest 18 months or net assets shall be less than 200 percent of pro forma preferred stock.

‖ Boston Edison's obligation is a purchase fund whereby the company is required to offer to purchase 200,000 shares annually at not more than $10 plus accrued dividends provided there was a period of 45 consecutive days in the preceding 12 months when the preference shares traded at less than $10.

Redemption premium declines to $0.25 on January 16, 1991 and thereafter.

¶ Michigan Wisconsin may not issue additional senior or parity preferred unless (1) gross income available for interest and dividends for any 12 consecutive months of the latest 15 months is at least one and one-half times actual interest and pro forma preferred dividends and (2) net assets are at least 225 percent of liquidation preference of the preferred.

** Consent of holders of two thirds of preference shares required to incur funded debt or issued preferred unless net income for the preceding calendar year is at least equal to three times pro forma interest and preferred dividends.

†† Votes with common in election of directors at all times.

‡‡ No vote but certain parity stock issuance tests must be met.

§§ Two thirds consent required to issue additional preferred unless net investment income is three times sum of interest and preferred dividends.

‖‖ Majority consent required to issue additional preferred unless (1) shareholders' equity equals liquidating preference, (2) net income for 12 of 24 months is two times preferred dividend requirements, and (3) net earnings available for 12 of 24 months is one and one-half times fixed charges.

Exhibit 3 (continued)

Comparison of terms for public offerings with warrants to purchase common stock:

DESCRIPTION OF ISSUE	Am. Tel. & Tel Co. (3)	Amerada Hess Co.	Government Employees Insurance Co.‡	Chrysler Financial Corp.
Amount	$1,569,327,000	$150,000,000	$39,112,440	$90,000,000
Offering	8¾ percent debentures due May 15, 2000 with warrants to purchase 31,386,540 common shares	6¾ percent subordinated debentures due March 15, 1996 with warrants to purchase 900,000 shares of capital stock of Louisiana Land and Exploration Company	651,874 shares of common stock with warrants to purchase 651,874 shares of common stock	7⅞ percent subordinated debentures due May 15, 1986 with warrants to purchase 1,900,000 shares of common stock of Chrysler Corporation
Unit	One debenture ($100 principal) and warrants to purchase two shares of common stock of the company	One debenture ($1,000 principal) and warrants to purchase six shares of capital stock of LL&E	One share of common stock and warrant to purchase one share of common stock of the company	One debenture ($1,000 principal) and warrants to purchase 20 shares of common stock of Chrysler Corporation
Date of offering	April 13, 1970	March 23, 1971	May 5, 1971	May 11, 1971
DESCRIPTION OF WARRANTS				
General:				
Form	Registered	Registered	Registered	Registered
Antidilution provisions*	Yes	Yes	Yes	Yes
Voting rights	No	No	No	No
Preemptive rights	No	No	No	No
Where traded	NYSE	ASE	OTC	NYSE
TERM OF WARRANTS				
Dated	May 18, 1970	March 23, 1971	May 15, 1971	May 15, 1971
Distribution date†	November 15, 1970	June 15, 1971	August 1, 1971	August 15, 1971
First exercisable upon	November 15, 1970	Distribution date	August 1, 1971	Distribution date
Initial expiration	May 15, 1975	June 15, 1976	August 1, 1978	May 15, 1976
Extendable at company's option	No	No	No	No
Maximum term	5 years	5¼ years	7¼ years	5 years
Residual value upon expiration	None	None	None	None
EXERCISE FEATURES				
Warrant evidences right to purchase	1 share of the company	1 share of LL&E	1 share of the company	1 share of Chrysler Corp.
Exercise price	$52.000	$81.000	$73.000	$34.000
Last reported price of common stock	$50.750	$84.500	$72.500 (bid)	$30.625
Premium (discount) of exercise price to last reported price of common	2.46%	(4.14%)	0.69%	11.02%
Possible additional funds raised by exercise of warrants	$1,632,100,000	$72,900,000	$47,586,802	$61,200,000‖
Possible additional funds as a percent of offering	104.00%	48.6%	121.67%	68.00%
Potential theoretical dilution of common stock	5.41%	None§	7.71%	3.48%
Treatment of fractional shares	Sale or purchase of fraction to constitute full share	Sale of fraction to constitute full share	Sale of fraction to constitute full share	Sale of fraction to constitute full share
Exercise price payable in cash or securities	Cash	Cash	Cash	Cash

* The exercise price and number of shares purchasable upon exercise are adjusted upon occurrence of certain events.
† Distribution date may be advanced by agreement between underwriters and company.
‡ Rights offering.   § No dilution as warrants apply to the outstanding capital stock of LL&E.   ‖ Proceeds to Chrysler Corporation.

	The B. F. Goodrich Company	Occidental Petroleum Corporation	MCI Communications Corporation
DESCRIPTION OF ISSUE			
Amount	$75,000,000	$75,000,000	$9,600,000
Offering	7 percent subordinated debentures due August 15, 1997 with warrants to purchase 1,500,000 shares of common stock of the company	$2.50 cumulative preferred stock with warrants to purchase 3,000,000 common shares of the company	4,500,000 shares of common stock and warrants to purchase 4,800,000 shares of common stock of the company
Unit	One debenture ($1,000 principal) and warrants to purchase 20 shares of common stock of the company	One share of preferred stock and warrant to purchase one share of common stock of the company	four shares of common stock and warrants to purchase four shares of common stock of the company
Date of Offering	August 9, 1972	April 23, 1975	November 18, 1975
DESCRIPTION OF WARRANTS			
General:			
Form	Registered	Registered	Registered
Antidilution provisions*	Yes	Yes	Yes
Voting rights	No	No	No
Preemptive rights	No	No	No
Where traded	ASE	NYSE	OTC
TERM OF WARRANTS			
Dated	August 15, 1972	April 15, 1975	November 17, 1975
Distribution date†	November 15, 1972	July 22, 1975	February 25, 1976
First exercisable upon	Distribution date	Distribution date	Distribution date
Initial expiration	August 15, 1979	April 22, 1980	November 17, 1980
Extendable at company's option	Yes	Yes	No
Maximum term	Indefinite	10 years	5 years
Residual value upon expiration	None	Yes‡	Yes‡
EXERCISE FEATURES			
Warrant evidences right to purchase	1 share of the company	1 share of the company	1 share of the company
Exercise price	$30.000	$16.250	$2.500
Last reported price of common stock	$26.750	$14.125	$1.813 (bid)
Premium (discount) of exercise price to last reported price of common	12.15%	15.04%	38.44%
Possible additional funds raised by exercise of warrants	$45,000,000	$48,750,000	$12,000,000
Possible additional funds as a percent of offering	60.00%	65.00%	125.00%
Potential theoretical dilution of common stock	9.38%	5.11%	24.53%
Treatment of fractional shares	Sale or purchase of fraction to constitute full share	Sale or purchase of fraction to constitute full share	Sale or purchase of fraction to constitute full share
Exercise price payable in cash or securities	Cash	Cash	Cash

* The exercise price and number of shares purchasable upon exercise are adjusted upon occurrence of certain events.
† Distribution date may be advanced by agreement between underwriters and company.
‡ Upon expiration, one share of common stock is issuable for each 100 warrants unexercised.

Part tHree

Determining tHe appropriate discount rate: The cost of capital to private and public sector organizations

CASE 3-1

THE QUAKER OATS COMPANY: COST OF CAPITAL (A)

While the question of appropriate measures of the cost of capital had been under discussion within the Quaker Oats Company for several years, by mid-1973 considerable disagreement still existed among the people involved. Although it was widely accepted within the company that Quaker Oats' overall cost of capital was approximately 8 percent, some people believed the true cost to be much higher, particularly due to the company's recent aggressive diversification efforts. Quaker Oats' acquisitions in the toys and recreation field, the growth of its restaurant business and its chemical division, these people argued, have undoubtedly changed the nature of the company's business and the sources of its profits. Since these new areas have traditionally not been as stable as the grocery products business, they must have increased the risk associated with ownership of Quaker Oats shares. Therefore, the company's cost of capital is likely to have increased.

THE QUAKER OATS COMPANY

The Quaker Oats Company, incorporated in 1901, is a major world-wide producer and marketer of packaged brand-name food products, including cereals, mixes, table syrup, frozen foods, corn products, and pet foods. The company is also a major producer of furan chemicals, which are used in the foundry industry, the refining of petroleum and in the manufacture of a wide range of products such as plywood, rubber, and plastics. Operations are conducted through the following groups:

Grocery Products Group. Makes ready-to-eat cereals, sold mainly under the names Quaker, Cap'n Crunch, Quisp, Life, King Vitamin, Quangaroos, Puffed Rice, and Puffed Wheat; pet foods sold mainly under the brand names Puss'n Boots, and Ken-L Ration; hot cereals including regular and quick cooking oatmeal, flavored instant oatmeal, farina, and rolled wheat cereals, sold under the Quaker name; pancake mixes and table syrup under the Aunt Jemima brand name; frozen goods, including waffles and French toast under the Aunt Jemima name; frozen pizza and related products under the Celeste brand name, etc.

International Grocery Products Group. Manufactures and sells food products through subsidiaries in Argentina, Australia, Brazil, Colombia, Denmark, Mexico, the Netherlands, and Venezuela. It makes cereals and pancake mixes, and operates chocolate candy and beverage business in Mexico, sells food products through a subsidiary in Nicaragua, and makes and sells pet foods through subsidiaries in Australia and Europe.

Toys and Recreational Product Group. Makes preschool toys under the Fisher-Price name. Louis Marx & Co., Inc., a manufacturer of riding toys, games, trains, and other toys for children of broader age groups, was acquired in June 1972. In July 1972 the company entered the leisure-time fields for adults and older children by acquiring the operations of Needlecraft Corporation of America, a manufacturer of wool and synthetic yarns, needlecraft kits, and goods stamped for embroidery and other needlework (see Exhibit 3).

Exhibit 1

THE QUAKER OATS COMPANY
Consolidated Income Statements
($000)

| | Year ended June 30† | | | |
	1974	1973	1972	1971
Net sales	$1,227,345	$990,767	$795,240	$701,862
Income before extraordinary item	39,878	42,123	35,614	31,107
Extraordinary (charge) credit	—	—	—	(5,886)
Net income after taxes	$ 39,878	$ 42,123	$ 35,614	$ 25,221
Dividends:				
Preferred stock	429	452	484	490
Common stock	15,723	14,711	13,006	12,636
Reinvested earnings	$ 208,336	$184,610	$187,561	$165,437
Per common share*:				
Income before extraordinary item	$1.91	$2.04	$1.78	$1.56
Extraordinary (charge) credit	—	—	—	(0.30)
Net Income	$1.91	$2.04	$1.78	$1.26
Dividends declared	$0.76	$0.72	$0.68	$0.67

* Adjusted for stock splits.

† Results for 1972 through 1968 are restated to reflect the July 20, 1972 merger with Needlecraft Corporation of America, recorded as a pooling of interests. Prior years have not been restated because effect is not material.

Industrial and Institutional Product Group. Makes and distributes furan chemicals, made from agricultural by-products, for use in the foundry industry, in petroleum refining, and in making a variety of products such as plywood, rubber, and plastics. It also sells cookies and cracker products to the grocery trade and ice cream wafers to the dairy industry. As of November 1973, this group operated 13 restaurants under the name Magic Pan, featuring crepe specialties, in 11 U.S. cities and planned to open four more restaurants in fiscal 1974.

Exhibits 1 and 2 present audited financial statements for fiscal years ended on June 30, 1971, 1972, 1973, and 1974. A breakdown of

Exhibit 2

THE QUAKER OATS COMPANY
Consolidated Income Sheets
($000)

	June 30			
	1974	1973	1972	1971
Assets				
Current Assets:				
Cash	$ 2,092	$ 3,038	$ 8,009	$ 9,699
Marketable securities, at cost which approximate market	9,590	23,316	15,326	25,068
Receivables (less allowances of $3,546,000 and $2,613,000, respectively)	160,129	111,218	91,468	62,387
Inventories	225,172	169,607	126,732	86,546
Prepaid expenses	9,295	6,631	6,173	8,067
Current Assets	$406,278	$313,810	$247,708	$191,767
Other receivables and investments:	5,968	6,903	5,575	3,823
Property, plant and equipment at cost:				
Land	8,053	7,276	7,092	6,279
Buildings and improvements	135,147	113,284	101,544	88,993
Machinery and equipment	293,766	253,564	234,526	198,407
	$436,966	$374,124	$343,162	$293,679
Less accumulated depreciation (including reserve for estimated losses on plant dispositions of $4,020,000 in 1972)	117,645	102,047	99,234	95,208
Properties (Net)	$319,321	$272,077	$243,928	$198,471
Intangible Assets:				
Excess of cost over net assets of acquired businesses	38,210	30,004	27,747	26,389
Patents, trademarks, designs, less amortization	6,612	7,276	7,751	3,287
	$776,389	$630,070	$532,709	$423,737

Exhibit 2 *(continued)*

	June 30			
	1974	*1973*	*1972*	*1971*
Liabilities and Shareholders' Equity				
Current Liabilities:				
Short-term debt	$114,695	$ 65,893	$ 36,108	$ 18,880
Current maturities of long-term				
debt	3,998	3,447	4,285	2,390
Accounts payable and accrued				
expenses.	91,634	78,050	67,511	52,050
Income taxes payable	7,448	6,501	5,337	6,690
Dividends payable.	4,039	3,823	3,449	3,287
Current Liabilities	$221,814	$157,714	$116,690	$ 83,297
Long-term debt, less current				
maturities	171,427	123,821	131,521	95,294
Other liabilities	8,196	6,090	2,270	—
Deferred income taxes	36,511	29,650	22,613	15,404
Shareholders' Equity:				
Preferred, $50 par value, $3				
cumulative convertible	7,105	7,408	7,945	8,160
Common, $5 par value	104,745	104,464	67,105	64,390
Additional paid-in capital	23,882	22,359	3,350	1,710
Reinvested earnings	208,336	184,610	187,561	162,805
	$344,068	$318,841	$265,961	$237,065
Less treasury common stock, at				
cost.	5,627	6,046	6,346	7,323
Shareholders' Equity	$338,441	$312,795	$259,615	$229,742
	$776,389	$630,070	$532,709	$423,737

the company's sales and earnings before interest and taxes by operating group is given in Exhibit 3.

The extent and pace of Quaker Oats' recent diversification efforts is probably best evidenced by the fact that although sales of the Grocery Products Group, which has represented the company's traditional line of business, grew by 39 percent during the 1971–74 period (from $449.6 million in 1971 to $628.9 million in 1974), its share of total company sales dropped from 64 percent in 1971 to 51 percent in 1974 (see Exhibit 3).

THE ARGUMENTS

The debate within Quaker Oats over the company's cost of capital is summarized in the following series of intracompany correspondence.

Exhibit 3
Sales and ebit breakdown by operating group (millions)

Operating groups	Year ended June 30			
	1971	1972	1973	1974
Sales:*				
Grocery Products	$449.6	$484.1	$528.1	$ 628.9
	(64.0%)	(60.9%)	(53.3%)	(51.0%)
International Grocery Products	$ 87.0	$106.7	$133.9	$ 197.0
	(12.4%)	(13.4%)	(13.5%)	(16.0%)
Toys and Recreational Products	$ 81.9	$116.8	$224.7	$ 270.1
	(11.7%)	(14.7%)	(22.7%)	(22%)
Industrial and Institutional				
Products	$ 83.4	$ 87.6	$104.1	$ 131.3
	(11.9%)	(11.0%)	(10.5%)	(11%)
TOTAL	$701.9	$795.2	$990.8	$1,227.3
Ebit:				
Grocery Products	$ 43.2	$ 43.5	$ 51.1	$ 48.3
	(65.1%)	(56.3%)	(52.9%)	(49.4%)
International Grocery Products	$ 5.2	$ 5.3	$ 6.8	$ 14.1
	(7.8%)	(6.9%)	(7.0%)	(14.5%)
Toys and Recreational Products	$ 13.6	$ 22.8	$ 31.9	$ 25.4
	(20.5%)	(29.6%)	(33.7%)	(26%)
Industrial and Institutional				
Products	$ 4.3	$ 5.6	$ 6.7	$ 9.9
	(6.6%)	(7.2%)	(6.9%)	(10.1%)
TOTAL	$ 66.3	$ 77.2	$ 96.5	$ 97.7

* Prior years' data are restated to reflect the 1973 shift of organizational responsibility for industrial and governmental cereals business from the Industrial and Institutional Product Group to the Grocery Products Group, in the allocation of certain costs between groups.

June 19, 1973

TO: Mr. T. J. Curley, Jr. Copies to: Mr. E. J. Garneau,
FROM: Mr. T. D. Henrion Manager, Project
SUBJECT: *Cost of Capital* Evaluations

I feel that the debate within the company on our cost of capital is extremely important. Although it is impossible for anyone to say with certainty exactly what our cost of capital is, a relevant range is very important for decision making. The thing which concerns me most is that top management feels that our cost of capital is only 8 percent when it is actually much higher.

A large part of my concern is centered on our acquisition evaluations. Even though the debate is over only a few percentage points or less, a few percentage points can make a tremendous difference. As an example, when we were discussing if we should buy our own stock, an evaluation was done using our acquisition model. With the cost of capital assumed to be 8 percent, our stock was evaluated at $37.71 per share. Using 9 percent, our stock was evaluated at $31.77 per share. This represents a difference in evaluation of Quaker Oats of approximately $124 million, a sizable error in evaluation. This makes clear the importance of spending more time evaluating the cost of capital for projects and acquisitions. Even though we may continue to use 10 percent for project evaluations, management may have a false sense of security that marginal projects are profitable because they believe the cost of capital is only 8 percent.

I assume that those who will be reading this have some basic understanding of the latest theories of finance which in a large part are based on work done by Modigliani and Miller, and as I know has been presented to several people in the company by Joel Stern. Even if one has no prior knowledge of the subject, I hope that the following discussion of our cost of capital is clear and easy to understand.

QUAKER OATS COST OF CAPITAL

The true cost of capital represents the opportunity cost of capital; that is, the return that could have been obtained had the funds been invested elsewhere with the same amount of risk. There are two types of risk: business and financial risk. The return which could normally be expected from an investment in a particular industry is the return necessary to compensate the investors for the business risk. It is independent of the financing of the investment. On the other hand, financial risk is the risk arising from the method of financing. When the firm employs both debt and equity, the total risk is broken into two parts. The bondholders are accepting less than the full risk while the stockholders are accepting a larger share of the risk. The leverage associated with issuance of bonds will result in a greater fluctuation of the stockholders' returns, thus greater risk. It is apparent then that there is no financial risk associated with the ownership of common stock if there is no debt outstanding. All of the risk in this case would be what we are calling business risk.

The calculation of the cost of equity capital is one of the most difficult problems of corporate finance. There are at least five methods which have been used to compute the cost of equity capital. Of these, only one is theoretically and logically acceptable. All the others have glaring shortcomings which make them impractical for general use. The only acceptable method is the use of the risk-adjusted rate of return. Before discussing the risk-adjusted computation of the cost of capital, the shortcomings of the other methods will be briefly discussed.

1. Present price earnings method

This method assumes that the cost of equity capital can be estimated from the present price/earnings ratio. Using this method, the earnings/price ratio is taken as the measure of the cost of equity capital. This implies that a high P/E stock has a low cost of capital and implicitly should be willing to undertake projects which have low yields. In fact, the P/E ratio is high because the investing public believes that the company can invest at higher rates of return than the average company. This method also neglects future earnings and does not look at cash flows and the timing of the cash flows.

2. The present price/expected—earnings method

A second approach is to use the expected potential earnings or estimated average future earnings divided by the market price of the stock. This approach has two drawbacks. First, it looks at the earnings rather than the cash flows and second, the evaluation of a stock is dependent on many things, only one of which is earnings.

3. Dividend valuation method

A third approach is the evaluation of dividends. This approach would be acceptable except that earnings and dividends are only loosely related. The problem really becomes one of estimating the cash flows and the potential dividends in the future.

4. Past rate of return method

This method computes the return to Quaker Oats stockholders in the past and assumes that this is the return they deem necessary for the future. This is less than satisfactory because the return in the past is dependent on numerous factors which do not necessarily project into the future.

This leaves the risk-adjusted method as the only other alternative. It is not perfect, but it is much better than any of the other alternatives. One of the primary reasons it is better is that it uses the market return to common stocks as a base. This eliminates any of the problems associated with individual stocks. The price of a company's stock is usually relatively unstable while the adjustment to the market rate of return necessary to account for a company's risk should be relatively stable over time.

Risk and the cost of capital

The risk of owning an individual stock can be partially eliminated by owning a portfolio of stocks. This means that even though several individual stocks may be very risky ("risky" meaning a high fluctuation or variance in price), by holding a large portfolio this risk can be diversified away. Risk may be explained by looking at a frequency

Frequency A

10% rate of return

Frequency B

10% rate of return

distribution. If the frequency distributions in the illustration above are "standard normal," the height of the curve represents the probability of being at a particular return. In both cases the expected return is 10 percent, but in A it is much more likely that the return far exceeds 10 percent or that it is far less than 10 percent or negative. While

B has the same expected return, it is improbable that the return will be far from 10 percent.

The true risk of a stock is how its return is related to the total portfolio. If all the stocks moved up and down together then this risk would be eliminated by diversification. This relationship of the movement of stocks is called the covariance. If two stocks move in the same direction they have a positive covariance. If they move in opposite directions then they have a negative covariance, and if there is no relationship the covariance is zero.

The covariance is the risk which cannot be eliminated by diversification. Thus, if a portfolio of stocks has a high covariance with the total market, diversification will not eliminate the risk and, therefore, investors must be compensated with a higher rate of return. This is another way of saying that the cost of capital for a firm with a high covariance with the total market is higher than a firm with a low covariance.

The statistic which is used to describe the relationship of an individual stock to the total market is called the "beta" (B). If an individual stock's "beta" is equal to 1, when the market moves up or down 1 percent, this stock also moves up or down by 1 percent. A "beta" of 2 would indicate a 2 percent movement in an individual stock when the market has a 1 percent change. The *S&P 500 Stock Index* is usually used for movement in the market.

Since the beta measures the movement in the price of individual stock in comparison to the total market, it automatically takes into consideration the amount of leverage of the individual company.

The cost of equity capital for an individual stock can be determined by using the beta of that stock, the risk-free rate of return and the market rate of return. The treasury bill rate is usually used for risk-free rate, and for the market rate of return 9.3 percent is often used. This is the return found by Fisher and Lorie for all stocks listed on the New York Stock Exchange for the period 1928–65. Merrill Lynch, et al., have compiled the B statistics for most publicly traded stocks. The cost of equity capital, Y, can be computed by using the following formula:

$$Y = R_f + (R_m - R_f)B$$

where R_f is the risk-free rate of return, R_m is the market rate of return, and B is the beta of the individual stock.

The overall cost of capital (c^*) can then be computed using the weighted average cost of debt and equity capital. That is:

$$c^* = \frac{E}{D+E} \cdot Y + \frac{D}{D+E} \cdot (1-t)b$$

where E is the amount of equity, D is the amount of debt, Y is the cost of equity, b is the cost of debt, and t is the tax rate.

Before actually calculating the cost of capital for Quaker Oats, some additional discussion will be helpful in understanding the cost of capital and why it changes through time.

Inflation and the cost of capital

The cost of both debt and equity capital have built into them an inflation premium. For example, bondholders must be compensated for the loss in purchasing power and also receive some real rate of return. The nominal interest rate, i, is comprised of two parts such that it is usually referred to as $i = r + p$ where r is the real return and p is the anticipated rate of inflation over the life of the bond. Attached is a graph which shows the nominal interest rate less the Consumer Price Index. Note that the real rate has fluctuated within a very small band. Like bondholders, stockholders must also be compensated for the purchasing power lost through inflation. Thus, when estimating the cost of capital, care must be taken to explicitly state if this cost of capital includes or excludes the inflationary premium.

When the nominal rate of return is used for project evaluations or acquisitions, price increases should be assumed during the life of the project. If costs are increasing at the same rate as the prices, the operating income will also be increasing at the same rate. The nominal rate of return will be above the real rate of return by approximately the rate of price increases assumed. For example, if a project indicated a DCF rate of return of 13 percent when prices were assumed to be increasing by 5 percent per year, the real rate of return would only be 8 percent.

The implications of this for project evaluations and acquisitions are obvious. First, if a discount rate which included the inflationary premium is used, it should be assumed that prices are increasing by the same amount as the premium. Second, if the discount rate does not include the inflationary premium, the cost of capital is much lower but no price increases should be assumed. Third, as inflation and inflationary expectations change, the computation of the nominal cost of capital will be changing. Thus, it is dangerous to use one fixed rate for the cost of capital without periodic review.

Cost of capital for foreign acquisitions

For domestic acquisitions, there is general agreement that the seller's cost of capital is the appropriate rate of discount to be used for evaluation. For foreign acquisitions the exact same principles apply.

Because a small domestic acquisition has very little effect on the parent company and can be financed at our cost of capital, it is tempting to say that our cost of capital is the appropriate rate for evaluation. However, when one realizes that if this policy were continually followed, several small acquisitions would start to change the company's financial position and the risk which the investment community associates with our stock. That is to say, a series of acquisitions could change the parent company's cost of capital. Likewise, one small foreign acquisition will have little effect on our financial structure and could be evaluated at our cost of capital. However, several such acquisitions would change our own cost of capital and the value of our stock. If one carried to an extreme the misguided logic of using our cost of capital for foreign acquisitions, almost all such acquisitions would look attractive. We would find that the foreign part of our business would be larger than our domestic, and our company's cost of capital would become the foreign cost of capital.

Most foreign countries have a capital scarce situation compared to the United States. The cost of capital in these countries should be determined not by our cost of capital, but by rates prevailing in that particular country. The rate of return would tend to equalize if it were not for higher risk in foreign countries and the barriers to capital and labor mobility. The associated risks are the uncertainty of future tax rates, the possibility of nationalization, and a less stable political and economic climate. The appropriate discount rate for foreign projects and acquisitions is something which needs more study, but from very rough estimates which have been done, I believe that the cost of capital for foreign projects and acquisitions is considerably higher than in the United States. Actually how much higher depends on the particular country. In Latin America I feel that the real cost of capital is approximately 4 percent above that in the United States.

Calculations of Quaker's cost of capital

Calculations of Quaker's cost of capital have been made using three different approaches: (1) the "standard" cost of capital calculation which might be done by just plugging numbers into a formula without taking into consideration the current market conditions, (2) the cost of capital considering the current market conditions, and (3) the cost of capital in real terms.

Merrill Lynch calculates the B for Quaker's stock and most other listed stocks on a monthly basis. When our cost of capital was previously calculated, a B of .79 was used based on the December 1971 issue of "Security Risk Evaluation" published by Merrill Lynch. This B was based on the previous five years using monthly observations. Using the previous 60 monthly observations for B, and assuming the riskless rate of return is 6.0 percent and using the 9.3 percent that Fisher and Lorie found to be the market rate of return, Quaker's equity cost of capital is:

$$Y = R_f + (R_m - R_f) \text{ B}$$
$$Y = 6.0 + (9.3 - 6.0) .79$$
$$Y = 6.0 + 2.6$$
$$Y = 8.6$$

Quaker's current bond yield is approximately 7.5 percent, thus our aftertax nominal cost of capital using 8.6 percent as the cost of equity is:

$$c^* = \frac{E}{D+E} \cdot Y + \frac{D}{D+E} \cdot (1 - t)b$$
$$c^* = .68(8.6\%) + .32 (.5) (7.5\%)$$
$$c^* = 5.8 + 1.2$$
$$c^* = 7.0$$

Taking into consideration the current market considerations, there are two factors which have changed: (1) Quaker's B, and (2) the market rate of return.

Quaker's beta has changed considerably in the last few years. Our acquisitions in the toys and recreation field, the growth of our chemical division, and our restaurant business have considerably changed the nature of our business and the sources of our profits. These areas are not as stable as the grocery products business and have increased the risk associated with ownership of our stocks. This is the same thing as saying that our "beta" and, thus, our cost of capital, have increased.

For evidence of this, several methods were used. First, an update of Merrill Lynch's "Security Risk Evaluation" was obtained from the treasurer's department. The April 1973 issue showed our beta as .87. This reflected the price movement of our stock from March 1968 to March 1973. Even though the B had increased from the previously calculated .79, a large part of the recent calculation was from a period which did not properly reflect the recent changes which have taken place in the company. As a result, I calculated our B for increasingly shorter time periods to see what the result would be. Using data through May 31, 1973, if the time period is shortened to four years, the beta is .98, three years .95, two years 1.75 and one year 2.3. The high beta for the most recent year reflects the fact that since December 1972, the price of Quaker stock has dropped 22.5 percent while the S&P 500 has declined 11 percent.

One year or even two years is too short a period to accurately measure a company's beta. However, the above does yield some evidence that our beta and our cost of capital have increased in recent years. What is our B today? As can be seen, a case for almost any number could be made. A better perspective can be obtained by looking at our individual sources of profit. If the International sector is deleted, our planned F-74 profit is 49 percent from Grocery Products, 10 percent from Industrial and Institutional, and 41 percent from Toys and Recreational. Since 90 percent of Industrial and Institutional's profit will come from Chemicals, the B of the chemical industry would be a good approximation for that part of our business. The average B of 16 chemical companies is 1.2. The average B of four toy manufacturers (Ideal, Mattel, Milton Bradley, and Tonka) is 1.4. If we assume grocery products is a low risk, stable industry with a B of .8, we can calculate a weighted average "B" for Quaker Oats.

$$
\begin{array}{ccc}
 & \text{Weight for} & \text{Weight for} \\
\text{Weight for} & \text{Toys and} & \text{Industrial and} \\
\text{Quaker B} = \text{Grocery Products} \times B + \text{Recreation} \times B + \text{Institutional} \times B
\end{array}
$$

Quaker B = .49 (.8) + .41 (1.4) + .10 (1.2)
Quaker B = 1.1

I feel that with the recent radical changes in the nature of our business and on the basis of all calculations made that a B of 1.1 for Quaker is a good estimate.

The second changed factor is the market rate of return. The Fisher-Lorie study was done for the years 1928–65. During this period the average rate of inflation (CPI) was only 1.7 percent. Fisher and Lorie found the market rate of return to be 9.3 which means that the real rate of return over this period was 1.7 percent less or 7.6 percent. The recent inflation rates have resulted in an inflationary expectation far in excess of 1.7 percent. The average rate of increase in the Consumer Price Index has been 4.1 percent since 1965. The current level long-term interest rates would indicate that investors are estimating a rate of inflation in the future of approximately 4 to 4½ percent. If we assume a 4 rate of inflation for the future, then the nominal market rate of return will be equal to the real rate of 7.6 percent plus 4 percent or 11.6 percent. Using the new B of 1.1 and the new market rate of return, Quaker's cost of capital is:

Cost of equity
$Y = 6.0 + (11.6 - 6.0)\ 1.1$
$Y = 6.0 + 6.2$
$Y = 12.2\%$

Aftertax overall cost of capital
$c^* = .68\ (12.2\%) + .32\ (.5)\ (7.5\%)$
$c^* = 8.3 + 1.2$
$c^* = 9.5\%$

It should be noted that this figure includes the inflationary premium discussed earlier. However, some project evaluations and almost all acquisitions assume price increases. Evaluations of acquisitions assume that profits and prices will continue to increase in the future based on past changes which include inflationary increases. Thus, when a rate of discount of 10 percent is used to evaluate these acquisitions, the value derived should be the maximum Quaker is willing to pay, and if this price is paid it will not yield any substantial additional value to our stockholders.

In order to find the cost of capital in real terms, the market return and the bond yield must be adjusted for inflation. If we assume that the anticipated rate of inflation is 4 percent, then the real cost of capital is simply the nominal cost of capital 9.5 percent, less the 4 percent inflationary premium, or 5.5 percent.

The large effect which a small change in B has on the cost of capital should be noted. Table A shows the different costs of capital for different assumptions. For acquisitions and project evaluations some attempt should be made to take into consideration the cost of capital for each particular case. The total cost of capital to Quaker Oats is really a moot question. What is important is the cost of capital for different segments for our business. If a single rate is used, the projects or acquisitions that will look most attractive will be those which have the highest risk. This would change our cost of capital and decrease the value of our stock. This is a lesson which should be easy for us to see when we look at our own company and how it has changed in the last few years. I do not mean to imply that the recent acquisitions have not been good ones, only that they have increased the volatility of our stock and, thus, the risk associated with holding it.

Table A
Cost of capital—Assuming 4 percent inflation

			B	
R_m	.9	1.0	1.1	1.2
10.6%	7.9	8.4	8.7	9.0
11.6%	8.7	9.1	9.5	9.8
12.6%	9.3	9.8	10.2	10.7

B = Beta.
R_m = The market rate of return.
R_f = The riskless rate is assumed 6 percent.
Best estimate is 9.5 percent.

Finally, I would like to discuss the necessity for reviewing the cost of capital over time. As indicated above, the cost of capital of a company will change as the company changes. Very few companies have changed as radically as Quaker Oats has in such a short time. However, as mentioned above, the cost of capital for the company is unimportant. The important thing is to estimate the cost of capital for individual projects and acquisitions. Real rates of return change very little over time. Thus, the importance of reviewing the cost of capital is to be certain that the rate of inflation assumed corresponds to the rate of inflation assumed when the cost of capital was last calculated.

T. D. Henrion
Financial Analyst

DATE: July 3, 1973   Copies to: Mr. W. F. Guinee,
TO: Mr. Thomas J. Curley, Jr.   Senior Vice President
FROM: Peter B. Fritzsche   Mr. R. A. Bowen
SUBJECT: Cost of Capital   Vice President &
                                                                Corporate Controller
                                                                Mr. R. D. Denison
                                                                Vice President,
                                                                Corporate Planning
                                                                & Analysis
                                                                Mr. E. J. Garneau
                                                                Manager, Project
                                                                Evaluations
                                                                Mr. T. D. Henrion
                                                                Financial Analyst

We have reviewed Tom Henrion's memorandum on the cost of capital and have the following comments:

We are in agreement with the proposition that a company's cost of capital should be reviewed from time to time to determine if it is increasing or decreasing and what effect this might have on our project evaluations. In addition, we agree with the idea that for acquisitions in particular, it is the sellers' cost of capital (assuming Quaker's debt to equity ratio) that should be used as the minimum cutoff rate which in turn determines the maximum purchase price we could afford to pay. Finally, we are also in agreement with the proposition that foreign acquisitions tend to have higher costs of capital primarily because of higher costs of debt as well as higher market rates of return.

In terms of Quaker's current cost of capital, we disagree with the assumptions made by Tom, although we agree with the methodology used. Specifically, our disagreements are as follows:

1. It's inappropriate to use a weighted average beta based on the corporate mix of business. The market will take into account the different businesses you're in and it's the long-term, actual market beta that should be used, not a weighted average of the different industries in which you operate. Only a long-term beta should be used, because a short-term beta can be affected by unnatural and unrealistic factors. In Quaker's case, the appropriate beta to use would be the most recent four or five years' average. The past two years, Quaker's beta (and that of many others) has been affected by the unrealistic and unnatural affects of the price freeze while at the same time the *S&P 500* appears to have been much more stable. In Quaker's case the current beta that should be used should be either .87 or .98, not the weighted average of 1.1.
2. The most significant change in Quaker's cost of capital in Tom's analysis, however, is caused by the supposed increase in market rate of return from 9.3 percent to 11.6 percent to take into account the effects of inflation. The 9.3 percent rate is the market rate of return for the years 1928–65. While the average rate of inflation during this period was only 1.7 percent, it did include several periods where the inflation rate was close to 4 percent, i.e., just after World War II and the Korean

War. As such, the market rate of return of 9.3 percent includes periods of high inflation as well as periods of low inflation or actual deflation. The Fisher-Lorie figure should be updated to include the latest period, but the long-term rate of return would not be significantly different from the 9.3 percent. As a matter of fact the market rate of return in the past three years, which have been periods of very high inflation, has been very poor in terms of stock prices. Such was not the case in prior periods of high inflation. In addition, the effects of inflation in the calculation of the cost of equity is taken care of in the short-term risk-free rate of return which is currently slightly in excess of 6 percent.

3. Based on your own calculations, the cost of capital for Quaker currently is 7.5 percent. The mathematics are as follows:

   a. Cost of equity

$$Y = 6.3 + (9.3 - 6.3)\ .98$$
$$Y = 6.3 + 2.9 = 9.2$$

   b. Aftertax cost of capital

$$c^* = .68\ (9.2\%) + .32\ (.5)\ (7.5\%)$$
$$c^* = 6.3 + 1.2$$
$$c^* = 7.5$$

The real difference in our numbers comes from the fact that Tom is adjusting the cost of capital primarily through changes in market rates of return based on the current inflation rate, while our approach would be to have the current rate of inflation be one small piece of the long-term average market rates of return. As you can see the different assumptions have a very significant effect on our cost of capital.

Peter Fritzsche
Vice President
Business Development

DATE: July 13, 1973
TO: File
FROM: T. D. Henrion
SUBJECT: Response to Peter Fritzsche on the Cost of Capital

There seems to be a growing agreement on the different issues associated with the cost of capital. This makes it necessary to concentrate only on the areas of contention. With that in mind, I address the issues which Peter Fritzsche raised with respect to my cost of capital memorandum.

Using a weighted average beta is quite appropriate for estimating the cost of capital, especially considering the recent changes in the company's structure due to acquisitions. It is becoming more apparent among academicians and the investment community that using the beta calculated for an individual stock can be misleading. Most beta calculations have very high standard errors (that is, they are very unreliable) and can be affected by "unnatural and unrealistic factors" in the short run which will have enough impact on the beta to make it unreliable. Thus, there has been a tendency to look at betas from a "risk class" point of view.

I would, however, be in general agreement that using a period as long as five years should eliminate most of the distortions associated with random "unnatural" movements in the price of a stock. On the other hand, one should never plug numbers into a formula and assume the results are reasonable. For evaluating the cost of capital for Quaker some adjustment must be made to take into consideration the fact that a large part of our business has changed.

On the basis of the estimates I ran for our beta, in a year or two the Merrill Lynch service will be estimating our beta at something higher than 1.1 which I estimated. At that time I will probably be arguing that the Merrill Lynch figure is too high. However, it will depend on the market conditions at that time, not on just what a formula says it is. As an example, the wage-price controls have had an injurious effect upon us and have probably had a tendency to raise our beta. If the danger of additional price controls is no longer present in a year or two some adjustment should be made to our calculated beta.

The second area of contention is how to handle inflation. The point I was trying to make is that the cost of capital must be adjusted for inflation if we have estimates which include inflation. The adjustment should have nothing to do with historical data, but should be adjusted in conjunction with the assumptions being made about future price increases used in the project and acquisition evaluations.

I believe Peter feels past rates of inflation are good predictors of future rates. While I don't feel this is true, the important point is to include inflation (regardless of the specific expected rate used) in the cost of capital and the project projections. If this is handled in a consistent fashion, the specific rate of inflation used doesn't matter. Any consistent treatment will result in the same answers.

The 6 percent used as the risk-free rate and the 7.5 percent used for our borrowing rate both have inflationary expectations built into them. I am simply contending that the same adjustment needs to be made for the market rate of return.

Another argument is that the addition of Fisher-Price, Marx, and Needlecraft have reduced the company beta through diversification. From an investor's point of view this does not reduce the beta because this is diversification he could get himself through buying several similar stocks. Beta is the risk which cannot be diversified away. These acquisitions reduce our beta only if the acquired company's beta is lower than our beta.

In summary, let me again emphasize that the company's cost of capital is a moot question; the specific rate of inflation to use is also a secondary consideration. What is important is the cost of capital we should use for project evaluations and acquisitions. In order to do this, two adjustments must be made. First, it is necessary to make an adjustment to the beta to take account of the market assigned risk to the type of business. Second, the cost of capital has to be adjusted to correspond to the inflation assumptions made in the projected sales.

Thomas D. Henrion
Financial Analyst

Exhibit 4
Yields on highest grade seasoned corporate bonds

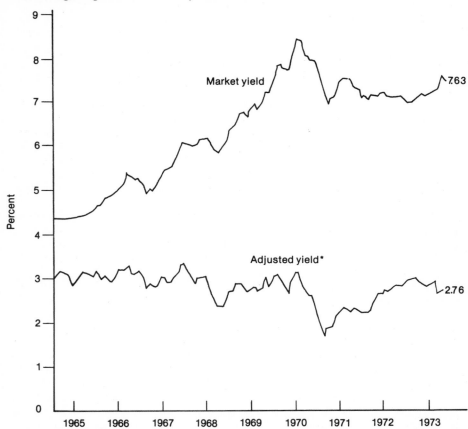

* Market yield less average annual rate of change in consumer prices over three previous years. Latest
data plotted: market yield-September; adjusted yield-September estimated.
  Source: Prepared by Federal Reserve Bank of St. Louis; published in *Monetary Trends,* October 1973.

Case 3-2

The Quaker Oats Company: Cost of Capital (B)

INTRODUCTION

In August of 1973, N. F. Guinee, senior vice president in charge of finance and planning for the Quaker Oats Company, was attempting to determine the minimum acceptable rate or rates of return to be required on new capital investments. Recently, Tom D. Henrion, financial analyst at Quaker Oats, had computed the cost of capital for the company using the "Capital Asset Pricing Model" for determining its cost of equity. Mr. Henrion had concluded that Quaker Oats' aftertax cost of capital was in the neighborhood of 9.5 percent (see Quaker Oats Company: Cost of Capital [A], Case 3–1).

A major issue under discussion was whether the company should use a single cutoff rate based on the company's overall weighted average cost of capital or if this minimum cutoff rate should differ for the various divisions or economic units according to their individual or profit-risk characteristics. E. J. Garneau, project evaluation manager of Quaker Oats, thought that the use of multiple hurdle rates, based on the approximate cost of capital that each economic unit would have if it were a separate business entity, would result in a more efficient and profitable allocation of capital among Quaker's divisions than the use of a single cutoff rate for Quaker as a whole. The use of a single cutoff rate, it was argued, tended to discriminate against projects of the more stable divisions and favor those of the more risky units.

Those favoring the use of a single, overall company cutoff rate argued that only through the use of a uniform hurdle rate could the company expect to maximize the return on its investments. In addition, they pointed out that not only would multiple hurdle rates lead to suboptimal investment decisions, but that estimates of cost of capital for the different economic units were illusory at best, because it was impossible to determine what their capital structure and individual cost components would be like if they were separate business entities.

COST OF CAPITAL OF THE MAGIC PAN DIVISION

The following correspondence illustrates the arguments made in favor of the use of multiple hurdle rates at Quaker Oats, as well as an attempt to compute the cost of capital for the Magic Pan Division.

DATE: August 15, 1973   Copies to: Mr. R. A. Bowen
TO: Mr. W. Fenton Guinee   Mr. P. B. Fritzsche
FROM: Mr. E. J. Garneau   Mr. R. D. Denison
SUBJECT: Cost of Capital Studies

Enclosed is the first in a series of studies we intend to conduct on the cost of capital of Quaker's various divisions. We are attempting to quantify these capital costs so that a series of "hurdle" or cutoff rates, which would vary according to the division/industry under consideration, can be used in individual project evaluations. We feel that the use of such multiple hurdle rates, rather than a single cutoff rate for Quaker as a whole, will result in more efficient and profitable allocations of capital among Quaker's divisions.

The enclosed study describes our attempt to find such an individual cutoff for our Magic Pan Restaurant Division. The major finding is that Magic Pan's cost of capital is approximately 7.5 percent, versus a 9.13 percent figure for Quaker as a whole. An attempt was made to sample data from those companies most closely resembling Magic Pan in terms of restaurant type, size, and operation. Thus Magic Pan's high calculated beta (1.83 versus Quaker's .79) and low cost of capital can be primarily attributed to the higher leverage ratios prevalent in the restaurant industry.

We recognize some of the present limitations and shortcomings of such analysis. Availability of full and accurate information, comparability of data from disparate entities, averaging techniques, and the state of the art of beta analysis all contribute to inaccuracies surrounding the estimated figure. It should be noted also that the figure derived for Magic Pan is a "future measure" rather than a current figure, for the data basic to the analysis was taken from established companies. Since Magic Pan is essentially in its "start-up" stage, it can be presumed that it will "grow" into figures that fall into the range encompassing the more mature measures derived herein.

Despite the difficulties inherent in such analysis, we feel that the large difference between the cost of capital figures derived for Magic Pan and Quaker exceeds any difference due to analysis inaccuracies alone and has direct implications for future investment proposals in terms of acceptable returns. We hope future studies of other divisions will yield similar differences and continue to point the way toward the use of accurate multiple hurdle rates, rather than a single cutoff rate, in the evaluation of Quaker's investment projects.

Prior to further work we would appreciate your comments and suggestions on the methods used and results obtained herein.

Emilio Garneau
Manager—Project Evaluation

Encl.

DATE: August 14, 1973
TO: Mr. E. J. Garneau
FROM: Mr. J. C. McCall, Jr.
SUBJECT: Magic Pan Cost of Capital

It is believed that the cost of capital for Magic Pan may be different than for Quaker as a whole. To explore this further I obtained information on a number of companies in the restaurant business. I excluded from consideration all restaurant chains that are part of a much larger company.

The cost of capital was calculated using the following two formulae:

$$Y = R_f + (R_m - R_f)\, B$$

$$c^* = \frac{E}{D+E} \cdot Y + \frac{D}{D+E} \cdot (1-t)b$$

where:

$Y =$ Cost of equity capital.
$R_f =$ The risk-free rate of return.
$R_m =$ The market rate of return.
$B =$ The beta of the individual stock.
$c^* =$ The cost of capital.
$t =$ The tax rate.
$b =$ The cost of debt.
$D =$ The sum of (1) all interest-bearing debt at the *market* value and (2) capitalized lease expense over 15 years. It does not include preferred stock
$D + E =$ The sum of (1) total assets including goodwill and (2) capitalized lease expense over 15 years.

The assumption was made that all of the companies analyzed have a bond yield *(b)* of 7.5 percent and a risk-free rate of return *(R_f)* of 6 percent. The market rate of return *(R_m)* was considered both as 9.3 percent and 11.6 percent (the latter assuming 7.6 percent real growth plus 4 percent inflation). The beta for each company was obtained from the April 1973 Merrill Lynch analysis of stock movement over the last five years. The debt and equity percentages were obtained from annual reports and investment research reports.

Exhibit 1 shows a comparison of cost of capital calculations for Quaker and for the sample of restaurants under different assumptions. It indicates that Magic Pan's cost of capital may be as low as 7.5 percent (compared to Quaker's calculated cost of capital of 9.13 percent). Exhibit 2 shows the effect on the restaurant sample's cost of capital of a 20 percent change in each factor used to calculate cost of capital.

Exhibit 1
Calculated cost of capital

	Quaker		Restaurants	
Beta	.79	1.1	1.83	1.83
Bond rate *(b)*	7.50%	7.50%	7.50%	7.50%
$D/D+E$	.36%	.36%	.70%	.70%
$E/D+E$	.64%	.64%	.30%	.30%
R_f	6.00%	6.00%	6.00%	6.00%
R_m	11.60%	11.60%	9.30%	11.60%
t	50.00%	50.00%	50.00%	50.00%
Y	10.42%	12.16%	12.04%	16.25%
c^*	8.02%	9.13%	6.24%	7.51%

Exhibit 2
Sensitivities

			Revised		Percent change	
	Original	+20 percent	Y	c^*	Y	c^*
Beta	1.83	2.20	18.32	8.13	13%	8%
Bond rate *(b)*	7.50%	9.00%	16.248	8.02	—	7
$D/D+E$	.70%	.84%	16.248	5.75	—	23
R_f	6.00%	7.20%	15.252	7.21	6	4
R_m	11.60%	13.92%	20.494	8.78	26	17
t	50.00%	60.00%	16.248	6.97	—	7
$E/D+E$	.30%	.16%	16.248	8.25	—	10
Y	16.248%	—	—	—	—	—
c^*	7.51%	—	—	—	—	—

Because sensitivity analyses have indicated that leverage $(D/D + E)$ has a sizable impact on the cost of capital, and in addition the capitalization of leases have a significant impact on the leverage ratio, we were careful to include in the leverage ratio only those companies for which this information was available (in this case four companies). Annual lease commitments were capitalized over 15 years using a yield of 9 percent. Exhibit 3 shows detail on how $D/D + E$ values were determined.

Exhibit 4 shows the beta value for all companies for which a figure was available and the $D/D+E$ value for four companies. The arithmetic mean beta from the 17 values in Exhibit 4 is 1.77. Of the 17 restaurants for which beta measures were available, 6 were selected as being closest to Magic Pan with respect to the types of restaurants operated and absence of other types of business as part of the company. The six are indicated by asterisks in Exhibit 4. The arithmetic mean beta for these six is 1.83. The arithmetic mean $D/D+E$ for the four companies with values shown in Exhibit 4 is .70. The mean beta of 1.83 and mean $D/D+E$ of .70 are the values that were used to calculate the cost of capital in Exhibit 1. Exhibit 5 provides a short description of each of the 18 companies included in the analysis.

Exhibit 3
Calculation of $D/D + E$ ($000)

1. *Quaker*
   Short-term debt (interest-bearing):
   Notes payable to banks .... $ 12,058
   Commercial paper 21,550
   Current maturities of LTD 4,136
   Long-term debt:
   Revolving credit 37,000
   3½% note 8,000
   6½% note 25,000
   7.7% debentures 50,000
   Foreign obligations 9,621
   Capitalized leases 31,630

   Total Debt $198,995
   Total assets 520,686
   Capitalized leases 31,630

   Total $552,316

$$D/D + E = 198,995/552,316 = .36$$

2. *Denny's*
   Short-term debt (interest-bearing):
   Notes payable to banks .... $ 173
   Current maturities 5,262
   Long-term debt:
   Long-term notes 19,319
   Debentures 14,108
   Capitalized leases:
   Lease obligations 12,929
   Capitalized lease commitments 84,895

   Total Debt 136,686
   Total assets 107,086
   Capitalized lease commitments 84,895

   Total $191,981

$$D/D + E = 136,686/191,981 = .71$$

3. *Sambos*
   Short-term debt (interest-bearing):
   Current portion of LTD .... $ 2,740
   Long-term debt 4,109
   Capitalized lease commitments 43,930

   Total Debt .... $ 50,779
   Total assets 21,921
   Capitalized lease commitments 43,930

   Total .... $ 65,851

$$D/D + E = 50,779/65,851 = .77$$

4. *Steak & Ale*
   Short-term debt (interest-bearing):
   Current portion of LTD .... $ 158
   Long-term debt 1,617
   Capitalized leases 17,572

   Total Debt 19,347
   Total assets 14,686
   Capitalized lease commitments 17,572

   Total .... $ 32,258

$$D/D + E = 19,347/32,258 = .60$$

Exhibit 3 *(continued)*

5. *Steak & Brew, Inc.*

Short-term debt (interest-bearing):

Current portion of LTD	$ 135
Long-term debt	790
Capitalized lease commitments	10,982
Total Debt	11,907
Total assets	5,905
Capitalized leases	10,982
Total	$ 16,887

$$D/D + E = 11,907/16,887 = .71$$

Exhibit 4
Beta and $D/D + E$ values for sample companies

	Beta	$D/D + E$
Full menu restaurants:		
*Denny's	1.42	.72
Frisch's	1.63	
Howard Johnson	1.48	
International Industries	2.63	
Morrison	.87	
*Restaurant Association	2.56	
Royal Castle	1.43	
*Sambo's	1.54	.77
Saga	1.26	
*Specialty Restaurants	1.97	
Steak restaurants:		
*Steak & Brew Inc.	2.47	.71
Steak & Ale Restaurants of America, Inc.		.60
Bonanza	2.89	
Ponderosa	2.34	
Gino's	.86	
*Valles	1.00	
Italian restaurants:		
Pizza Hut	2.06	
Mexican restaurants:		
Taco Bell	1.69	

Exhibit 5
Description of companies

DENNY'S

Owns and operates 85 percent of 811 Denny's restaurants and Winchell's Donut Houses; franchises the remainder.

FRISCH'S

Operates and franchises 92 restaurants, drive-ins, and coffee shops. Also operates two high-rise motor hotels in the Cincinnati area.

HOWARD JOHNSON

Operations include a Restaurant Group, Accommodations Group, Special Divisions Group and Manufacturing and Distribution. The company operates or licenses 910

Exhibit 5 *(continued)*

Howard Johnson, Red Coach Grill and Ground Round restaurants and 460 motor lodges. The company's Special Divisions Group includes grocery products, a small gift shop operation, and consultation services on motor lodge operation. The Manufacturing and Distribution Group includes four food-processing plants for candy, condiments, and ice cream.

INTERNATIONAL INDUSTRIES

Operates and franchises Orange Julius stands, Ice Cream Shoppes, Original House of Pies stores and Love's Wood Pit Barbeque Restaurants. Also franchises rental stores for party supplies, medical equipment, and camping and sporting goods. Operates Bryman schools for medicine and dentistry.

STEAK & BREW INC.

Steak & Brew operates 55 restaurants and has 10 under franchise. Offers a limited menu of steak, prime rib, and salad bar.

MORRISON

Eighty-nine percent of total revenue is from operation of cafeterias, restaurants, and food service business. Operate 70 public cafeterias and restaurants and service 184 industrial feeding facilities in the Southeast. The company owns seven motor inns and franchises five others.

RESTAURANT ASSOCIATION

Operates 75 specialty restaurants, coffee shops, cafeterias, luncheon clubs, and snack bars in 25 cities. Deluxe restaurants include Four Seasons, The Forum of the Twelve Caesars, and Tower Suite. Moderately priced include Brasserie, Tavern on Green, Mamma Leones, and Yard of Ale.

ROYAL CASTLE

Owns and operates a chain of 153 "24-hour-a-day" counter service and takeout hamburger facilities. They are in the process of extending these operations to campgrounds, pizza restaurants, and steak houses.

SAMBOS

Operates 250 Sambo's full menu restaurants in 23 states.

SAGA

Operates an educational, health care, business and industry, Straw Hat Pizza, and Saga Enterprises division.

Educational	—Food service to 270 schools.
Health care	—Manual and vended food services to hospitals.
Business and industry	—Food service to offices and plants.
Straw Hat	—Own 73 and franchise 69 restaurants.
Saga Enterprises	—Operate Velvet Turtle and Black Angus restaurants.

SPECIALTY RESTAURANTS

Operate a chain of 21 popular priced restaurants and two shopping villages.

BONANZA

Licenses and services a chain of franchised low-cost steak restaurants. The company operates 86 of the 307 restaurants themselves and features standard menu and rapid service.

PONDEROSA

Operates 68 steak houses directly and franchises 68 others.

Exhibit 5 *(concluded)*

GINO'S

  Operates 322 restaurants under names of Gino's and Gino's Steak House, Gino's Kentucky Fried Chicken, and Tops Restaurants.

VALLES

  Operates a chain of 14 steak houses and fast-food snack bars.

PIZZA HUT

  Develops, operates, and franchises Pizza Huts. The company owns 320 units and franchises 460.

TACO BELL

  Owns and franchises fast service restaurants featuring inexpensive Mexican foods. Of the 442 total units, 250 are in California.

STEAK & ALE RESTAURANTS OF AMERICA, INC.

  Company operates about 60 limited name steak restaurants under the names of "Steak & Ale" or "Jolly Ox."

Conclusion

It was not possible to find any one public company that closely resembles Magic Pan in size, operation, and kind of specialty restaurants. It also was not easy to find *both* beta and $D/D + E$ for each of the companies analyzed. A more detailed analysis would require an examination of 10K reports for each of the 18 companies in Exhibit 2.

I am very uncomfortable about placing much emphasis on beta values because we know that (1) they vary significantly depending on the number of years over which the calculation is made, (2) the makeup of many of the companies compared has changed considerably over the calculation period, and (3) many factors other than riskiness affect stock prices. This, coupled with the fact that the sample size was small prevent placing any significant degree of confidence in the results. However, assuming that Quaker's cost of capital is close to 9.13 percent (Exhibit 1), it would appear that Magic Pan's cost of capital is lower (maybe as low as 7.5 percent).

J. C. McCall, Jr.
Supervisor—Financial Analysis

JCMcD:ls

Case 3-3

The Dickey-Lincoln Dam Project

Robert Orr, legislative assistant to a New England senator, had barely settled into his seat in the House Gallery when Congressman Edward Boland (D–Mass.) rose to address the question of why a discount (interest) rate of 3¼ percent was used by the House Public Works Committee for the proposed Dickey-Lincoln School Dams in Northern Maine.

> **Mr. Boland (D–Mass.):** The question has been raised: what about the discount rate? I am looking across this Chamber here at members from the great Southwest, the great Northwest, the South, the Midwest, and I am looking at members in whose districts projects have been built for years at 3¼ percent.
>
> Does the gentleman from Connecticut or the gentleman from Massachusetts or do any of those who oppose this project suggest that New England ought not to be treated on the same basis as every project that has been heretofore built by the Corps of Engineers, or by the Bureau of Reclamation? Do they suggest that we now ought to pay 6⅞ percent? This project meets all of the criteria of the Corps of Engineers at the 3¼ percent discount rate.
>
> **Mr. Giamo (D–Conn.):** The purpose of stating the interest rate at 3¼ percent . . . is merely to point out the fiction of these interest charges and to show that they are not the true and actual costs of these projects . . . if they ever used the real interest rates and really told the American people what they were paying for a lot of these projects, they would never get them approved.
>
> **Mr. Whitten (D–Miss.):** Will the gentleman yield? . . . if we are submitting the interest rate of some years ago, that the same increase in the front end products has changed in the same manner, so while it may have been 3¼ percent back yonder, the end

127

result of the end product increases at the same ratio. So the relative comparison is the same.

Mr. Myers (D–Penn.): It is true that the cost of interest which is now being used is not current as to rate, but also the benefits are not being brought up to date either. The benefits we can realize from the project are worth a whole lot more than the Corps is using today. The low-interest rate and the low benefits used in the benefit-cost ratio is relevant.

Mr. Boland: The gentleman is absolutely right, it is axiomatic that if costs increase, benefits increase also. There is no question about it.

As the congressmen broke for a quorum call, Orr scanned the fact sheet which an environmental lobbyist had given him:

. . . requested by the Department of Interior and authorized by Congress in 1965 [but without appropriations] . . . located near Dickey, Maine, on the Upper St. John River, one of the last wild rivers in the East. . . . Two miles long, 335 feet high: would be the 6th largest dam in the United States, 11th largest in the world—larger than the Aswan Dam in Egypt . . . would create an 86,000 acre reservoir . . . approved by the Senate year after year, defeated in Committee in the House, but this year was included in House Public Works bill for the first time. . . .

The lobbyist had predicted that Orr's boss might get a lot of favorable publicity if he led a pro-environmental fight against Dickey-Lincoln. But, as Orr listened to the debate, he began to think that while the environmental problems might be substantial, the economic and financial problems were even more intriguing. He was particularly interested in resolving this discussion of the appropriate discount rate, as it seemed to be crucial to the decision. He continued scanning the fact sheet looking for some economic data on the project. Just then, however, Congressman Boland rose to speak on that very point.

Mr. Boland: Dickey-Lincoln will have a total capacity production of 830 megawatts and will provide 740 megawatt hours of peaking power for New England. It will provide 1.2 billion kilowatt-hours annually of hydropower with no fuel costs and very low maintenance costs. . . . While Dickey-Lincoln, like all hydroelectric projects, will have an expensive price tag it will have virtually no fuel costs and very low maintenance costs. Although the initial costs of nonhydroplants, such as fossil fueled or gas turbine installations, is less, the high annual costs of fuel and maintenance makes their ultimate cost far greater.

. . . Dickey-Lincoln will have a minimum life span of 100 years compared to an approximate life of 35 years for nonhydroplants. Thus, all the project's costs will be fully reimbursed within 50 years. The only ultimate federal cost will be $14,500,000, which represents the project costs for flood control and one half of the recreational costs which are in any case nonreimbursable under federal law. Besides all this Dickey-Lincoln will save, in terms of comparable nonhydroplant fuel usage, 1.5 million barrels of oil or 600,000 tons of coal, or 9.2 billion cubic feet of gas annually. The value of saving those quantities over a 100-year period . . . ought to be, I think overwhelmingly evident to all.

. . . As prescribed by law, a rate of 3¼ percent has been used to discount the future benefits of the project to current investment costs. But even at 6⅞ percent, the benefit-to-cost ratio would be 1.3 to 1, more than sufficient to warrant its full funding.

Boland's arguments carried the day and the amendment to delete all funding for the controversial dam was beaten. But as Orr walked back to the Senate side he knew he had heard enough to know that the economics of the project—and more specifically the discount rate employed—merited closer scrutiny before the bill came before the Senate.

DICKEY-LINCOLN ANALYSIS

The Corps of Engineers' study was a straight forward benefit-cost analysis which incorporated the 3¼ percent discount rate prescribed by Congress for public works projects (Exhibit 1). The costs of building the project, plus interest at 3¼ percent, were amortized over 100 years. The annual interest and amortization payment, plus annual maintenance and annualized costs of major replacements were combined and converted into annual costs. Benefits included, as a savings, the full cost of an equivalent amount of power priced at private sector rates plus estimated annual flood control, recreation and redevelopment benefits. This analysis yielded a benefit:cost ratio of 2.6:1. The Corps also presented an "economic efficiency test" which considered the full cost of an equivalent amount of power as if an equivalent amount of capacity had been built at 3¼ percent by the private sector. Hence, they also included as a cost in this alternative the foregone flood control, recreation, and redevelopment benefits. This analysis also produced a favorable benefit:cost ratio.

Finally, the Corps constructed a financial analysis called a "repayment analysis," assuming the project would be repaid at 5⅞ percent over 50 years. This analysis showed savings to consumers generated by cheaper Dickey-Lincoln power of $11.7 million annually.

THE DISCOUNT RATE

After establishing that the senator for whom he worked would be willing to pursue the issue depending on what the research uncovered, Orr began to review the economics and finance literature on the topic of social discount rates. He also remembered that Senator William Proxmire (D–Wis.) had pursued this subject on the Senate Floor earlier in the year. He believed that Proxmire's statement would be a good gauge of how easily the Senate would accept any changes in this concept. (Exhibit 2.)

Orr began his research with the belief that the discount rate was simply the rate at which the federal government could borrow money. But, after he began reading opinions put forth by leading economists and financial experts, he realized that the subject was ever more complex than he had anticipated.

Orr felt that both the discount rate and the benefit:cost analyses were important issues to be clarified for this, and future debates. He wanted to provide his boss with a more useful basis for analysis and choice.

Exhibit 1
Dickey-Lincoln School Lakes, Maine
Fact Sheet

Project Economics

A. General

The project's average annual benefits are currently estimated as follows: (January 1, 1975 price levels)

Benefit	Amount
Power	$52,798,000
Flood control	77,000
Area redevelopment	983,000
Recreation	1,250,000
Total benefits	$55,108,000

The average annual cost of the project reflecting amortization of the initial investment and annual operation and maintenance cost totals $21,138,000. This results in a benefit-to-cost ratio of 2.6 to 1.

Source: *Congressional Record,* December 5, 1974, pps. 38929–38930.

Exhibit 1 *(continued)*

1. Power. As noted, power would be the principal benefit realized through construction of the Dickey-Lincoln School Lakes Project. On-site annual power generation of 1.2 billion kilowatt-hours would result from the total installed capacity of 830,000 kw. Additional power generation of 350 million kilowatt-hours would also be gained by downstream Canadian power plants due to regulated flows from Lincoln School Lake of which 50 percent would be allocated to the United States.

The peaking power output from the project would provide an estimated 10 percent of the New England peaking power generation required in the mid-1980s.

2. Flood control. The flood control benefit results from elimination of flood damages below the project site. Fort Kent, located about 28 miles below Dickey Dam, has experienced ten floods during the past 47 years of record. The most recent floods occurred in May 1961, May 1969, April 1973, and May 1974. The May 1974 flood stages exceeded the record flood of April 1973 and caused damages estimated at $3 million. These losses would be prevented by the project. In view of the uncertain status of Dickey-Lincoln School Lakes and the recurring flood problem at Ft. Kent, a small local protection project has been formulated under Section 205 of the 1948 Flood Control Act, as amended, that would provide some degree of protection to the Town of Ft. Kent. The proposed dike and pumping station would protect to a 100-year frequency flood level and would be limited principally to the commercial center of Ft. Kent. The proposal is presently under review by the office of the governor of Maine.

Dickey-Lincoln School Lakes would provide full protection to the Ft. Kent area.

3. Redevelopment. The Area Redevelopment benefit represents the effect of added employment resulting from the project. The Dickey-Lincoln School Project is located in the part of Aroostook County which is classified as a Title IV (1) Economic Development Area denoting an area of substantial and persistent unemployment. Numerous employment opportunities would arise and the associated wages related to project construction and future operation and maintenance would result in substantial relief to the economically depressed area.

4. Recreation. The recreation benefit is a preliminary estimate of general recreation, hunting and fishing use developed at the close of earlier preconstruction planning activity. As presently envisioned limited facilities such as campsites, comfort stations and boat launching ramps would be provided. A preliminary recreational master plan will be developed—in conjunction with appropriate state and federal agencies—in the early stages of current preconstruction planning effort.

B. Economic analyses

The justification for authorization of all Corp of Engineers' projects is measured in terms of the benefit-to-cost ratio. The economic analysis used to develop this yardstick is based on standards prescribed by Senate Document No. 97, 87th Congress, entitled "Policies, Standards and Procedures in the Formulation, Evaluation and Review of Plans for Use and Development of Water and Related Land Resources." Total project benefits for Dickey-Lincoln School Lakes are comprised of at-market power, total downstream energy, flood control, recreation and area redevelopment type benefits. The power benefits for Dickey-Lincoln School Lakes are equated to the cost of privately financed

Exhibit 1 *(continued)*

equivalent alternative sources of power. The unit power values, furnished by the Federal Power Commission, are based on gas turbines for that portion of project power expected to be marketed in the Boston area for peaking purposes and a base load fossil fuel steam plant as an alternative for that portion to be marketed in Maine.

The project cost is evaluated on an annual basis reflecting amortization of the investment and annual operation and maintenance expenses. The cost has been increased to provide for the transmission of power by adding 50 percent of the annual cost of a line between the project and Boston. It has been assumed that the remaining one half the annual cost will be derived from the wheeling by others of off-peak power. The interest rate used in the economic evaluation is 3¼ percent and the period of analysis is 100 years. Attached as Table 1 is a summary of the economic analysis.

The Corps of Engineers also uses a procedure referred to as an "economic efficiency test" to comprehensively evaluate proper resource development. The objective of an ideal system operation is to meet area power demands at least cost to consumers. Therefore the least costly addition to a region's capacity could be considered as a yardstick for purposes of making a decision regarding such additions. The "economic efficiency test" provides for such a determination. Basically the test provides for a comparison of the costs of providing an equivalent amount of power from the most feasible alternative, likely to develop in the absence of the project, evaluated on a basis comparable with the determination of the federal project costs (with respect to interest rate, i.e., 3¼ percent taxes and insurance). The Corps "economic efficiency test" indicates that the annual at-market charge for Dickey-Lincoln School Lakes power amounts to $21,138,000 while alternative equivalent power charges amount to $42,-759,000. This results in a ratio of 2.0 to 1 in favor of Dickey-Lincoln School Lakes. This means that even if private utilities could obtain financing equivalent to the federal rate, water resource benefits could be provided by Dickey-Lincoln School at half the cost of the private utility alternatives. The attached Table 2 illustrates the "economic efficiency test."

C. Repayment analysis

The above analyses are used to define the economic worth of the project. The financial value of power, however, is determined through the repayment analysis. Marketing of electric power from federal projects is the basic responsibility of the secretary of interior as authorized by Section 5 of the 1944 Flood Control Act. Repayment rates must be sufficient to recover costs of power production and transmission including annual operation and maintenance expenses. The total investment allocated to power must be repaid over a reasonable period of years. As a matter of administration policy, this period has been specified as 50 years. On January 29, 1970, the secretary of interior, under his administrative discretion to establish power rates, instituted new criteria for determining interest rates for repayment purposes for projects not yet under construction. The current interest rate used for Dickey-Lincoln School Lakes repayment under this revised criteria is 6⅛ percent. The resulting analysis shows that power from Dickey-Lincoln School Lakes could be marketed at 30.98 mills per kilowatt hour as compared to 40.90 mills per kilowatt hour for the private alternatives. On an annual basis this represents a savings of about $12.4 million.

Exhibit 1 *(continued)*

Table 1
Dickey-Lincoln School Lakes economic analysis—Annual costs and benefits
(based on 3¼ percent interest rate and 100-year project life)*

Total investment—Dams	
Construction costs of dams	$356,000,000
Interest during construction	28,800,000
Total Investment	$384,800,000
Annual costs—Dams	
Interest and amortization	$ 13,037,000
Operation and maintenance	1,500,000
Major replacements	248,000
Loss of land taxes	98,000
Subtotal Dams	$ 14,883,000
Total investment	
Construction costs of transmission line	$123,100,000
Interest during construction	6,000,000
Total Investment	$129,100,000
Annual costs—Transmission lines	
Interest and amortization	$ 4,374,000
Operation and maintenance	950,000
Major replacements	394,000
Subtotal Transmission Lines	$ 5,718,000
Total annual costs	
Dickey-Lincoln School Lakes	$ 14,883,000
Transmission (50 percent)	2,859,000
Annual costs	$ 17,742,000
Annual benefits (see below)	46,492,000
B/C ratio	2.62 to 1
Annual benefits	
Marketed in Maine:	
105,000 kw. × .95 × $54.25	$ 5,411,000
372,000,000 kwh. × .95 × $0.010	3,534,000
Marketed in Boston:	
725,000 kw. × .905 × $16.50	10,826,000
782,000,000 kwh. × .929 × $0.030	21,794,000
Downstream:	
350,000,000 kwh. × 0.008	2,800,000
Subtotal Power	$ 44,365,000
Prevention of flood damages	60,000
Recreation	1,250,000
Redevelopment	817,000
Total Annual Benefits	$ 46,492,000

Note: Figures have been rounded.
* Capital recovery factor 100-year life; .03388

Exhibit 1 *(continued)*

Table 2
Dickey-Lincoln School Lakes economic efficiency test
(based on 3¼ percent interest rate)

Annual benefits
Power marketed in Maine:

105,000 kw. × .95 × $25.00	$ 2,494,000
372,000,000 kwh. × .95 × $0.010	3,534,000

Power marketed in Boston:

725,000 kw. × .905 × $6.50	4,265,000
782,000,000 kwh. × .929 × $0.030	21,794,000

Downstream:

350,000,000 kwh. × $0.008	2,800,000
Subtotal	34,887,000
Adjustment for flood control*	60,000
Adjustment for recreation*	1,250,000
Adjustment for redevelopment*	817,000
Total Benefits	$37,014,000
Annual costs	17,742,000
Comparability ratio	2.1 to 1

Note: Figures have been rounded.
* Flood control, recreation, and redevelopment benefits which are provided incidentally to construction of Dickey-Lincoln School would be foregone by the alternative. Therefore, the values of these benefits are added to the alternative in order to obtain a valid comparison.

The difference between the economic analyses previously described and the repayment analysis warrants further clarification. This has caused a considerable amount of misunderstanding and misinterpretation. The economic analyses—both for the benefit-to-cost ratio determination and the "economic efficiency test" are economic parameters measuring a project's worth. These analyses are not unique to Dickey-Lincoln School Lakes. The benefit-to-cost ratio is employed universally by the Corps in measuring a project's economic justification. The "economic efficiency test" is also universally used by the Corps in conjunction with projects having generation of electric power as a project purpose. The economic analyses utilize a 3¼ percent interest rate and 100-year period of evaluation. On the other hand, the repayment analysis—which will ultimately be computed by the Department of Interior—is a financial analysis which determines the appropriate charge at which power costs must be marketed to return the total annual investment allocated to power. For this analysis an interest rate of 6⅛ percent and a 50-year repayment period are used.

Exhibit 1 *(concluded)*

Table 3
Dickey-Lincoln School Lakes

I. Repayment analysis (50-year period—5.875 percent interest rate)

	Dam and appurte-nances	Trans-mission	Total
A. First costs:			
1. Construction costs allocated to power*	$341,235,000	$123,100,000	$464,335,000
2. Interest during construction (at 5.875 percent)	50,008,720	10,848,000	60,856,720
Total investment	$391,243,720	$133,948,000	$525,191,720
B. Annual cost (50 years at 5.875 percent):			
1. Interest and amortization	$ 24,390,100	$ 8,350,300	$ 32,740,400
2. Operation and maintenance	1,500,000	950,000	2,450,000
3. Major replacements	165,000	262,000	427,000
Total annual cost	$26,055,100	$ 9,562,300	$ 35,617,400
C. Repayment requirement:			
1. System transmission revenues from wheeling off-peak power (50 percent)		$ 4,781,100	$ 4,781,100
2. Net amount to be recovered by power revenues	$ 26,055,100	4,781,200	30,836,300
3. Energy revenues†	12,461,500	0	12,461,500
4. Amount to be recovered by capacity	13,593,600	4,781,200	18,374,800
5. Capacity value (at-market 756 megawatt)	17.98	6.33	24.31
D. Total capacity charge:			
Capacity value			$24.31
Administration charge for marketing			0.50
Total capacity charge (per kilowatt)			$24.81

* Remaining construction costs have been allocated to flood control, recreation, and area redevelopment.
† Energy value fixed at 10 mills per kilowatt-hour equivalent to value for Maine market area.

II. Comparison of cost
(Dickey-Lincoln School versus privately financed alternatives)

	Capacity dollars per kilowatt	Energy (mills per kilowatt-hour)	Composite (mills per kilowatt-hour)
A. Composite values:			
Private alternatives:*			
Gas turbine (Massachusetts)	16.50	30.00	44.90
Fossil fuel (Maine)	54.25	10.00	25.35
Combined private	21.49	21.39	34.43
Dickey-Lincoln School	24.81	100.0	25.05
B. Annual savings:			
Private alternatives (1,246,150 kwh × 34.43)			$42,905,000
Dickey-Lincoln School (1,246,150 kwh × 25.05)			31,216,000
Annual savings (say $11,700,000)			$11,689,000

* Based on values furnished by the Federal Power Commission.

Exhibit 2

Mr. Proxmire: The purpose of this amendment is straightforward. It would permit the executive branch to apply the 6.875 percent discount rate—agreed upon by the U.S. Water Resources Council last October after extensive hearings—to all public works projects heretofore authorized by the Congress, but not yet under construction. It would require the application of this rate to projects authorized by the pending omnibus rivers and harbors bill.

Each of my colleagues has on his desk an information sheet prepared by my office explaining why this amendment should pass. In my remarks I will elaborate on this barebones presentation and show why Senate endorsement of this legislation is essential if we are to see that the tax-payer's dollars are spent wisely on the basis of objective fact, rather than through the politics of the pork barrel.

To begin with let us look at exactly what we mean when we discuss the discount rate as applied to federal public works projects. This is an essential ingredient in determining whether or not the benefits to be realized by a project exceed the costs. Of course, if benefits do not exceed costs—if the benefit-cost ratio is not greater than 1 to 1— then the project is not authorized by the Congress.

In determining benefits we have to look at the present value of future benefits.

That is very complicated, because the benefits overwhelmingly come at a future time, sometimes as much as 5, 10, 20, 40, or 50 years in the future.

This is where the discount rate comes in and why the discount rate is critical— crucial—in determining whether the project should go ahead. I think it is possible to justify almost anything if the discount rate is very low. On the other hand, it is possible to exclude everything if the discount rate is too high. So it is the discount rate that is the determining factor on the amount to be spent on public works projects.

What is the value today, for example, of a benefit worth $5 million in the year 1984? Such future benefits have to be discounted because, just as $1 invested today would be worth a great deal more in 10 years, so $1 in benefits accruing several years from now is worth a great deal less than that dollar is worth today. A bird in the hand is worth two in the bush.

As chairman of the Joint Economic Committee I have held a series of hearings on the discount rate issue. For example, in January of 1968, the committee held hearings on "Interest Rate Guidelines for Federal Decision-making." In May of 1969, I chaired additional hearings entitled "Guidelines for Estimating the Benefits of Public Expenditure."

The vast majority of economists and other experts who testified at these hearings concluded that the best standard for discounting the value of benefits over time is the interest rate representing opportunities foregone in the private sector. There is a good reason for this substantial agreement. If we remove funds from the private sector through federal taxes and these funds would have yielded 12 percent if privately invested, we only waste these resources if we invest them in a federal project yielding a 4 percent return. We are overinvesting in an activity that yields less real economic benefits than its alternatives. This is a clear misallocation of resources.

The professionals unanimously agree among themselves that this is a waste of our economic resources. Whether the economists are conservative or liberal, they all come down hard on the assertion that in the past our public works expenditures have not been based on a correct allocation of our resources and have, indeed, been wasteful.

Exhibit 2 *(continued)*

The Nation cannot afford such waste when we have so many high priority public investment needs.

What is the current private sector rate? It is generally considered to hover somewhere between 8 and 12 percent. As a matter of fact, it is around 12 percent if we take the return before taxes, and that is a fair comparison. The prime commercial lending rate has been well above 9 percent over the past few months. This is the cost of money in the private sector. The Office of Management and Budget in budget circular A-94, discount rates to be used in evaluating time-distributed costs and benefits, states that a discount rate of 10 percent is to be used to evaluate programs subject to the circular.

In any event the generally accepted discount rate is well above the rate that would apply to public works projects if my amendment were to be accepted. As I indicated earlier the rate set by my amendment would be a modest—very modest—6⅞ percent.

Even if we consider the federal long-term borrowing rate, the rate under discussion today is extraordinarily reasonable. In my estimation the long term borrowing rate is too low a standard to apply, by and large. But even this rate—which is the minimum standard rate we could rationally apply to evaluating federal projects—is no lower than the discount rate I am proposing today. In fact it is currently hovering around 7 percent.

Now the U.S. Water Resources Council originally proposed a discount rate of 7 percent—somewhat higher than the standard they finally settled on. What was the reaction to this proposal? Over half of those responding favored the application of a higher discount rate to federal public works projects. The following conservation groups, concerned as they are by a rate so low as to minimize the value of protecting the environment, favored a discount rate of 10 percent:

Citizens Committee on Natural Resources.

Environmental Action.

Environmental Defense Fund.

Friends of the Earth.

Izaak Walton League of America.

National Parks & Conservation Association.

National Audubon Society.

National Wildlife Federation.

National Resources Defense Council.

Sierra Club.

Trout Unlimited.

Wilderness Society.

Wildlife Management Institute.

They are all in favor of a higher discount rate than the discount rate my amendment provides.

Former Secretary of the Interior Stewart Udall responded to the Council's proposed 7 percent rate in these words:

Exhibit 2 *(continued)*

Especially noteworthy are the proposals to set the discount rate at a much more realistic level than exists under present guidelines and the much greater recognition given to preserving environmental guidelines.

I think that we all recognize that Mr. Udall was not only a great secretary of the interior who understood the importance of these projects, because he came from a state that benefited greatly from these projects, but he is also one of the most outstanding environmentalists in this country or anywhere else. And, as I say, he favors a discount rate of 7 percent or higher.

The next question is why should we apply this rate to past and present public works projects as well as future authorizations? Frankly, a much more reasonable question would seem to be why shouldn't we? Why should we give a public works project a break simply because it was authorized in, say, 1962, while a project authorized next year suffers?

Certainly there is no excuse for not applying the 6⅞ percent rate to the projects authorized by the pending bill. The new standard was promulgated last October. Why in the world shouldn't it apply to projects approved since that date?

Frankly I can think of only one answer to this last question, and it is not a very good answer. If we applied the new higher rate to projects included in the pending bill a number of marginal projects simply would not qualify. Of course, they should not qualify. If they cannot meet a standard considerably more lenient than the one used in the marketplace, there is no reason in the world why the taxpayer should be asked to subsidize them. They are economic cripples and should be treated as such.

Even at a lower rate many of these projects are very questionable. Why? Because certain benefits are added to the total picture that should not be counted at all. A sterling example is future flood control benefits. Many of the projects included in the bill are promoted on the ground that they would result in more intensive flood plain development. For example, the basic justification of the Days Creek Lake project comes from development related to construction that will take place at a later date and will be located in the former flood plain. Yet the use of flood plain development benefits violates sound land use principles. It also happens to run counter to the recommendations of the National Water Commission.

But how about projects authorized before the effective date of the newly approved 6⅞ percent discount rate? Why should they have to be reevaluated in terms of the new rate?

First let me make it clear that my amendment does not require these older projects to be reevaluated. It simply permits it. The language of my amendment would allow the executive branch to reevaluate the older projects if such a reevaluation was felt to be appropriate. This is in sharp contrast to the language of the bill as it was reported from committee, which would require the use of discount rates as low as 3¼ percent and, in effect, prohibits a reevaluation.

Over 80 percent of those commenting on the new standards proposed by the U.S. Water Resources Council believed that these standards should be applied to projects previously authorized as well as future projects. This is the way the Council summarized comments on retroactivity:

Projects are not ends in themselves, but means for achieving our national goals. These Principles and Standards reflect the fact that our goals have changed.

Exhibit 2 *(continued)*

> Our public works program must now dovetail with these new goals; otherwise, the program ceases to serve its national purpose. This, it seems is elementary . . . Projects which do not conform with the new goals do not serve the national interest.

This, it seems to me, is elementary.

There is also a good dollars and cents reason why a realistic discount rate should be applied to all authorized public works projects—whether the projects were authorized ten years ago or yesterday. It would save the taxpayer literally billions of dollars. The Water Resources Congress has estimated that a 7 percent discount rate would kill 50 percent of the projects already authorized. Since the dollar value of these authorizations is $11.9 billion the savings to the American public could be more than $5 billion. Keep in mind that these are projects that simply cannot be justified as providing benefits equal to their cost under current standards.

Should we fail to pass my amendment some projects will be built on the bais of a 3¼ percent discount rate. This is a ludicrously low figure when we consider that the federal government has to pay almost 7 percent—twice as much—to borrow the money that finances these public works projects. The return on those dollars would be only half what we pay for them.

This brings me to my next point. Let us consider the fact that projects authorized on the basis of discount rates ranging from 3¼ to 5⅝ percent will have to compete with future projects based on a 6⅞ percent discount rate. Does this make any sense in allocating scarce federal dollars? Why should a state or region suffer because the discount rate applied to a project in that region is twice the discount rate applied to a competing project that never should have been authorized, and would not have been if the higher discount rate had been in effect at the time of authorization? The answer is obvious. This is economic discrimination of the worst sort. And I might add that any of my colleagues shortsighted enough to vote against my amendment because it would have an adverse impact on one or two projects in their state may find that they are sowing the seeds of destructive public policy in the future as good projects in their state go by the boards while less justifiable programs are pursued.

Some may argue that my amendment would adversely affect projects authorized many years ago as part of a system of water resource projects, thus adversely affecting an entire program. Or it may be possible to point to communities that have relied on a previously authorized project, to their detriment if the project is not constructed. That is exactly why I left it up to the executive branch agencies to make the decision as to whether or not to apply the new discount rate of older projects. This will permit the flexibility needed to take account of mitigating circumstances.

Finally let me point out that the death of an inefficient project does not mean that a particular erosion or flood control problem can never be resolved. There are many ways to skin a cat. There are all sorts of solutions to individual flood control problems. Some of them may be less costly and have a lesser impact on the environment than a project authorized five or ten years ago. My amendment would focus attention on these alternative solutions.

Before I conclude I want to make it clear that my amendment articulates and represents the administration's position on the subject. In order to drive this point home I would like to quote from a news release put out by the Water Resources Council last

Exhibit 2 *(concluded)*

August announcing the new planning criteria for the Nation's water resources. These criteria include the discount rate formula implemented by my amendment—the formula that the Senate Public Works Committee has attempted to nullify through the language contained in section 65 of the bill. Here is what the president said about the new standards, including the new discount formula:

> [The Principles and Standards] . . . represent the culmination of several years review by the Water Resources Council to develop improved planning criteria to achieve our goal of wise use of the Nation's water and related land resources with full consideration to the protection of our environment. I commend the Water Resources Council for accomplishing such a difficult task.

Secretary of the Interior Morton had this to say about the new discount rate formula:

> It is felt that the discount rate provision will foster the planning of better programs and projects for a given level of federal investment.

In order to make it crystal clear that my amendment and the administration's position are identical I would like to quote one final segment from the aforementioned news release:

> A planning discount rate to reflect the relative value of beneficial and adverse effects occurring in the future as compared with the present has been established by the council. This rate is consistent with the cost of government borrowing concept which is based on the assumption that the government's investment decisions are related to the cost of money to the government. The rate has been established at 6⅞ percent and will change up or down, as appropriate, not more than or less than ½ of 1 percent per year. The 'Principles and Standards' will be applied to all currently authorized by unfunded projects on a selective basis to be determined by the head of the agency.

There is absolutely no difference between this language and the impact of my amendment on water resources projects.

I earnestly hope that the Senate will adopt this amendment, and I reserve the remainder of my time.

Source: *Congressional Record,* January 22, 1974, pp. 303–305.

PART FOUR

THE INTERACTION OF INVESTMENT AND
FINANCING CHOICES

Case 4-1

Bougainville Power Station

Bougainville Island lies at the eastern end of the territory of Papua and New Guinea. While it is only 30 miles wide, it rises from the ocean to a central mountain range 8,000 feet high. In 1964 Conzinc Riotinto of Australia, Limited (CRA), began exploration work on the island, hoping to uncover new mineral deposits. Working on rugged volcanic terrain, in areas covered with dense jungle and soaked by rainfall of more than 200 inches per year, the exploration group soon located a massive body of low-grade copper ore.

In 1967 CRA incorporated a subsidiary company, Bougainville Copper Pty., Ltd., to develop and mine the new copper deposit. Terms and conditions under which this could be done were negotiated in 1967 between the company and the New Guinea government, and in early 1969 CRA decided to begin construction of the mine, scheduling full commercial production for some time early in 1972. Total cost of the construction and development program was estimated at $375 million— an amount that would cover not only the mining facilities but infrastructural investments such as roads, ports, towns, and power and water supplies as well. When completed, the Bougainville mine would be one of the largest open-cut mines in the world, yielding 80,000 tons of rough copper ore to the ore crushers and concentrators every day. CRA estimated that annual production would be 150,000 tons of refined copper and 500,000 ounces of gold.

The Bougainville project was to be levered in debt-to-equity proportions of 2:1. A Credit Agreement negotiated between Bougainville Copper and the Bank of America (acting on behalf of several banks and financial institutions) limited total loans to $250 million. One third this amount was to be a medium-term loan at a fixed interest rate of 10 percent; the remainder was to be a shorter term loan that would have a floating rate based on the London Eurodollar market rate.

Development of the mining area depended heavily upon adequate sources of electric power, and CRA placed high priority on completion of a 135-megawatt steam power station consisting of three turbine generator units. Management invited bids on the turbines from suppliers in a number of countries.

The standard evaluation procedure for equipment bids involved an appraisal of technical quality, delivery, performance, and overall cost. In general, the cost appraisal was straightforward; management simply measured the different levels of capital and operating costs for each bid, and discounted aftertax cash flows at 15 percent, being a rate which was regarded as reasonable, to determine the net present value of these costs. Generally, the equipment that offered the minimum costs was recommended for purchase, assuming its technical quality and delivery were acceptable.

In July 1969, John Browne, the financial analyst on CRA's engineering team, had received bids from companies in Switzerland, England, and Japan, who wished to supply equipment for the power station. The equipment specified in each of the bids complied fully with the technical and operating requirements of the power station. When Mr. Browne made a preliminary economic evaluation of the equipment enders, however, he realized that these offers would require more than the usual equipment purchase analysis. Not only were the capital and operating costs of the three bids different, but because the Japanese and British governments offered export subsidies to manufacturers, two of the bids included attractive financing proposals. Mr. Browne was not sure how these financing packages should be evaluated, but he knew that many similar evaluations could be expected by the CRA Group over the next few years. Because of this, he knew it was important not only to analyze the power station problem itself, but to draw from this decision a method of analysis that could be used in similar situations by companies throughout the CRA Group. Details of the bids, including the financing proposals, are shown in Exhibit 1.

Cash flows and net present value cost for the three bids are shown in Exhibit 2. Mr. Browne considered that 40 percent might be a reasonable tax rate to assume, in light of the Agreement provisions, and depreciation would be tax deductible using the sum-of-the-years'-digits method over 20 years. The equipment specified in the Japanese proposal required additional operating costs for service and maintenance; terms of their contract specified that the Japanese perform this service for a

Exhibit 1
Details of equipment bids

	Swiss	English	Japanese
Equipment cost	$3,412,000	$3,770,000	$3,086,000
Variation in building costs*	—	(50,000)	(275,000)
	$3,412,000	$3,720,000	$2,811,000
Variation in operating costs per year	—	—	+125,000

* These differences between the bids were expressed as deviations from a common base.

Financing terms offered by suppliers

Japanese:	Advance: Total cost of the equipment
	Interest rates: 7 percent
	Repayment: Ten equal annual installments of principal and interest, due 1972 through 1981
English:	Advance: Total cost of the equipment
	Interest rate: 5 percent
	Repayment: Ten equal annual installments of principal and interest, due 1972 through 1981
Swiss:	No special financing terms were offered.

Exhibit 2
Cash flows and present values ($000)

Year	Swiss	English	Japanese
1971 Equipment cost	($3,412)	($3,770)	($3,086)
1971 Decreased equipment need	0	50	275
1972–1991 Depreciable assets	3,412	3,720	2,811
1972–1991 Additional operating costs	0	0	125
Total present value costs:			
at 15 percent	$2,818	$3,073	$2,791

Note: Assets are depreciated by sum-of-the-years'-digits method; the applicable tax rate is 40 percent.

period of 20 years at a stated cost of $125,000 per year. Salvage values in 20 years were expected to be the same for all three proposals. The cash flows associated with the financing packages for the Japanese and English bids are shown in Exhibit 3.

When making his final decision, Mr. Browne felt he should resolve several analytical problems. It was important that he be able to do more than simply rank the three bids in descending order of costs; he needed to produce more precise estimates of the cost differences among bids, for several reasons. If the bids were quite close in cost, the engineering group might wish to select a supplier with whom they had enjoyed previous successful dealings. If the cost differentials were large, such an approach would be less justified. Also, since the power station was

Exhibit 3
Loan payment schedules ($000)

	English bid			Japanese bid		
	Total payment	Interest	Principal	Total payment	Interest	Principal
1972	$ 488	$ 188	$ 300	$ 439	$ 216	$ 223
1973	488	173	315	439	200	239
1974	488	158	330	439	184	255
1975	488	141	347	439	166	273
1976	488	124	364	439	147	292
1977	488	105	383	439	126	313
1978	488	86	402	439	104	335
1979	488	66	422	439	81	358
1980	488	45	443	439	56	383
1981	488	23	465	439	29	410
Totals	$4,880	$1,109	$3,771	$4,390	$1,309	$3,081

on the "critical path" of the entire mine project, CRA might be willing to pay a premium for early delivery of the turbine equipment.

Since it was expected that $80 million of the equipment purchases for the Bougainville mine project would involve special financing arrangements, Mr. Browne wanted to derive a general method of analysis to aid in making future decisions of this type.

Mr. Browne was also unsure of the discount rate he should use in evaluating the equipment bids. A colleague had suggested that the 15 percent rate might be inappropriate, because of the inclusion of special financing in the Japanese and English bids.

Case 4-2

Energy and Mineral Resources, Inc.

In the late 1930s Matthew Loft, a former oil wildcatter, organized a group of oil industry executives to begin refining operations in Tennessee and Mississippi. His company, Greenville Refining, became a prosperous regional refinery. In 1959 Matthew's son, Nathan, joined Greenville's management after receiving his M.B.A. Because the cash flows of Greenville were both large and stable. Nathan believed the company was in an excellent position to move into new, rapidly growing markets. Attracting bright aggressive managers and venture capital through his contacts, Nathan embarked on a program of what he termed "intelligent risk taking."

Under Nathan's leadership, Greenville Refineries purchased a number of retail gasoline outlets and several fleets of trucks and became Energy and Mineral Resources, Inc. (EMR). Using sophisticated transportation management and control techniques, EMR achieved substantial profit and cash flow benefits from the newly integrated operations.

In 1965 Nathan successfully urged two of his business school classmates to join him at EMR. Mark Effrey was a petroleum engineering specialist with management experience in a large oil company. Jason Byrd was a mining engineer with a strong record of success in operations management at the largest copper company in the United States. The three MBAs began mapping out a strategy to expand EMR's product and service base.

In 1967 EMR acquired a medium-sized copper mine which had capabilities for refining gold and silver extracted with the copper ore. Through reorganization and engineering developments, the mine began to generate profits well beyond EMR's expectations. Shortly thereafter, EMR established a road paving materials plant near their largest refinery.

The plant used refinery by-products to produce asphaltum which was then transported by EMR's fleet of trucks.

Because the company was growing so rapidly, EMR's management team felt they needed some specialized expertise in organizational control. Mark Effrey recalled that his former company had much success following the advice of Allison Voler, a nationally recognized consultant. Mark suggested that EMR invite Ms. Voler to join the company. Ms. Voler welcomed the offer of active management, and in 1970 she left consulting to join EMR.

By 1973 the four members of the management team were working together very effectively. They had tightened up the now very complex EMR organization, realized sizable profits through efficiency and innovation, and recruited a highly motivated and responsive group of executives to manage EMR's subsidiaries. This record of success and the availability of internally generated funds inspired the four managers to continue their strategy of sensible risk taking. They began to research new markets in depth, looking for potentially very high profit opportunities in areas related to their existing businesses. Their primary goal was to use present operations as profit and cash flow cushions to penetrate other markets. Ms. Voler in a presentation to the board of directors, said they were looking for "portfolio effects"—high profit ventures with enough diversification effect so that overall company risk would be limited.

In early 1974 Mark Effrey heard of a technical paper delivered before the Society of Naval Architects and Marine Engineers describing a recent innovation in nautical materials hauling—the integrated tug-barge concept. After some additional research into the subject, Mark felt this presented an ideal opportunity for EMR's managers to continue their expansion objectives. The four managers began gathering further information on the integrated tug-barge and in a month had concluded that indeed this was a prime candidate for a major diversification effort.

Until recently, most tug hauling had been done by conventional methods; a tug would link up to one or more shallow barges by means of a tow hawser and chains. This arrangement limited the total tonnage capacity of each raft of barges and caused problems of maneuverability and stability, especially in rough weather and narrow channels. Some conventional barges had been constructed with a slightly U-shaped hollow in the stern, into which a conventional tug could move, gaining some stability. However, when seas swelled to 10 or 12 feet, the tug would begin to churn within the barge and would have to back off, using the hawser once again.

The integrated tug-barge system gained tremendous competitive advantages over conventional systems through simple but ingenious technical innovations. Like some of the modified conventional barges, the Ingram tug-barge was built with a U-shaped hollow in the stern. The Ingram tug, however, could move two thirds of its length into the notch with very little space between the tug and the barge. A hydraulic ram system and a series of steel and elastic cushions would then lock the barge and tug tightly together, allowing the vessel to operate in heavy seas and to withstand swells of up to 50 feet. While conventional tugs required several deck hands and much maneuvering to dock or pick up barges, the locking and unlocking of the integrated tug took only two to five minutes and could be performed by one man at a central control panel on the tug's bridge. In transit, the tight fit between tug and barge allowed maximum thrust efficiency and maneuverability since little energy would be lost through the conventional hawser system. This meant integrated tug barges could carry much higher payloads with shorter load-unload times, resulting in very advantageous operating efficiencies. In addition, a tug-barge with a crew of 14 hands could do the job of a conventional vessel requiring 34 hands.

Several companies currently employed integrated tug-barges ranging in capacity from 15,000 to 65,000 tons, and their experience confirmed that the ships gave substantial economies and flexibility. One company used the system to haul crude oil in one direction, newsprint in another, and during slack time they employed the tug in salvage operations.

The manufacturer of the system had recently completed and tested a very large tug-barge, costing $23 million, which was able to carry 100,000 tons of cargo while only drawing 43 feet of water. The unique shape of the barge and its shallow draft would allow it to enter almost any U.S. port with substantially larger cargoes than had been possible in the past. By reducing the payload to 80,000 tons, the tug-barge could negotiate many inland waterways with very large and cost-efficient payloads.

In this tug-barge EMR saw the greatest opportunity for new market penetration and high profits. The flexibility of the vessel could ultimately allow shallow draft tugs to pick up tanker-sized loads of oil anywhere in the world and return directly to inland U.S. ports without the costly and treacherous transfer process currently required at ocean ports. EMR felt they could immediately begin to ship crude oil from Mexican Gulf rigs to their Mississippi and Tennessee refineries, and they could swiftly expand their tug hauling subsidiary using the cost-efficient integrated tug to penetrate the Gulf area bulk-shipping market. It seemed highly probable that EMR could capture enough of this market to run the first tug at or near 100 percent capacity year round.

The managers calculated that in one or two years they could acquire another tug, station it in Jacksonville, Florida, and undercut many competitors in the East Coast shipping market. EMR's efficient management techniques and the substantial economies of the new tug made this seem a highly profitable venture, suited to EMR's expansion goals. Nathan Loft said it would even be conceivable to add a third tug in two or three years and exploit its open-sea capabilities by shipping between the United States and many Latin American and Caribbean ports. He noted that the only real constraint facing EMR was availability of expansion capital, since EMR faced extremely heavy demand for funds for other new ventures. It was also clear to the four managers that to successfully penetrate this new market, they would require management expertise in shipping operations.

For this reason, Nathan approached another business school classmate, Lars Bakken, who was now director of a large family-owned shipping firm in Oslo. Bakken's firm had extensive experience in transoceanic shipping between the East Coast of the United States, the Great Lakes, and many European ports. Nathan turned his research data over to Lars for review and asked him to consider joining forces with EMR. In a week, Lars called Nathan expressing strong interest in the proposal and explaining that he believed the economies and market advantages of the venture to be very sound. The Norwegian said that he would participate as the primary manager of the new project in return for 25 percent equity interest; he would not, however, be able to make an actual cash investment in the proposed subsidiary.

EMR's lawyers advised Nathan that under U.S. law any ship operating intercoastally or on inland waterways must be a U.S. flag vessel, and that it could not be more than 25 percent foreign-owned. For a variety of reasons, it was clear that the new venture would have to be organized as a subsidiary legally separate from the parent company. EMR's management agreed that the 25 percent equity participation which Lars requested seemed somewhat high, but necessary in order to capture the full benefits of his expertise.

Once Lars expressed such strong interest, the major problem remaining for the EMR team was financing the first vessel in such a way to make this and future tug acquisitions most economical and advantageous.

As they had done in past ventures, Nathan and Allison went to the corporate finance department of a large midwestern bank for advice on the matter. Lars had helped Nathan work out the most probable ranges of operating margins for the vessel (profits before taxes, depreciation and financing charges). While they disagreed on some details, they strongly agreed that the vessel would generate a cash flow of from $3.8 million to $5.8 million per year. EMR's primary contact at the bank, Mr. Richard Williamson considered the data Nathan gave him and laid out two basic financing options. He recommended that EMR finance the acquisition with either a private placement of U.S. government guaranteed Ship Financing Title XI bonds, or a leveraged lease transaction. After describing the general nature of the two options, Mr. Williamson agreed to have his staff prepare a detailed analysis.

In about a week EMR received the letter and the analysis shown in Exhibit 1. Nathan called the managers together to discuss the bank's analysis before making a final decision. He explained that time was short since they would have to receive delivery of the tug in time to get the best marketing advantages. Funds were presently available within EMR to provide the 12.5 percent additional equity investment in the subsidiary if they chose the Title XI debt, but the management committee agreed that, given the many other profitable opportunities and the demand for capital by other subsidiaries, any equity funds invested in the tug should return an aftertax minimum of 18–20 percent.

Lars and Mark both raised the question of the vessel's residual value. Under the lease arrangement EMR would lose any residuals, and Mark wondered if this wouldn't be a significant amount. Lars was convinced that the economic life of the vessel would be much greater than that assumed in the banker's report. The five committee members agreed to think about the questions they had and get together shortly to reach a final decision.

Exhibit 1
Lease versus buy analysis

August 21, 1974

Mr. Nathan Loft
Energy and Mineral Resources
Greenville, Mississippi

Dear Mr. Loft:

I have completed and enclose a lease versus buy analysis for a $23 million vessel assuming operating margins of $3.8 million to $5.8 million in $500,000 intervals. The assumptions I used are basically those we discussed in our last meeting and are summa-

Exhibit 1 *(continued)*

rized in the "General Assumptions" section of the analysis. I should point out that the assumed equivalent interest rate to the lessee of 300 basis points below the effective debt cost is a very conservative lease rate. It is likely that a more finely tuned lease bid instead of a "ball park" rate, would be somewhat lower. In light of using a conservative lease bid, the analysis might be slightly weighted towards the buy alternative.

Based on the pure economics of the project as summarized in "Summary of Advantage (Disadvantage) of Leasing," it appears that leasing is attractive for assumed operating margins of $3.8 million and $4.3 million. At a level of $4.8 million of operating margin, the buy alternative is attractive for discount rates below 12.5 percent. At a 15 percent discount rate leasing remains attractive. With operating margins of $5.3 million or more the buy alternative becomes clearly more attractive at any discount rate.

Of course as we discussed the analysis assumed no residual value. Assessing the impact of a residual is a somewhat difficult task due to the great uncertainty as to the asset's value in year 25. Although no consideration of residual value is reflected in the "Summary of Advantage (Disadvantage) of Leasing," I have included an attempt to get a feel for the potential impact of residual value in the section entitled "Analysis of Present Value of Residual Value." This schedule could be used in conjunction with the "Summary of Advantage (Disadvantage) of Leasing" by subtracting the present value of the residual from the advantage of leasing at the same discount rate after choosing an assumed residual value and an assumed operating margin. For example, the advantage of leasing at an operating margin of $4.3 million discounted at 10 percent is $473,000. The present value of a 20 percent residual discounted at 10 percent is $314,000. The net advantage of leasing therefore would be $159,000. The only caution I would suggest in using such a figure is that there is a higher degree of certainty in realizing the $473,000 advantage of leasing than there is in realizing the $314,000 from the residual.

I hope this analysis has focused on the variables you wished to explore and will be of assistance to you. I have sent the analysis rather than presenting it in person so that you might have the results as soon as you could. I would still be glad to meet with you to discuss this analysis and determine what further analysis or service we could provide at this stage.

Best regards,

Richard Williamson
Financial Analyst
Corporate Finance Division

Enclosure

Exhibit 1 *(continued)*

LEASE VERSUS BUY ANALYSIS

Prepared for:

Energy and Mineral Resources, Inc.

CORPORATE FINANCE DIVISION

August 21, 1974

General Assumptions
Equipment cost: $23,000,000
EMR tax rate: 50 percent
Length of financing: 25 years

Buy Alternative
Depreciable cost: $23,000,000
Marad actual cost: $22,750,000
Title XI debt: $19,900,000 (87½ percent of actual cost)
Amortization: 50 level semiannual principal payments
Interest and principal payable: semiannually

Rate: Bond coupon rate: 9⅝ percent
      Guarantee premium: ⅝ percent
      Effective rate: 10¼ percent
      (Note: For computer runs effective rate of 10.148 was used to adjust for effect
      of semiannual principal payments)

Required initial investment: $3,100,000
ADR guideline: 14.5 to 21.5 years

Depreciation: As specified in summaries for each assumed level of operating margin.
In general accelerated depreciation (double-declining balance switching to sum-
of-the-years'-digits) over 14.5 years is used. In cases in which DDB/SOYD over
14.5 years prevents use of all available I.T.C. ($1,610,000) a slower method of
depreciation is also presented which allows all of the I.T.C. to be used before
the end of year 7.

Salvage value: None assumed

Lease Alternative
Equipment cost: $23,000,000

Debt rate: Bond coupon rate: 9⅝ percent
           Guarantee premium: ⅝ percent
           Effective rate: 10¼ percent

Exhibit 1 *(continued)*

Equivalent interest rate to lessee of the lease: 7¼ percent

Length of lease: 25 years

Payments: 50 level semiannual payments of $1,002,787

Summary of advantage (disadvantage) of leasing ($000)

	Advantage (disadvantage) of leasing*				
Assumed Operating Margin:	*$3,800*	*$4,300*	*$4,800*	*$5,300*	*$5,800*
Discount rate					
5%	492	(54)	(856)	(1,248)	(1,318)
7.5%	1,140	89	(529)	(917)	(1,318)
10%	1,347	473	(239)	(622)	(735)
12.5%	1,581	694	18	(356)	(485)
15%	1,685	889	248	(119)	(258)

* Present value of aftertax cash flows from leasing minus present value of aftertax cash flows from buying equipment.

Analysis of present value of residual value

The impact on the buy analysis of the present value of a residual value of the equipment in year 25 can be analyzed in two ways:

1. At the end of year 25 it could be assumed that the equipment is sold at "fair market value" with the cash flow from the sale taken as an inflow in period 25. The cash inflow from the sale will equal the "fair market value" less applicable capital gains taxes.
2. Assume that the equipment is retained in the firm and that the value of the equipment in year 25 is approximated by what it would cost to purchase the asset at "fair market value" from an outside party (such as a purchase back from a leasing company). The cost in year 25 of purchasing a 25-year-old asset is not simply the "fair market value" but is more accurately the "fair market value" reduced by the present value in year 25 of tax savings in subsequent years from purchasing a depreciable asset. Another way of saying the same thing is that it provides no depreciation and no tax benefits in years 25 on, but if you orginally leased the asset and purchase it at "fair market value" in year 25 you will have the tax benefits of some depreciation in the years 25 and on. The analysis below uses this second approach.

Exhibit 1 *(continued)*

Calculation of present value of residual ($000)

	Assumed residual value in year 25			
	10%	*20%*	*30%*	*40%*
Equivalent "fair market value" in year 25	$2,300	$4,600	$6,900	$9,200
Value in year 25 of tax savings from depreciation*	600	1,200	1,800	2,400
True value of residual in year 25†	1,700	3,400	5,100	6,800
Present value of residual (year 0) discounted at:				
5%	502	1,004	1,506	2,008
7.5%	279	558	837	1,116
10.0%	157	314	471	628
12.5%	89	178	267	356
15.0%	52	104	156	208

* Assumes "fair market value" is depreciated straight line over 14.5 years. Tax savings equal depreciation times an assumed tax rate of 50 percent and are discounted back to year 25 at a discount rate of 10 percent.

† Equivalent "fair market value" less value in year 25 of tax savings.

Lease analysis

Assumptions

Equipment cost: $23,000,000
Number of years: 25
Debt rate: Bond coupon rate: 9⅝ percent
Guarantee premium: ⅝ percent
Effective rate: 10¼ percent

Equivalent interest rate to lessee: 7¼ percent
Tax rate: 50 percent
Semiannual payments: $1,002,787

Exhibit 1 *(continued)*

Calculation of annual cash flow ($000)

Margin	$ 3,800	$4,300	$4,800	$5,300	$5,800
Lease payment	2,006	2,006	2,006	2,006	2,006
Pretax profit	$ 1,794	$2,294	$2,794	$3,294	$3,794
Aftertax cash flow	897	1,147	1,397	1,647	1,897
25 years of aftertax cash flow discounted at					
2.5%	16,527	21,133	25,739	30,345	34,951
5.0	12,642	16,166	19,689	23,213	26,736
7.5	9,999	12,786	15,572	18,359	21,146
10.0	8,142	10,411	12,681	14,950	17,219
12.5	6,798	8,693	10,588	12,483	14,377
15.0	5,798	7,414	9,030	10,646	12,262

Lease versus buy analysis for operating margin = $3,800,000 per year ($000)

		Discounted cash flow from	
Discount rate	Lease	Buy (1)	Buy (2)
5.0%	$12,642	$11,741	$12,150
7.5	9,999	8,859	8,821
10.0	8,142	6,795	6,493
12.5	6,798	5,271	4,817
15.0	5,798	4,113	3,597

Remarks: Buy (1) assumes maximum depreciation is used (i.e., DDB/SOYD over 14.5 years) No I.T.C. is usable. $1,458,000 of N.O.L. carry forwards expire unused.

Buy (2) assumes straight-line depreciation over 20 years. The full amount of I.T.C. available ($1,610,000) is taken over seven years.

Advantage of lease over buy is as follows:

Discount rate	Advantage (disadvantage) of leasing*
5.0%	$ 492,000
7.5	1,140,000
10.0	1,347,000
12.5	1,581,000
15.0	1,685,000

Note: See "General Assumptions" for listing of all assumptions. Detailed cash flow analyses for the "Buy (1) and Buy (2)" options at an operating margin of $3.8 million are attached. In the interest of brevity, the detailed analyses for higher margins are not included. These are, of course, available to you if you wish to seem them.

  * Over best buy alternative.

Exhibit 1 *(continued)*

Lease versus buy analysis for operating margin = $4,300,000 per year ($000)

Discount rate	Lease	Discounted cash flow from Buy (1)	Buy (2)
5.0%	$16,166	$16,220	$16,615
7.5	12,786	12,560	12,697
10.0	10,411	9.938	9,897
12.5	8,693	7,999	7,836
15.0	7,414	6,525	6,279

Remarks: Buy (1) assumes maximum depreciation is used (i.e., DDB/SOYD over 14.5 years). Only $308,000 of I.T.C. is usable and is taken in years 6 and 7.

Buy (2) assumes straight-line depreciation over 14.5 years. The full amount of I.T.C. available ($1,610,000) is taken over seven years.

Advantage of lease over buy is as follows:

Discount rate	Advantage (disadvantage) of leasing*
5.0%	$ (54,000)
7.5	89,000
10.0	473,000
12.5	694,000
15.0	889,000

Note: See "General Assumptions" for listing of all assumptions.
* Over best buy alternative.

Lease versus buy analysis for operating margin = $4,800,000 per year ($000)

Discount rate	Lease	Discounted cash flow from Buy (1)	Buy (2)
5.0%	$19,689	$20,545	$20,493
7.5	15,572	16,101	15,942
10.0	12,681	12,920	12,698
12.5	10,588	10,570	10,310
15.0	9,030	8,782	8,503

Remarks: Buy (1) assumes maximum depreciation is used (i.e., DDB/SOYD over 14.5 years). Only $1,219,000 of I.T.C. is usable and is taken in years 3 through 7.

Buy (2) assumes DDB/SOYD depreciation over 18.0 years. The full amount of I.T.C. available ($1,610,000) is taken over seven years.

Advantage of lease over buy is as follows:

Exhibit 1 *(continued)*

Discount rate	Advantage (disadvantage) of leasing*
5.0%	(856,000)
7.5	(529,000)
10.0	(239,000)
12.5	18,000
15.0	248,000

Note: See "General Assumptions" for listing of all assumptions.
* Over best buy alternative.

Lease versus buy analysis for operating margin = $5,300,000 per year ($000)

	Discounted cash flow from	
Discount rate	Lease	Buy
5.0%	$23,213	$24,461
7.5	18,359	19,276
10.0	14,950	15,572
12.5	12,483	12,839
15.0	10,646	10,765

Remarks: Buy assumes maximum depreciation is used (i.e., DDB/SOYD over 14.5 years). The full amount of I.T.C. available ($1,610,000) is taken over seven years.

Advantage of lease over buy is as follows:

Discount rate	Advantage (disadvantage) of leasing
5.0%	($1,248,000)
7.5	(917,000)
10.0	(622,000)
12.5	(356,000)
15.0	(119,000)

Note: See "General Assumptions" for listing of all assumptions.

Lease versus buy analysis for operating margin = $5,800,000 per year ($000)

	Discounted cash flow from	
Discount rate	Lease	Buy
5.0%	$26,736,000	$28,054,000
7.5	21,146,000	22,157,000
10.0	17,219,000	17,954,000
12.5	14,377,000	14,862,000
15.0	12,262,000	12,520,000

Remarks: Buy assumes maximum depreciation is used (i.e., DDB/SOYD over 14.5 years). The full amount of I.T.C. available ($1,610,000) is taken over five years.

Exhibit 1 *(continued)*

Advantage of lease over buy is as follows:

	Advantage (disadvantage) of leasing
Discount rate	
5.0%	($1,318,000)
7.5	(1,011,000)
10.0	(735,000)
12.5	(485,000)
15.0	(258,000)

Note: See "General Assumptions" for listing of all assumptions.

Exhibit 1 *(continued)*

Cash flow analysis (operating margin = $3,800,000; buy alternative 1; $000)

Assumptions

Investment	$23,000	Depreciable Investment	$23,000
Periods	25	Salvage value	0
Current tax rate	50%	Number of years	14.5
		Method	DDB/SOYD
Title XI Financing	$19,900		
Interest rate (per year)*	10.148%	Tax credit	0†
Number of years	25	Number of periods	0
Payment	$796	Starting in period	0

Discounted cash flows

Discount rate	Present value
2.500%	$15,906.53
5.000	11,741.19
7.500	8,858.73
10.000	6,795.28
12.500	5,271.25
15.000	4,113.39

Year	Margin	Depreciation	Interest	Principal	Taxes	I.T.C.	Net cash flow
0	0	0	0	0	0	0	$−3,100
1	$ 3,800	$ 3,172	$ 2,019	$ 796	0	0	985
2	3,800	2,735	1,939	796	0	0	1,065
3	3,800	2,529	1,858	796	0	0	1,146
4	3,800	2,326	1,777	796	0	0	1,227
5	3,800	2,124	1,696	796	0	0	1,308
6	3,800	1,922	1,615	796	0	0	1,388
7	3,800	1,719	1,535	796	0	0	1,469
8	3,800	1,517	1,454	796	0	0	1,550
9	3,800	1,315	1,373	796	$ 515	0	1,116
10	3,800	1,113	1,292	796	698	0	1,014
11	3,800	910	1,212	796	839	0	953
12	3,800	708	1,131	796	981	0	893
13	3,800	506	1,050	796	1,122	0	832
14	3,800	303	969	796	1,264	0	771
15	3,800	101	889	796	1,405	0	710
16	3,800	0	808	796	1,496	0	700
17	3,800	0	727	796	1,537	0	741

18	3,800	0	646	796	1,577	781
19	3,800	0	565	796	1,617	821
20	3,800	0	485	796	1,658	862
21	3,800	0	404	796	1,698	902
22	3,800	0	323	796	1,738	942
23	3,800	0	242	796	1,779	983
24	3,800	0	162	796	1,819	1,023
25	3,800	0	81	796	1,860	1,063
	$95,000	$23,000	$26,252	$19,900	$23,603	0

* Includes guarantee premium.
† Not usable.

		N.O.L. carry forward ($000)			
Period	Pretax profit (loss) ($000)	Used	Lost	Cumulative	Taxes paid ($000)
1	$(1,392)	—	—	$1,392	—
2	(874)	—	—	2,266	—
3	(586)	—	—	2,852	—
4	(304)	—	—	3,156	—
5	(20)	—	—	3,176	—
6	262	$262	$1,130	1,784	—
7	546	546	328	910	—
8	828	828	—	82	—
9	1,112	82	—	—	$515

Exhibit 1 (concluded)

Cash flow analysis (operating margin = $3,800,000; buy alternative 2; $000)

Assumptions

				Discounted cash flows	
Investment	$23,000	Depreciable investment	$23,000	Discount rate	Present value
Periods	25	Salvage value	0	2.500%	$17,055.34
Current tax rate	50%	Number of years	20	5.000	12,149.91
		Method	Straight line	7.500	8,820.73
Title XI Financing	$19,900	Tax credit	$1,610	10.000	6,492.61
Interest rate (per year)*	10.148%	Number of periods	7	12.500	4,817.35
Number of years	25	Starting in period	1	15.000	3,579.06
Payment	$796				

Year	Margin	Depreciation	Interest	Principal	Taxes	I.T.C.	Net cash flow
0	0	0	0	0	0	0	$-3,100
1	$ 3,800	$1,150	$2,019	$796	$315	$170	840
2	3,800	1,150	1,939	796	356	190	899
3	3,800	1,150	1,858	796	396	210	960
4	3,800	1,150	1,777	796	436	230	1,021
5	3,800	1,150	1,696	796	477	250	1,081
6	3,800	1,150	1,615	796	517	270	1,142
7	3,800	1,150	1,535	796	558	290	1,201
8	3,800	1,150	1,454	796	598	0	952
9	3,800	1,150	1,373	796	638	0	992
10	3,800	1,150	1,292	796	679	0	1,033
11	3,800	1,150	1,212	796	719	0	1,073
12	3,800	1,150	1,131	796	760	0	1,114
13	3,800	1,150	1,050	796	800	0	1,154
14	3,800	1,150	969	796	840	0	1,194
15	3,800	1,150	889	796	881	0	1,235
16	3,800	1,150	808	796	921	0	1,275
17	3,800	1,150	727	796	962	0	1,316
18	3,800	1,150	646	796	1,002	0	1,356
19	3,800	1,150	565	796	1,042	0	1,396
20	3,800	1,150	485	796	1,083	0	1,437
21	3,800	0	404	796	1,698	0	902
22	3,800	0	323	796	1,738	0	942
23	3,800	0	242	796	1,779	0	983
24	3,800	0	162	796	1,819	0	1,023
25	3,800	0	81	796	1,860	0	1,063
	$95,000	$23,000	$26,252	$19,900	$22,874	$1,610	

* Includes guarantee premium.

Exhibit 2
Federal Ship Financing Program, March 1974

INTRODUCTION

The Federal Ship Financing Program, established pursuant to Title XI of the Merchant Marine Act, 1936, as amended, provides for a full faith and credit guarantee by the U.S. Government of debt obligations issued by U.S. citizen shipowners for the purpose of financing or refinancing U.S. Flag vessels constructed or reconstructed in U.S. ship-yards. The program is administered by the secretary of commerce acting by and through the assistant secretary for maritime affairs (secretary). The guarantee of the U.S. government under this program provides for the prompt payment in full of the interest on and the unpaid principal of any guaranteed obligation in the event of default by the shipowner in the payment of any principal and interest on the obligations when due or for other specified defaults. The Federal Ship Financing Fund established pursuant to Title XI is used by the secretary as a revolving fund for the purpose of underwriting the government's guarantee and to pay the expenses of the Program. In addition, the secretary is authorized to borrow from the U.S. Treasury in the event the Fund is insufficient for the purpose of making prompt payments under its guarantee.

PURPOSE

The primary purpose of the Program is to promote the growth and modernization of the U.S. Merchant Marine by issuing guarantees of obligations to enable the financing and refinancing of vessels constructed in the United States and owned and operated by citizens of the United States. The Program enables owners of eligible vessels to obtain long-term financing on favorable terms and conditions and at interest rates that are comparable to those available to large and financially strong corporations. Such favorable financing terms are usually not available to the average shipowner.

ELIGIBILITY REQUIREMENTS

Vessels eligible for Title XI assistance generally include vessels designed principally for research or commercial use and over five net tons. However, any towboat, barge, scow, lighter, car float, canal boat, or tank vessel, to be eligible, must be more than 25 gross tons and floating drydocks must have a capacity of 35,000 or more lifting tons and a beam of 125 feet or more between the wing walls.

The design of the vessel must be adequate from an engineering viewpoint for its intended use, and the delivered vessel must be in American Bureau of Shipping class A-1, or meet other standards acceptable to the secretary. The shipowner must be a U.S. citizen and have sufficient operating experience and the ability to operate the vessel on an economically sound basis. The shipowner must meet certain financial requirements with respect to working capital and net worth, both of which are based on such factors as the amount of the guaranteed obligations, the shipowner's financial strength, intended employment of the vessel, etc. These factors also affect the terms of the guarantee with respect to continuing Title XI financial covenants, guarantee fees, reserve fund, etc. No guarantee under this program can be legally entered into unless the project is determined by the secretary to be economically sound.

Exhibit 2 *(continued)*

PROCEDURE

Application forms for Title XI (Form MA-163) may be obtained upon request from the Maritime Administration at the address given at the end of this brochure. Attached to the application is a copy of General Order 29, Revised, which constitutes the rules and regulations governing the operation of Title XI. Twelve completed sets of the application, including schedules and exhibits as required, should be sent to the Maritime Administration accompanied by a filing fee of $100 which is not refundable.

Approval of the application will be contingent upon the determination by the secretary as to whether the vessel(s) and the project meet all the applicable requirements of the existing statutes and regulations. If the application is approved, a conditional letter commitment to guarantee the obligation will be issued, stating the requirements necessary for final approval. If the application is not approved, the applicant will be notified in writing. Final approval of the application is accomplished after the formal documentation of the transaction and all the conditions in the letter commitment are satisfied. At such time the secretary will enter into a formal Commitment to Guarantee and guaranteed obligations (notes or bonds) may be issued and sold and a secured interest or a mortgage on the vessel(s) recorded.

AMOUNT GUARANTEED

The amount of the obligation guaranteed by the government is based on the "actual cost" of the vessel as determined by the secretary. The actual cost of a vessel includes those items which would normally be capitalized as vessel costs under usual accounting practices, such as the cost of construction, reconstruction, or reconditioning (including designing, inspecting, outfitting and equipping) of the vessel, together with commitment fees and interest on the related loan during the period of construction. All items of actual cost must be determined to be fair and reasonable by the secretary. Some costs are excluded from actual cost (and are sometimes considered capitalizable costs) such as legal and accounting fees, printing costs, guarantee fees, vessel insurance and underwriting fees and any interest on borrowings for the shipowner's equity in the vessel(s).

The secretary is authorized to guarantee an obligation which does not exceed 75 percent of the actual cost of most eligible vessels. However, obligations may be guaranteed in an amount not exceeding 87.5 percent of the actual cost of (1) passenger vessels, designed to be of not less than 1,000 gross tons and capable of a sustained speed of not less than 8 knots, to be used solely on inland rivers and waterways, (2) oceangoing tugs of more than 2,500 horsepower, (3) barges, (4) vessels of more than 2,500 horsepower designed to be capable of a sustained speed of not less than 40 knots, and (5) other vessels of not less than 3,500 gross tons and capable of a sustained speed of 14 knots. Vessels built with construction-differential subsidy or vessels other than barges and passenger vessels in (1) above engaged solely in the transportation of property on inland rivers and canals exclusively are eligible only for a guarantee not exceeding 75 percent of their actual cost.

If a Title XI guarantee of an obligation for a vessel is documented after delivery or for refinancing, the actual cost must be depreciated from the date of delivery to the documentation date of the guarantee.

Exhibit 2 *(continued)*

SOURCE OF FUNDS

Since the Federal Ship Financing Program is a guarantee program and not a direct loan program, funds secured by the guaranteed debt obligations and used for the financing of the vessel(s) are obtained in the private sector. The main sources for such funds include banks, pension trusts, life insurance companies and bonds sold to the general public.

AMORTIZATION AND INTEREST RATE

The maximum guarantee period is 25 years from the date of delivery; however, if the vessel has been reconstructed or reconditioned, the life may be extended by the secretary to include the remaining useful years of the vessel as determined by the secretary. Amortization in equal payments of principal is usually required; however, other amortization methods such as level debt (equal payments of principal and interest) may also be approved if sufficient security is offered such as long-term charters, reduction of the amount of guarantee and/or length of guarantee period.

The interest rate of the obligation guaranteed, for both new and refinanced vessels, must be within the range of interest rates prevailing in the private market for similar loans and risks and must be determined to be fair and reasonable by the secretary.

INVESTIGATION FEE

An investigation fee, not exceeding one half of 1 percent of the original principal amount of the obligation to be guaranteed, is charged for the investigation of applications, including related appraisals and inspections. Generally, a fee of only slightly in excess of one eighth of the 1 percent is charged. If the application is not approved, one half of the fee is refundable.

ANNUAL GUARANTEE FEES

The fee for the guarantee of an obligation for a delivered vessel will be not less than one half of 1 percent or more than 1 percent per annum, of the average principal amount of the outstanding obligation, or not less than one quarter of 1 percent or more than one half of 1 percent per annum, of the principal amount of an obligation relating to a vessel under construction, reconstruction or reconditioning. Amounts on deposit for the vessel in an escrow fund held by the U.S. Treasury pursuant to Title XI are excluded in the computation of this charge. The fee is required by law to be paid annually in advance.

Unless otherwise determined by the secretary, the annual premium rates are based on a ratio of net worth to long-term debt of the shipowner, and are subject to annual adjustment except during the construction period.

"BUY AMERICAN" POLICY

The Maritime Administration's long-standing policy has been that vessels built with the aid of Title XI are subject to the "Buy American" provision of Section 505 of the act which states in part:

> "In all such construction the shipbuilder, subcontractors materialmen or suppliers shall use, so far as practicable, only articles, materials, and supplies of the growth, production, or manufacture of the United States as defined in paragraph K of Section 401 of the Tariff Act of 1930."
>
> Pursuant to Title XI the shipowner may be permitted to use components of foreign manufacture providing (1) the performance of the vessel will not be adversely affected, and (2) the incorporation of such foreign components into the vessel will not impair its entitlement to operate in the coastwise trade of the United States or to carry preference cargoes. However, if foreign components are used, the cost thereof will be excluded from actual cost if the secretary determines that suitable American domestically produced components are available. This reduction in actual cost will increase the owner's share of the total cost of the vessel and reduce the amount of the guaranteed obligation.

REFINANCING

Amounts outstanding on existing Title XI obligations, or amounts outstanding on obligations not previously insured or guaranteed (provided they had been issued for the purposes contained in Title XI) may be refinanced under the Title XI program up to the amount of the depreciated actual cost of the vessel(s) but not exceeding the amount of the existing obligations being refinanced. Such refinancing under Title XI must meet all the applicable requirements of the existing statutes and regulations, and the original obligation must have been issued within one year after vessel delivery. Vessels purchased as "used" vessels are not eligible under this provision. However, under certain conditions the proceeds of guaranteed obligations issued with respect to any eligible vessel may be used for the construction of a new vessel or for the purchase of certain marine equipment.

ADDITIONAL INFORMATION

This brochure is intended as general guide to the Federal Ship Financing Program (Title XI) and its basic provisions. Additional or more specific information, and applications (Form MA-163) may be obtained from:

Chief, Division of Ship Financing Guarantees
Office of Subsidy Administration
Maritime Administration
Department of Commerce
14th & E Streets, N.W.
Washington, D.C. 20230

CASE 4-3

U.S. Navy: Tanker Lease Program

In August 1973, Jim Mortenson, a staff analyst for the Senate Budget Committee, was asked to examine a report from the comptroller general's office. The report investigated a recent Build and Charter program under which the navy was proposing to acquire nine new oil tankers. (See Exhibit 1.) Since the charter payments would come from Operations and Maintenance funds, the proposal did not require specific authorization from Congress. The total capitalized cost, however, was over $500 million, which had aroused some concern over:

1. The appropriateness of using funds requiring no outside approval.
2. The method of analysis used in evaluating the lease proposal, particularly the discount rate used.

The comptroller general had therefore investigated the proposal and supporting analysis.

Jim believed that federal agencies ought to be consistent in:

1. Using a conceptual framework for evaluating the relative costs and benefits of investment proposals.
2. Determining the level/levels in government from which the costs and benefits ought to be viewed.
3. Setting criteria by which such proposals ought to be approved.

He was aware that the Congressional Subcommittee on Economy in Government had prepared a report on the Economic Analysis of Public Investment Decisions [Exhibit 2]. He was also aware that this had caused considerable controversy (as evidenced by dissenting congressional opinions) [Exhibit 3].

Jim hoped that a thorough analysis of the navy proposal and comptroller general's report would serve to highlight important policy issues. Not only could it help clarify some traditionally confusing issues, but it could also lead to the development of specific policy guidelines for all government agencies. In the future, proposals like this could then be completely and appropriately analyzed.

Exhibit 1

COMPTROLLER GENERAL'S
REPORT TO THE CONGRESS

BUILD AND CHARTER PROGRAM
for
NINE TANKER SHIPS

Military Sealift Command
U.S. Department of the Navy

BUILD AND CHARTER PROGRAM

In June 1972 the Military Sealift Command, Department of the Navy, entered into the Build and Charter program to acquire the use of nine new tankers. Private interests were to provide for their construction and financing, with a commitment from the Navy, that it would lease the tankers, with renewal provisions, for 20 years.

By renting instead of purchasing, the navy can apply Operation and Maintenance (O&M) funds which, unlike procurement funds, do not require specific authorization and approval by the Congress.

Need for tankers

One of the navy's activities is to arrange for Department of Defense (DOD) ocean transportation of bulk petroleum, oil, and lubricant (POL) products. Almost all of the demands placed upon the navy for this liquid-cargo transportation are for long distances, generally from the refineries, where crude oil is converted into POL products, to established military distribution terminals. Throughout the world, there are 117 distribution terminals: 26 army, 31 air force, and 60 navy. To service these terminals, the navy employs a fleet of both government-owned and commercially chartered tankers.

The tankers are civilian-manned, contract-operated, commercial-type ships. The principal products carried are (1) navy special fuel oil, a product used as ship fuel, (2) jet aircraft fuel, (3) gasoline for piston aircraft, (4) motor gasoline, and (5) diesel fuel.

As of October 1971, when the navy briefed DOD officials on its proposed Build and Charter program, the Military Sealift Command tanker fleet consisted of 56 tankers having a total capability of 1,316,000 dead weight tons (DWT).* Of the 56 tankers, 32 were commercial charters, representing about 75 percent of the total DWT capability.

* Dead weight ton (DWT) is the measurement of a ship's total carrying capacity in tons weight including cargo, fuel, passengers and crew, when fully loaded down to its permitted load line.

Exhibit 1 *(continued)*

The remaining 24 tankers were government owned: 10 were T-1 or T-5 tankers, representing about 9 percent of the total DWT capability, and 14 were T-2 tankers, representing about 16 percent of that capability. On the basis of navy and DOD studies made from 1965–69, navy officials stated they needed 9 new tankers to replace the 14 T-2 tankers which were of World War II vintage. Because the T-2 tankers were more than 25 years old, the navy believed operating and repair costs had increased to the point where it was not cost effective to continue their operation.

According to navy officials, U.S.-flag tankers with the specifications needed by the navy are not available for long-term charter and, furthermore, new tankers with these specifications are not being built commercially in the United States. Tankers of the desired size are available under foreign flags, but the Cargo Preference Act of 1904 requires that all DOD material be shipped under the U.S. flag, if available. If the navy chartered foreign-flag vessels on a long-term basis, a problem would develop each time a U.S.-flag vessel became available for charter hire. To obtain tankers meeting its specifications, the navy concluded that new tankers must be built.

Navy officials told us that, since 1958, they have requested procurement funds to purchase new tankers to replace the T-2 tankers. The requests were denied at higher budget review levels within the navy or DOD because procurement funds were needed for higher priority combatant ship construction programs. The Build and Charter program was designed to meet the need for new tankers without spending procurement funds.

The program contemplates 20 years of fixed, biweekly charter payments (rent) for the exclusive use of nine tankers. Because the money is for rent payments and not for outright purchase, O&M funds can be used. Furthermore, because O&M funds are used, specific line-item congressional approval is not mandatory.

The tankers are operated under the Navy Industrial Fund, a revolving fund reimbursed from the appropriated O&M funds of the army, air force, marine corps, and navy. Industrial fund operations allow the navy to spread costs to the other military services using the POL transported in the tankers. The POL transportation rates are set annually on the basis of forecasted costs, and the military service customers are billed at these rates for services received. Thus, the costs of operating the tanker fleet—including charter costs—are ultimately passed on through the Navy Industrial Fund to the O&M accounts of the military services receiving the transported POL products.

Before awarding contracts, the navy requested and obtained two key rulings. The first, from the General Accounting Office and Department of Justice, stated that the charters would constitute a valid general obligation of the United States which is secured by its full faith and credit. The second, from the Internal Revenue Service, allowed owner participants to be treated as a partnership for tax purposes and allowed the tankers to be depreciated in 14½ years by either the double-declining balance method or the sum-of-the-years'-digits method. One of the material representations relied on for this ruling was that, at the end of the charter term, the tankers should have an estimated value of not less than 15 percent of cost.

NAVY BUILD AND CHARTER PROGRAM

After obtaining bids from 14 construction companies, the navy entered into a series of principal financing documents for the construction and leasing of nine tankers on

Exhibit 1 *(continued)*

June 20, 1972. The navy executed contracts with two special-purpose corporations, Marine Ship Leasing Corp. and Marine Vessel Leasing Corp. (Since Marine Transport Lines, Inc., will act as the fiscal agent for the two special-purpose corporations and to simplify discussion of this transaction, Marine Transport can be considered—for purposes of this report only—the owner of the tankers.) In essence, the navy, in these contracts, promises to lease the nine tankers when they are built, tested, and delivered. The lease period, with renewal options, is 20 years. The type of lease is called a bareboat charter, which means that only the ship is leased; the navy is to bear other operating costs for such things as crew, fuel, maintenance, and insurance. The transaction can be divided into three phases: (1) construction, (2) delivery and long-term financing, and (3) charter.

Construction phase

Marine Transport executed construction contracts simultaneously with Todd Shipyards Corporation for building four tankers and with Bath Iron Works Corporation for building five tankers. The navy and the shipbuilders have no direct contractual arrangement. The fixed-price construction contracts' prices are shown in the following table.

Contractor	Unit price	Units	Total
Bath	$16,031,000	5	$ 80,155,000
Todd	16,595,000	4	66,380,000
Total		9	$146,535,000

These commercial-type tankers, built to standards of the maritime industry, are not of a military design. The contractual delivery dates, by hull or ship number, are given in Schedule 1.

Schedule 1. Build and charter ship delivery schedule

Delivery date		Hull number	Shipbuilder
1. June	15, 1974	100	Todd Shipyards
2. July	5, 1974	360	Bath Iron Works
3. July	27, 1974	101	Todd Shipyards
4. October	19, 1974	361	Bath Iron Works
5. October	26, 1974	102	Todd Shipyards
6. November	16, 1974	362	Bath Iron Works
7. November	30, 1974	363	Bath Iron Works
8. December	7, 1974	103	Todd Shipyards
9. December	7, 1974	364	Bath Iron Works

Since government progress payments will not be available to finance the construction, Marine Transport will obtain construction loans from the interim lenders, the Chase Manhattan Bank (Todd's banker) and the First National City Bank (Bath's banker). The annual interest rate on the construction loans, which is not fixed, will be 115 percent of the bank's base rate on 90-day loans to substantial and responsible commercial

Exhibit 1 *(continued)*

borrowers in effect at the opening of the first business day of the calendar quarter when funds are made available.

From time to time, and as needed during the construction period, Marine Transport will borrow money from the interim lenders and provide it to the shipbuilders as they progress on the construction of the tankers. The interim lenders will obtain liens against the tankers until the loans, plus interest, are repaid.

Delivery and long-term financing phase

After the construction phase is completed, the ships are delivered to Marine Transport and the previously agreed-to, long-term financing arrangements become operative. Until the ships are delivered, the total cost cannot be determined. The navy estimate of total or capitalized costs is shown in Schedule 2.

Capitalized costs are fundamental to determining (1) the amount of both borrowed and equity funds to be invested through selling bonds and ownership rights, (2) the amount of the navy's charter payments, and (3) all other miscellaneous dollar flows related to the Build and Charter program. Although the February 1973 navy estimate of capitalized costs is $158.5 million, we have assumed that the December 1974 actual capitalized costs will be $160 million. This assumption facilitates our calculating estimated dollar flows later in this report but does not distort the analysis.

When Marine Transport obtains the tankers in the second half of 1974, it must pay back the money (principal plus interest) it borrowed to make progress payments during the construction phase. The bond purchasers are then called on for 75 percent, or $120 million, of the assumed $160 million capitalized cost and the owner participants are called on for 25 percent, or $40 million, of this amount.

The bonds to be purchased bear 7⅞ percent interest and are called "First Preferred Fleet Mortgage Bonds." The bond purchasers, 35 institutional investors, will receive interest only during the first ten years after bond purchase. During the second ten years they will receive interest plus purchase price.

The 14 owner participants invest 25 percent of the capitalized cost ($40 million) plus an added 2 percent of capitalized cost ($3 million). The $3 million is a fee to Marine Transport Lines, Inc.; Citicorp Leasing; and Salomon Brothers for arranging the Build and Charter transaction. In return the owner participants receive a paper loss for tax purposes during the first 13 years due primarily to the rapid depreciation of the ships. This loss, used to offset income from other sources, thereby reduces their tax liability in that year.

The net effect is that the owner participants are buying a tax loss, or Marine Transport is selling depreciation expense. The transaction does not allow the companies to avoid paying taxes; it defers payment of taxes to the later years of the contract. To the owner participant, as a 48 percent taxpayer, every dollar of tax deferral translates into 48 cents of interest-free money which can be reinvested.

The analysis of estimated dollar flows resulting from this transaction assumes that the original 14 owner participants will remain parties to the agreement for the full 20-year lease period. The analysis would change depending on such factors as (1) the original owners' decision to sell their rights, (2) the sale proceeds from the transactions, (3) the gain or loss on the sale, and (4) the depreciation to be allowed to subsequent owners.

Exhibit 1 *(continued)*

Schedule 2. Military Sealift Command estimate of capitalized cost, February 1973

	Bath		Todd		Total
	One tanker	Five tankers	One tanker	Four tankers	(nine tankers)
Construction price	$16,031,000	$80,155,000	$16,595,000	$66,380,000	$146,535,000
Supervisory fee	64,444	322,220	64,445	257,780	580,000
Performance bond*	25,000	125,000	25,000	100,000	225,000
Commitment fee (½ of 1 percent)†	100,194	500,970	103,719	414,874	915,844
Interest on loan 6 percent per year	1,118,160	5,590,800	1,157,493	4,629,974	10,220,774
Total	$17,338,798	$86,693,990	$17,945,657	$71,782,628	
Total estimate of capitalized costs					$158,476,618

* Paid by Bath and Todd.
† Paid to bond purchasers.

Exhibit 1 *(continued)*

Charter phase

When Marine Transport accepts the tankers, they are immediately chartered to the navy. The navy pays the charter hire on the 15th and last days of each month. The initial charter period is for five years with options to renew for three additional five-year periods. At the end of the 20-year period, the tankers are to be returned. The terms of the contracts prohibit the navy or any other government agency from ever purchasing these tankers. This prohibition was needed so that, for income tax purposes, the transaction could not be considered as a deferred sale to the government.

The navy's charter payments are structured so that, during the first ten years, the amount paid is exactly equal to the interest that the owners must pay to the bond purchasers. After the tenth year, the Navy's charter payments are more than double because, during the second ten-year period, principal and interest must be paid to the bond purchasers. Assuming a total cost of $160 million, the charter payments for nine tankers would be about $9 million each year for the first ten years and about $22 million each year for the second ten years.

Termination features

Construction period. If the navy terminated the Build and Charter program during the construction period, the government would be obligated to pay:

1. Construction costs incurred up to the termination date.
2. Costs incurred for settling termination claims.
3. $180,000 for each ship terminated for expenses and profit to the parties arranging the Build and Charter program.
4. To the extent not covered above, expenses paid and interest thereon to the owner participants, interest to the interim lenders, and unpaid commitment fees to the bond purchasers.

Total termination costs to the government cannot exceed the construction contract price, less payments already made, less any work not terminated.

Lease period. If the navy terminates for convenience during the lease period, the government must pay (1) the termination value of the ships, less net sales proceeds, and (2) final fees and expenses of the trustees. Termination value for the first 12 years of charter is 122.5 percent of capitalized costs; it declines in the later years of the contract and reaches 42.5 percent of capitalized costs in the 20th year of charter. If termination occurs due to loss at sea or seizure, a stipulated loss value, approximately the same as the termination value of each year, is applied.

LEASE VERSUS PURCHASE ANALYSIS

The navy, in evaluating the economics of leasing versus purchasing tankers, used the criteria established in DOD *Instruction 7041.3*. This instruction provides that a 10 percent discount rate be applied. This rate represents an estimate of the average return on private investment, before taxes and after inflation. The source cited for this instruction is OMB *Circular A-94*.

Circular A-94 prescribes the discount rate for evaluating government decisions con-

Exhibit 1 *(continued)*

cerning the initiation, renewal, or expansion of programs or projects. However, *A-94* states that its provisions do not apply to the evaluation of government decisions concerning the acquisition of commercial-type services. The circular states that guidance for making these decisions is contained in *Circular A-76.*

Circular A-76 prescribes that the yield on long-term Department of the Treasury borrowings be used in evaluating lease versus purchase alternatives. This rate, at the time the transaction was entered into, was about 6 percent.

Whether leasing or purchasing is the more economical alternative depends upon the discount rate applied. Table A summarizes the cost of lease and purchase alternatives when *A–94* (10 percent) and *A–76* (6 percent) criteria are applied. An 8 percent discount rate and an undiscounted column are also included to show the sensitivity at various discount rates.

Table A

	Present value at various discount rates ($ millions)			
	Undiscounted	6 percent	8 percent	10 percent
Cost to government to lease:				
Adusted charter payments to reflect tax effects	$314.1	$160.7	$132.4	$110.9
Cost to government to purchase:				
Capitalized cost	$160.0	$136.9	$130.2	$124.0
Less residual value	−24.0	−6.3	−4.1	−2.7
	$136.0	$130.6	$126.1	$121.3
Cost advantage of leasing	−$178.1	−$ 30.1	−$ 6.3	+$ 10.4

Under *A-76* criteria (6 percent) purchasing would have been the more economical alternative by about $29.6 million. Under *A-94* criteria (10 percent) leasing would have been the more economical alternative by about $10.4 million.

Each of the cost elements is discussed below.

Cost to government to lease

To show the cost to the government, we have adjusted the navy charter payments to reflect the tax effect. The adjusted charter payments totaling $314.1 million are made up of (1) the actual cash payment of charter hire by the navy and (2) the taxes that are deferred (not paid until later years)—shown as an addition—in the early years of the contract and taxes paid—shown as a subtraction—in the later years of the contract.

For example, in the fourth year the estimated navy charter payment is $9.5 million and the deferred taxes are $9 million, thus the adjusted charter payment is actually $18.5 million. In the 20th charter year the estimated navy payment is $21.6 million and the taxes paid are $8.3 million; a subtraction results in an adjusted charter payment of $13.3 million. We have made this calculation for each of the 23 years, and the total adjusted charter payments are $314.1 million. (See Schedule 3.)

Exhibit 1 (continued)

Schedule 3. Estimated* dollar flows resulting from Military Sealift Command's Nine Tanker Build and Charter program ($000)

Tax year	(1) Charter payments	(2) Interest income	(3) Interest expense	(4) Depreciation expense	(5) Other expense	(6) Charter tax loss (−) or profit	(7) Charter taxes deferred or paid (−)	(8) Adjusted charter payments to reflect tax effects col. 1(+) or (−)col. 7
1	—	—	$ 399†	—	$ 790	$ −1,189	$ 571	571
2	—	—	3,021†	—	41	−3,062	1,470	1,470
3	$ 2,156	—	8,689†	$ 9,713	3,246	−19,492	9,356	11,512
4	9,450	$ 65	9,450‡	18,756	61	−18,752	9,001	18,451
5	9,450	65	9,450	17,416	61	−17,421	8,358	17,808
6	9,450	65	9,450	16,076	61	−16,072	7,715	17,165
7	9,450	65	9,450	14,737	61	−14,733	7,072	16,522
8	9,450	65	9,450	13,397	61	−13,393	6,429	15,879
9	9,450	65	9,450	12,057	61	−12,053	5,786	15,236
10	9,450	65	9,450	10,718	61	−10,714	5,143	14,593
11	9,450	65	9,450	9,378	61	−9,374	4,500	13,950
12	9,450	65	9,450	8,038	61	−8,034	3,857	13,307
13	9,450	65	9,450	6,698	61	−6,694	3,213	12,663
14	21,628	149	9,290	4,287	61	8,139	−3,907	17,721
15	21,628	149	8,626	1,272	61	11,818	−5,672	15,956
16	21,628	149	7,908	—	61	13,808	−6,628	15,000
17	21,628	149	7,133	—	61	14,583	−7,000	14,628
18	21,628	149	6,296	—	61	15,420	−7,402	14,226
19	21,628	149	5,391	—	61	16,325	−7,836	13,792
20	21,628	149	4,413	—	61	17,303	−8,305	13,323
21	21,628	149	3,358	—	61	18,358	−8,812	12,816
22	21,628	149	2,218	—	61	19,498	−9,359	12,269
23	21,628	149	985	—	7,564	13,228	−6,350	15,278
	$312,936	$2,140	$162,227	$142,543	$12,800	$ −2,494	$ 1,200	$314,136

* The estimated dollar flows are based on the following assumptions: capitalized cost of nine tankers will be $160 million; federal tax rate will be 48 percent; average delivery date of nine tankers will be October 1974; total time will be 23 years— 3 years for construction, 20 years for charter; other income in years 1 to 13 will offset tax losses.
† Interest on construction loans, years 1 through 3.
‡ Interest on bonds, years 4 through 23.

Exhibit 1 *(continued)*

Cost to government to purchase

Capitalized costs. Assuming the navy could, or wanted to, justify applying procurement funds for the purchase of the nine tankers, we used the same capitalized
costs ($160 million) in our analysis as were used for the Build and Charter program.
We recognize that, to purchase the tankers, the navy would have to pay some amount
more than the $146.5 million to the shipbuilders because the navy would have to
administer the shipbuilding contracts and make progress payments. The difference of
$13.5 million should be more than enough to cover costs of administering the contract
and of borrowing funds to make progress payments during the three-year construction
period.

Residual value. We recognize that it is highly conjectural to attempt to project,
23 years into the future, a value of nine not-yet-built tankers; however, the estimate
given to Internal Revenue Service for its ruling on depreciation was 15 percent ($24
million) of original costs ($160 million).

Conclusions

Discount rates. As stated ealier, whether or not leasing is more economical than
purchasing depends on the discount rate used to calculate the present value of future
payments.

The navy used criteria comparable to that contained in *Circular A-94* and evaluated
the lease versus purchase decision using a discount rate of 10 percent. Under this
criteria, the decision to lease appeared more economical than purchasing by $10.4
million.

We believe that the *A-94* criteria was not appropriate for evaluating the lease versus
purchase decision and that criteria comparable to that contained in *Circular A-76* would
have been appropriate. Under *A-76* criteria the decision would have been evaluated
using the yield on long-term Treasury obligations which was about 6 percent at the
time of the navy's decision to lease. Using a discount rate of 6 percent, the decision
to purchase would have been more economical by $29.6 million.

DOD's advance notification to the Congress. The navy has authority to
enter into long-term lease programs by using O&M funds appropriated by the Congress,
but in so doing the authorizing prerogatives and oversight responsibilities of the Congress
are diminished. In this instance we believe the Congress was not assured an opportunity
to evaluate and participate in a decision-making process which resulted in the commitment of more than $300 million in public funds.

According to the commanding officer, Military Sealift Command, the only written
communication provided to the Congress was a press release on January 4, 1972,
stating the construction costs of $66.4 million to build four ships at Todd Shipyards
and the construction costs of $80.1 million to build five ships at Bath Iron Works.

The navy selected the Build and Charter program, not as the result of a lease versus
purchase analysis, but because it could not obtain procurement funds to purchase
new tankers and would rather conserve its procurement funds for combatant ships.
The navy analysis of charter payments does not take into account the direct tax effects
of this transaction. However, the tax shelter was a key factor in arranging this transaction.

Exhibit 1 *(continued)*

Navy officials agree that the manner in which the Congress was informed of this program could be improved.

Recommendations

We recommend that the Secretary of Defense revise DOD instructions to provide for application of the guidelines set forth in *Circular A-76* in evaluating long-term leasing of assets such as ships.

To improve congressional visibility of future build and charter programs, the secretary of defense should assist the Congress by

1. Providing it with information on the proposed method of acquisition (long-term leasing or purchasing).
2. Providing, to the appropriate congressional committees, a detailed cost analysis showing full impact on future budgets when long-term leasing is the proposed acquisition method.
3. Requiring analyses of long-term leasing arrangements to be made on a total-cost-to-the-government basis, including the direct effects of delayed payments of income taxes.

Agency comments and our evaluation

Both DOD and the navy generally concur in our recommendations for providing Congress full information on future build and charter programs (Exhibit A). DOD also agrees that appropriate congressional committees should be provided with detailed cost analyses showing full impact on future budgets when long-term leasing is the proposed acquisition method.

The navy did not concur, however, in our treatment of deferred taxes. The navy believes that a lease versus purchase analysis should not recognize the value of deferred payment of income taxes as a cost. Instead, the navy considers the only true identifiable cost to the government to be the charter hire payments. Further, it is the DOD position that the effects of tax deferral do not represent a readily identifiable cost to the government and that it should not be included in the cost attributed to the Build and Charter program unless it can be identified with some precision.

We included the effect on taxes in our comparison because this was a key factor in the agreement, and the deferral of taxes represented the return to the owner participants on their investment of about $40 million. We believe that capital investment decisions should be made on a total-cost-to-the-government basis, including the effect of tax revenues.

In addition, DOD did not concur in our recommendation that DOD instructions be revised to provide for application of the guidelines set forth in OMB *Circular A-76* in evaluating long-term leasing assets such as ships. DOD stated that it employs the 10 percent rate specified in DOD *Instruction 7041.3* and disagreed that a 6 percent rate indicated in OMB *Circular A-76* would be more appropriate.

In our report, we pointed out that OMB *Circular A-94*, the basis for DOD *Instruction 7041.3*, is not applicable to the acquisition of commercial-type services and that guidance for making such decisions is contained in OBM *Circular A-76*. DOD, along with

Exhibit 1 *(continued)*

OMB, should determine the appropriateness of *Circular A-76* criteria for use in lease versus purchase analyses.

DOD also believes that the residual value of the ships should be shown as 5 percent, instead of 15 percent, of cost. We used 15 percent because this was the estimate given by the owners to the Internal Revenue Service for its ruling on depreciation.

Finally, DOD also points out that:

> ". . . tankers financed through the appropriation, Shipbuilding and Construction, Navy, had customarily represented military designs with special features which made them more costly than the commercial design called for in this program."

Although this may be true, navy officials said that commercially designed ships could be obtained under either arrangement.

MATTER FOR CONSIDERATION BY THE CONGRESS

Since the navy's Build and Charter program is similar to government programs for leasing buildings, the Congress should evaluate the need for legislation similar to Public Law 92–313 of June 16, 1972, which amended the Public Buildings Act of 1959, to require congressional approval of building leases greater than $500,000 a year and to require that a prospectus containing the details of the transaction be provided to the Congress. Similar legislation may be appropriate for long-term leasing of such assets as ships.

Since the Build and Charter program can be considered as setting a precedent (the navy is considering acquiring other types of vessels, such as dry cargo ships, in this manner) legislation could be an effective tool to insure congressional cognizance of future long-term leasing programs.

Exhibit A

ASSISTANT SECRETARY OF DEFENSE
Washington, D.C. 20301

INSTALLATIONS AND LOGISTICS

July 9 1973

Mr. James H. Hammond
Deputy Director, Procurement
  and Systems Acquisition Division
U.S. General Accounting Office
Washington, D.C. 20548

Dear Mr. Hammond:

This is in response to your letter of April 12, 1973, to the Secretary of Defense which forwarded copies of your draft report entitled "Build and Charter Program for Nine Tanker Ships Department of the Navy."

Exhibit 1 *(continued)*

The Department of Defense (DOD) concurs in the recommendations that Congress should be provided full information regarding the proposed method of acquisition (long-term leasing as well as purchasing). DOD also agrees that appropriate congressional committees should be provided with detailed cost analyses showing full impact on future budgets when long-term leasing is the proposed acquisition method. Advance notification of concerned Committees by DOD respecting proposed build and charter programs has occasionally been informal in the past. At this time formal procedures providing for the systematic transmission of appropriate information on proposed programs are being developed in my office.

Regarding the recommendation of the draft report—that "analysis of long-term leasing arrangements . . . be made on a total-cost-to-the-government basis <u>including the direct effects of delayed payments</u> of income taxes to the government," there is some disagreement on the part of DOD respecting the portion which I have underlined. It has been stated in DOD that:

  a. . . . the Navy considers the only true identifiable cost to the Government to be the charter hire payments by [the Military Sealift Command] MSC;
  b. The valuation of tax deferrals is very complex and could be subject to much dispute. . . . An accurate assessment of tax impact would require solicitation of data which most taxpayers consider privileged.
  c. OMB guidance does not require a determination of deferred taxes. . . . It is believed that Congress is the proper body for determining whether certain provisions of the Internal Revenue Code, which have the effect of deferring taxes, are in the public interest.

It should be noted that the question in hand is not one which has been decided upon with finality by recognized professional authorities. Therefore, it is suggested that our dissenting view be presented in the GAO paper to give due recognition to both sides of the issue. This might be done through the incorporation of two additional points stating that:

  It is the DOD position that the effects of tax deferral do not represent a readily identifiable cost to the government and that they should not be included in the cost attributed to build and charter unless they can be identified with some precision. When the effect of tax deferral is excluded from the cost comparison presented in Table 1, the break-even point between purchase and lease occurs where the discount rate used in computing present value is approximately 6 percent.

This compares with a value between 9 and 10 percent in the GAO presentation. The draft report also "recommends that the Secretary of Defense revise DOD instructions to provide for application of the guidelines set forth in (OMB) *Circular A-76* in evaluating long-term leasing arrangements." This refers to the money valuation criteria advanced in *Circular A-76*. These criteria provide for an effective discount rate of about 6 percent, which yields a preference for purchase over lease in the draft report formulation.

The DOD employs the 10 percent rate specified in DOD *Instruction 7041.3,* and disagrees with the draft report's stated conclusion that the 6 percent rate indicated in *Circular A-76* would be more appropriate. The draft report includes no analysis of the derivation or applicability of specific discount rates as such, and hence provides

Exhibit 1 *(concluded)*

no basis for the selection of one rate over another. In this sense, the stated preference for a 6 percent rate appears to be a matter of opinion. Furthermore, there are other provisions of *Circular A-76,* not recognized in the draft report, which, if applied, would tend to shift the cost preference in the direction of build and charter.

Another observation in DOD is that the 15 percent residual ship value assigned in the draft report to the purchase approach is higher than the normal residual value of MSC ships when they are retired since they are normally held until their residual value is scrap value (at about 5 percent). Finally, it has been observed that there are potential secondary effects in terms of income to the government from taxes on the interest income generated through the build and charter transaction which could be applied as credits against the cost of that option, thereby improving its position relative to the direct procurement approach. It is recognized that there are also other potential secondary tax effects. It is clear from our staff discussions that the GAO is aware of these extensive potential effects and it is suggested that if they are not to be taken into account the reasons for excluding them be explicitly stated in the report.

It should be noted that, as of the inception of the nine-tanker build and charter program, tankers financed through the appropriation, Shipbuilding and Construction, navy, had customarily represented military designs with special features which made them more costly than the commercial design called for in this program. Furthermore, there is a question as to whether this would not continue to be the case in the future.

It is the general DOD feeling that, with the reservations noted, this is potentially a very useful report.

Sincerely,

Assistant Secretary of Defense
(Installations & Logistics)

Exhibit 2

ECONOMIC ANALYSIS OF PUBLIC INVESTMENT DECISIONS: INTEREST RATE POLICY AND DISCOUNTING ANALYSIS

Interest rate policy and discounting analysis—an abstract

In this report, the Subcommittee on Economy in Government presents its conclusions on the application of discounting procedures in federal government bureaus and agencies and submits its recommendations on this matter. The subcommittee accepts without qualification the proposition that consistent discounting procedures and appropriate interest rate policy must be adopted throughout the federal government if wise and economic investment decisions are to be made. Testimony presented to the subcommittee demonstrated that such consistency is not now present. The subcommittee recommends that no public investment be deemed "economic" or "efficient" if it fails to yield overall benefits which are at least as great as those which the same resources would have produced if left in the private sector. Currently, the rate of return on alternative minimum-risk private spending is at least 5 percent. Indeed, some of the economists appearing before the subcommittee argued for substantially higher interest rates—rates in the 7 to 12 percent range.

On the basis of the testimony presented, the subcommittee recommends that—

1. The Bureau of the Budget insist on the adoption of consistent discounting procedures by all agencies.
2. The Bureau of the Budget, in conjunction with an appropriate government agency, immediately undertake a study to develop a method for estimating the weighted-average opportunity cost of private spending displaced by government investment. This method should recognize that the financing of the federal government entails a reduction in both private consumption and private investment spending.
3. An appropriate federal agency undertake the ongoing publication of this weighted-average opportunity cost interest rate as guidance to those agencies applying discounting analysis to public investment decisions. This interest rate calculation and publication should be pursuant to and based upon the above-mentioned study.
4. The proposal of the Water Resources Council which ties the interest rate to the yield on government securities with long terms to maturity be adopted. The subcommittee judges that the yield on long-term federal government securities is the lowest possible rate consistent with the minimum-risk opportunity cost of displaced private spending.
5. The Bureau of the Budget and the program evaluation staffs of all federal agencies intensify their efforts to formulate accurate monetary estimates of the benefits and costs of public investments.
6. The Congress review, with the purpose of relaxing, existing legal and institutional constraints on agency efforts to implement sound economic evaluations of proposed investments. These constraints are especially severe in the area of transportation investments.

This report, then, deals with the optimum discounting procedures to be used in evaluating the economics of public investments. It does not argue that the democratically chosen representatives of the people should ignore the noneconomic impacts of public spending or refrain from placing a high value on them. The subcommittee, however,

Exhibit 2 *(continued)*

does urge that when and if a program warrants funding because of these noneconomic effects, the cost of attaining these other objectives be clearly recognized. It is only with the accurate evaluation of the real national economic impacts that the costs of securing these other social objectives can be recognized and appraised.

THE DISCOUNTING PROCEDURE MUST BE USED IF GOOD PUBLIC INVESTMENT DECISIONS ARE TO BE MADE

Sound investment policy in both private business and the government requires that the decision maker know the expected rate of return on the alternative projects competing for a share of his budget. For the decision maker in private business, this knowledge enables him to allocate his budget among the competing claims so as to obtain the maximum difference between the revenues and outlays for his firm. The public decision maker, however, does not focus on these financial flows. Rather, he is concerned with the social returns and costs attributable to his investment undertakings. His objective is to gain the maximum difference between social benefits and costs for each dollar which he spends. For investments in which both benefits and costs are evaluated in monetary terms, procedures must be sought to capture all social returns and losses in the quantitative estimates. However, even when confronted with public investments whose benefits cannot be accurately measured in dollar terms or expenditures whose impacts spill over onto third parties in some unknown way, the public decision maker must undertake discounting analysis to determine the effectiveness of alternative expenditures in satisfying objectives.

A characteristic of investments—whether public or private—is that they commit resources in the future and carry an expectation of gains which only materialize over time. It is the expectation of gains and costs which will be realized only in the future which poses the crucial problem for investment analysis. Because a dollar expected a decade from now is not worth as much as a dollar expected tomorrow, even if the price level does not change, some procedure must be found for placing streams of benefits and costs with different time patterns on a common basis. Only then can they be accurately compared.

The procedure recommended by both economists and businessmen for accomplishing this common-time-basis adjustment is known as discounting. It works by ascertaining how much a dollar held today could be turned into in future years if invested wisely and by then applying this adjustment to dollars of gains and costs not expected to be received or incurred until future years. For example, if one could, through properly investing it, transform $100 to $105 next year, then it is clear that $105 expected next year is worth only about $100 today. In this case, dollars not expected to materialize until future years get reduced through the discounting procedure by 5 percent for each year which they are deferred. Thus, an individual who spends $100 of his income on consumption goods today, foregoes the $105 which he could have received and spent next year if he had foregone current consumption today.

The following table presents a simple example of the impact of the discounting procedure on the economic evaluation of an investment. Investment X is expected to cost $5 million next year. The project is expected to yield benefits or revenues of $600,000 per year for the next 25 years which if simply added up, total $15 million. It requires the continued expenditure of $100,000 per year to keep it in operation.

Exhibit 2 *(continued)*

The effect of discounting on the evaluation of a typical investment, using discount rates of 0, 3, 5, and 10 percent ($000)

	Interest rate (percent)			
	0	*3*	*5*	*10*
Value today of total benefits	$15,000	$10,448	$8,456	$5,442
Value today of total costs	$7,500	$6,741	$6,409	$5,906
Benefit-cost ratio	2.00	1.45	1.32	0.92
Value today of excess of benefits over costs	$7,500	$3,707	$2,047	−$468

From the calculation displayed in the table, the necessity for accurate and consistent discounting is clear. The expected benefit-cost ratio of the example project is 2 if no discounting is applied. The ratio drops to 1.3 with an interest rate of 5 percent and to below unity with a rate of 10 percent. If the costs and benefits are added with no account taken of the time factor, the project shows an excess of benefits over costs of $7.5 million. If an interest rate of 10 percent is applied, costs are estimated to exceed benefits by nearly $0.5 million.

CURRENT DISCOUNTING PRACTICES IN THE FEDERAL AGENCIES ARE NEITHER CONSISTENT NOR ADEQUATE

From the testimony of the comptroller general and agency representatives, the subcommittee learned of current discounting practices in the federal agencies. As the report of the comptroller general so clearly demonstrated, discounting practices are neither consistent across agencies nor, in all cases, are they appropriate. In the subcommittee's judgment, substantial room for improvement remains in both the application of the discounting technique and in the appropriate interest rate used for discounting. Accepting as an ideal the situation in which all agencies apply the discounting technique to all expenditures which involve either benefit or cost commitments extending into the future and utilize an appropriate interest rate in performing the discounting, the subcommittee found substantial weaknesses in federal government practice. We nave conciuded the following:

1. The application of economic analysis to public expenditures will be of primary importance in assisting the decision maker to choose among alternative expenditures designed to accomplish similar objectives and of substantially less help in determining the optimal size of the government budget or its allocation among programs with divergent objectives. The practice of accurately and appropriately discounting future benefits and costs is an essential element in the economic analysis of investment alternatives. It is of crucial importance in assisting the decision maker both to choose effectively among alternatives that accomplish the same objective and, where feasible, to make cross-program evaluations.
2. While most agencies are aware of the importance of discounting and are applying the technique when appropriate, there are notable exceptions. These exceptions occur where agencies are either constrained by law from doing benefit-cost analysis or report the application of a zero interest rate in evaluating proposed investments.
3. Some of the most effective applications of the discounting technique are found in

Exhibit 2 *(continued)*

agencies whose program benefits (and sometimes costs) are among the most difficult to accurately measure. For example, in evaluating alternative defense expenditures with the same objective but with different time profiles of future cost commitments, discounting practice has been consistent and effective. As representatives of the Department of Defense noted, while cost-effectiveness analysis is regularly one of the factors considered in reaching program decisions, it is an aid to judgment and not a substitute therefore. Similarly, in evaluating human resource projects, the Office of Economic Opportunity has tested the sensitivity of the computed value of invest-ments by using a number of different interest rates in the analysis. While citing the progress in economic analysis displayed in these areas, the subcommittee is not to be interpreted as passing judgment on program decisions in these departments.

4. Significant inconsistencies exist among agencies and among departments and bureaus in the same agency regarding discount rate policy for use in public investment analysis. For those agencies performing discounting analysis, the range of interest rates applied extends from about 3 percent to more than 15 percent. This range is not explained nor is it defended on economic grounds. Its existence is judged to result from a lack of consistent interest-rate policy. The effect of this discrepancy is to bias the decision process in favor of the sectors using low (or zero) interest rates and against those sectors using higher rates. Moreover, where the rate of interest used is lower than that used in the private sector, funds are being guided from uses bearing a higher return to uses bearing a lower return. The result of both of these effects is to depress the size of the national income and to sacrifice potential economic growth.

5. While substantial progress has been made in instituting analysis in the agencies, some agency personnel resist the application of economic criteria to programs in their departments. The record of the hearings shows, for example, the statement of the Director of the Bureau of Public Roads claiming that the "Bureau of Public Roads does not use discounting techniques in administering the Federal aid and direct Federal highway construction programs. In addition, we do not plan to use discounting techniques in the future." This is in contrast to the position of the repre-sentative of the Bureau of the Budget who argued that economic analysis and dis-counting should be consistently applied to investments undertaken by all agencies of the federal government. It likewise contradicts the testimony of the other experts that discounting analysis applied to the highway program would be especially useful.

6. The water resource agencies are currently applying an interest rate of 3¼ percent to both future benefits and costs. This rate is among the lowest in the federal govern-ment and is generally conceded to be too low by observers both in the government and outside. The application of this interest rate implies a substantial diversion of high return funds owned by private citizens to lower return public investments.

7. The proposal of the Water Resources Council for a new interest rate policy is to be commended. The subcommittee states its full support of the revised procedure. The proposed formula yields a current rate of 4⅝ percent which is based on the yield of government long-term securities. This procedure, which includes the provi-sion that the rate may be increased or decreased by not more than 0.25 percent per year to reflect the trend in the yield on long-term government securities, is defended by the Water Resources Council as being a more appropriate formula. The subcommittee, however, notes the position of the Bureau of the Budget and

Exhibit 2 *(concluded)*

the prevailing judgment of economic experts that this rate is at the floor of the acceptable range. The subcommittee also notes the need for additional efforts to accurately measure and quantify the real benefits and costs of investment in this and other public investment areas.

Exhibit 3

SEPARATE VIEWS OF REPRESENTATIVE PATMAN

I would like to express my disagreement with the conclusions presented in this committee report concerning the discount rate yardstick for the evaluation of public investments. The essence of the report's conclusions is that public investments can be evaluated in a manner similar or identical to that which is relevant for private investments. I believe that this is not true, and that once this premise is abandoned, the remainder of the conclusions can no longer be valid.

A Joint Economic Committee study estimated that in the decade 1966–75, public facilities costing $500 billion—half a trillion dollars—will be needed in communities across our land. Many of these facilities will provide services which will substantially improve the quality of life in our society, but these are improvements not easily measured in dollars and cents. Furthermore, many government activities may have few direct economic benefits, but may have indirect, or long-term, economic and social effects which will expand the productive capacity of our economy over the long run and greatly increase the national welfare. Reliance on profit-oriented business criteria to evaluate government investments would inevitably result in the abandonment of projects with more potential and far-reaching benefits, such as I described above, in favor of those which showed an immediate financial return. I believe this would be disastrous to the fulfillment of a whole range of the goals of our society.

The committee report recommends, in particular, that public projects be evaluated with the use of a discount (interest) rate which reflects the potential return on private sector spending which has been displaced by the public investment. This private sector rate would be higher than that generally used by government agencies today in the evaluation of alternative public investments.

According to the report ". . . where the rate of interest used [by the government] is lower than that used in the private sector, funds are being guided from uses bearing a higher return to uses bearing a lower return. The result . . . is to depress the size of the national income and to sacrifice potential economic growth."

This finding would be conclusive support for the recommendations of the report only if several conditions were met: *(a)* if the noneconomic benefits of government projects could be included in the measure of returns from these projects to make them fully comparable to measurements in the private sector; *(b)* if the measure of return from government projects could also include all the longer term indirect economic benefits, which do in fact contribute to the productive capacity of our economy, and *(c)* if we were all agreed that the size of our national income were the single and uppermost goal of our society. I believe that none of these three arguments can currently be supported.

I think we should also bear in mind the implications of accepting strict, business-

Exhibit 3 *(continued)*

oriented criteria for government activity. Do we mean to say that we believe society will benefit more from a new gadget than from the construction of a new school or sewage system because the immediate financial return on the former might be 6.5 percent as opposed to 5 percent on the latter?

The argument for judging the value of public investments on the basis of rates of return, or interest rates, in the private sector is further weakened when we realize what sort of factors go into determining the private sector rates. The discussion on appropriate interest rates in the committee report, itself, is begun with the admission that the capital market in our economy is far from being a perfectly competitive one. The interest rates established in this market are influenced not merely by the regular forces of supply and demand, but also, among other factors, by the policies adopted by various government units. In particular, the Federal Reserve System plays a major role in the determination of interest levels, and these levels have been maintained at an artificially high level for many years. Indeed, as I have pointed out on numerous occasions, the Fed is the beneficiary of a $50 billion portfolio on which it collects these inflated interest rates. The Congress, itself, has been lax in acting to allow interest rates to fall to levels which would better accommodate the needs of our economy.

One of the distressing aspects of our economic and social development as a society is that there are serious imbalances. We have neglected human resources in the interest of material things too often. One reason for this is that the public sector is on the low end of the scale so far as the credit of the Nation is concerned. Whenever money is tightened and interest rates boosted, our public facilities suffer, along with the small businessman and homebuilders. That is what is happening right now. Not only do the public facilities have much more difficulty in obtaining credit when scarcity prevails, but they must increase their expenses to pay high interest charges. This is a grievous burden for them and involves a transfer from the ordinary citizen to the wealthier class who have the lending power.

I must, therefore, disagree with the conclusions expressed in this committee report with respect to the appropriate discount rate for evaluating government investments. Our society has many objectives which could never be shown on a profit and loss statement, and our government has obligations to its citizens which cannot be dismissed by reference to a profit maximizing rate of return.

SEPARATE VIEWS OF SENATOR SPARKMAN

Unquestionably, the many demands of the people upon their government for facilities and services make it necessary that government establish priorities for the investment of public funds. It is equally true, however, that a system of priorities which is appropriate for investment in the private sector may not necessarily be appropriate for the investment of public funds. This is true because private investment seeks only economic efficiency, whereas public investment seeks objectives which are a mix of economic and social goals. It is this fact which prevents my endorsement of the committee report.

The committee report, and the record of the hearings upon which it is based, place far too little emphasis upon the need for a more effective system of measuring the direct and indirect benefits accruing from public investment designed to meet these economic and social goals. This is particularly true in the case of investment in water resource projects, where low rates of economic return prevail in early years, and the

Exhibit 3 *(concluded)*

mushrooming benefits of area development in later years are whittled away to insignificance by the kind of discount rate and procedure advocated by the committee report.

While there may be a need for a more efficient system of establishing public investment priorities, and while there may be a need for some degree of uniformity in the application of such a system by various public agencies, I am not prepared to advocate specific findings and recommendations in these areas until such time as a more thorough and balanced investigation of the matter has been made.

SUPPLEMENTARY VIEWS OF SENATORS SYMINGTON, JORDAN, AND PERCY

We recognize that there is wide variance and inconsistent policy among the federal agencies with respect to the use and application of discounting analysis in evaluating public expenditures. We endorse the finding, outlined in the report, of the need for improved and consistent application of sound economic analyses in the decisionmaking process with regard to public investments.

However, from our experience in the business world, we know that what often appears to be sound theory is not always sound in practice or acceptable in impact. We have basic agreement with many of the recommendations of the report and believe the attempt should be made, after thorough study by the agencies of the federal government under the supervision of the Bureau of the Budget, to develop a sound and consistent discounting analysis policy and especially to develop a method of quantifying and evaluating the social benefits of public investment which thus far have been either inadequately measured or determined immeasurable. The subcommittee has not addressed itself to the full consideration of what the impacts may be of specific application of the policies and procedures to be developed, particularly in the areas where grants-in-aid, matching funds, and other financial programs are involved in the federal-state relationship.

Therefore, we cannot at this time concur with the immediate implementation of the procedures and policies recommended to be developed, without first having opportunity to review and determine the impacts thereof.

CASE 4-4

LillEE-ThOMSON INdUSTRIES

One evening in late 1975, Greg Chappell, a young financial analyst, sat at his desk trying to sort out the events of the meeting that afternoon between the Executive Committee of Lillee-Thomson Industries, Inc., a British diversified company, and the group's Finance Unit.[1] The meeting had been called to discuss a proposal to invest substantial additional funds in the firm's shipping division.

It seemed to Chappell that communications had broken down immediately after the managing director had asked how much money the group was making on its current investments in shipping, apparently expecting a reasonably concise answer. Instead, what followed was a difficult discussion during which it became clear that no one could agree on what the financial performance of the division had been, how its performance should be measured or, even if it could be measured, what level of return was to be considered satisfactory. The meeting had been embarrassing for the finance people and Chappell was asked to untangle the issues raised in the meeting, to prepare a "valid" financial appraisal of the performance and contribution of the shipping division for top management and to devise a method for appraising the new investments.

The appraisal report was particularly important because the Executive Committee of Lillee-Thomson was contemplating a substantial further investment in shipping. Eight new vessels, an investment of around $200 million, were required if the group was to maintain its competitive position in the shipping market. Many competitors had already begun to upgrade their fleets. As such an investment would be the first major investment in the group for several years and would increase shipping's share of total group capital employed from around 10 percent to 40 percent, the issue was being treated very seriously. Chappell was aware

---

[1] In British parlance, "group" is synonomous with "head office" or "headquarters."

188

that there was considerable uncertainty among management over whether the original investment in shipping had been a profitable one and whether future investments could be expected to be financially attractive.

The shipping division had been an area of continual concern because of its presumed riskiness. Three basic areas of risk characterize the economic environment of the industry. First, the shipping market had been historically very unstable. Freight rates fluctuated widely with capacity utilization and market demand. The best security in the industry was to be locked into a long-term charter. However, charters didn't permit reaping the huge profits available in boom years, such as 1973. Under inflationary conditions, the best charter was a bareboat charter under which the charterer meets operating costs and the owner is responsible only for capital costs. Bareboat charters are, however, becoming increasingly rare. Scrap and resale values also fluctuated with the industry's cycle. When capacity was being fully utilized resale value was very high and when capacity utilization was low the bottom fell out of the used vessel market.

Second, the technological risk in vessel purchases had become more severe in the past decade. New technology and innovative marketing were resulting in the development of new transportation concepts. The container ship systems, such as the liquified gas carriers, and LASH ships were threatening the viability of the more traditional vessels.

Finally, the market was highly competitive, usually on the basis of freight rates. The best example of this competition is the fact that tankers had grown in size from 100,000 deadweight tons (DWT) in the early 1960s to sizes of almost 400,000 DWT in the 70s. The economies of scale in transportation were large and unit freight rates had dropped correspondingly. The smaller, older vessels could not compete on price. In order to help alleviate some of the industry's inherent riskiness, governments around the world subsidized vessel purchases.

Gregg recalled that the meeting had begun with the managing director asking how much money the group was making out of its current investments in the shipping division. He did not expect what followed: a series of inconclusive discussions in which some members stated that the shipping division had been a loser; some calculated that returns had exceeded 70 percent; and others weren't prepared to commit themselves. The principal responses were:

> ***Joe Hall (group accountant):*** The shipping division's return on capital employed (ROCE) has barely averaged 8 percent before

tax over the past five years [Exhibits 1 and 2]. As you know, ROCE is the standard performance measure we use throughout our group and, on this basis, shipping's performance has been dismal! Our group's overall ROCE has averaged 14 percent before tax in recent years and we believe that this excellent performance will continue. However, if 40 percent of our group's capital were to return only 4 percent after tax, I see no way we can keep our average return at 14 percent. Consequently, I feel that increasing our investment in shipping is very unwise, particularly given that

Exhibit 1
Shipping Division: Financial history ($000)

Earnings summary

	1970	1971	1972	1973	1974	1975
Trading profit	$ 1,580	$ 1,080	$ 2,520	$ 7,260	$10,440	$ 240
Depreciation*	(667)	(1,000)	(2,000)	(3,333)	(3,333)	(3,333)
Government grants†	133	200	400	667	667	667
Profit before interest and tax	$ 1,046	$ 280	$ 920	$ 4,594	$ 7,774	$ (2,426)
Interest	(216)	(516)	(888)	(1,536)	(1,806)	(1,566)
Profit before tax	$ 830	$ (236)	$ 32	$ 3,058	$ 5,968	$ (3,992)
Tax‡	(415)	—	—	(1,427)	(2,984)	—
Net profit	$ 415	$ (236)	$ 32	$ 1,631	$ 2,984	$ (3,992)

Balance sheet summary§

Assets	1970	1971	1972	1973	1974	1975
Cash in bank (O/draft)	$ 564	$ (487)	$ (1,255)	$ 469	$ 3,676	$ (4,634)
Net fixed assets	9,333	13,333	26,333	43,000	39,667	36,334
Loans to group‡	3,837	5,955	12,439	17,816	16,150	19,818
Total assets	$13,734	$18,801	$37,517	$61,285	$59,493	$51,518
Liabilities						
Tax currently payable	415	—	—	1,427	2,984	—
Long-term debt§	7,200	10,000	19,600	31,600	27,600	23,600
Deferred tax†	3,837	5,955	12,439	17,816	16,150	19,818
Government grants†	1,867	2,667	5,267	8,600	7,933	7,266
Shareholders funds	415	179	211	1,842	4,826	834
Total liabilities	$13,734	$18,801	$37,517	$61,285	$59,493	$51,518

* For accounting depreciation purposes, vessels were written off straight line over 15 years.

† Government cash grants equal to 20 percent of the asset purchase price were received at the time of vessel purchase. In the accounts, these grants were written into earnings over the first 15 years of vessel life. If a vessel was sold, the unwritten-down amount would be repaid to the government.

‡ Tax amounts in the Shipping Division financial statements reflected complex group adjustments and are summarized and simplified here. In practice, each of the vessels had been written off wholly (100 percent) in the first year against other group income. The deferred tax provision represents the value of the tax credits taken elsewhere in the group and in the summarized shipping accounts this amount is offset by an equivalent "loan" to the group. The effective tax rate was 50 percent.

§ The net of shipping's receivables and payables was adjudged to be negligible and accordingly was not extracted from the consolidated group data.

‖ Favorable credit terms of 80 percent of the asset cost, repayable on extended terms over ten years and at submarket interest rates of 6 percent were available to investors in shipping.

Exhibit 2
Pretax return on capital employed*

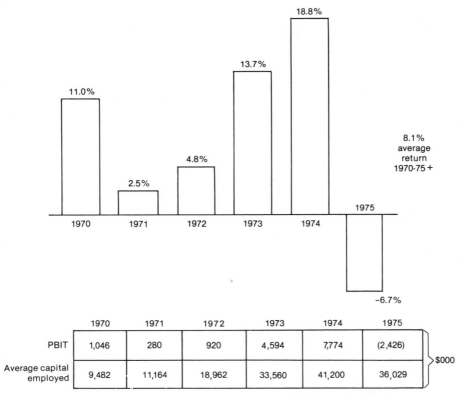

Returns on capital employed averaged only 8 percent between 1970 and 1975 . . .

* ROCE is defined as PBIT/average long-term capital employed in the year. Long-term capital includes debt, grants, and shareholder funds. Deferred tax is excluded from this calculation—because the income earned on these funds elsewhere in the group has not been included in the return.
† Based on average long-term capital employed throughout six years.

there is little evidence suggesting that shipping returns can be expected to be better in the future than in the past.

Steve Simons (financial staff member): But Joe, you know that ROCE is only an earnings measure and, because our assets are relatively new [Exhibit 3], such a measure understates *real* profitability in the early years. The use of ROCE in this case is inappropriate. A fairer view of shipping's performance is found by calculating the annual cash return. I ran these figures by taking annual operating cash flows (profit before interest and taxes plus all depreciation charges) as a percentage of gross fixed assets plus

Exhibit 3
Gross investment in fixed assets (vessels)*

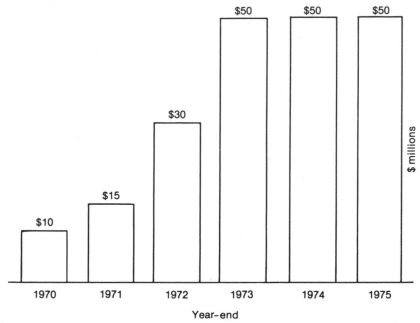

Year–end

Most of the assets are quite new. . .

* I.e., purchase cost of owned vessels.

working capital and found an average cash return on our original investment of 13 percent per year [Exhibit 4]. This is substantially higher than the ROCE figure and, if maintained over the 20–25 year life of the vessels it would give the division a discounted cash flow yield of 13 percent. I don't think this investment in shipping should be so simply discarded.

Hall: Cash is a fine thing for all you analysts to quibble about, Steve, but this group gets evaluated on its ROCE!

Simons: But cash is what really matters. Another problem is that the accounts understate the value of the government grants which amount to 20 percent of asset cost. The accounting practice is to write these grants into earnings over 15 years but the cash benefits are received in full at the time the vessels are purchased. This is "free-money" and should be deducted from the gross value of fixed assets in calculating the cash yield. This brings shipping's

Exhibit 4
Adjusted return on capital invested: Operating cash flow/gross fixed assets and net working capital

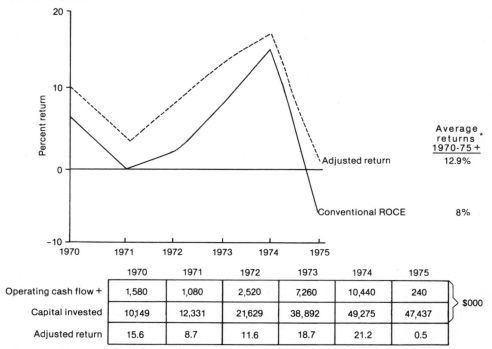

	1970	1971	1972	1973	1974	1975	
Operating cash flow +	1,580	1,080	2,520	7,260	10,440	240	$000
Capital invested	10,149	12,331	21,629	38,892	49,275	47,437	
Adjusted return	15.6	8.7	11.6	18.7	21.2	0.5	

Cash returns appear considerably higher than ROCE indicates . . .

* Based on average investment throughout six years.
† Operating cash flow = PBIT plus depreciation less grant write-down.

returns up to 16 percent [Exhibit 5] which compares quite well to the group average.

Hall [_grumbling_]: Sixteen percent is still miserable for this company overall—particularly in aftertax terms. . . .

Jill Mackay (tax specialist): No, on an aftertax basis the shipping investment should show better returns than the group averages. Everyone seems to be ignoring the fact that government policy toward shipping investments provides substantial tax benefits. These have real value! The group can write off the total cost of its investments in ships immediately against income earned anywhere in the group. . . .

Hall: But tax write-offs appear as losses in our financial statements. The rating agencies will throw a fit.

Exhibit 5
Cash return on funds at risk*

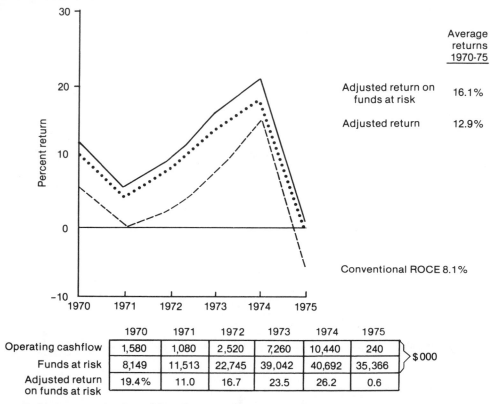

Cash returns on funds at risk to the group have averaged 16 percent. . .

* Funds at risk are debt plus equity, but excluding grants.

Paul Jacobs (executive committee member): It is true that none of our other investments receive the favorable tax treatment that shipping does, but I don't understand how that affects the division's operating returns.

Mackay: I disagree that operating returns are the only thing that should be considered in an investment decision. The shipping division also contributes tax benefits to the company as a whole and I believe their value should be included in any appraisal of shipping investments. Because a tax credit equal to 50 percent of the asset cost can be taken in the year after purchase, the aftertax return on the ships is roughly equal to the pretax return. A simple example illustrates this clearly. [Exhibit 6.]

Exhibit 6
A typical investment

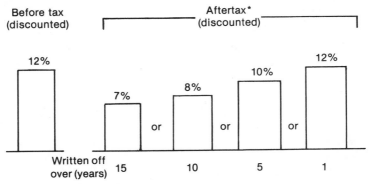

A. Immediate tax write-offs boost aftertax returns . . .

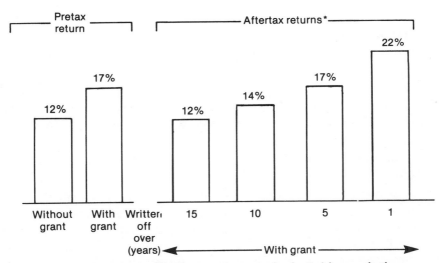

B. Investment grants amplify aftertax returns on funds at risk even further . . .

* One-year lag assumed in tax payments.

Jacobs [**skeptical but interested**]: Let me see those figures, that's hard to believe. . . It's certainly true, however, that our other investments receive much less favorable tax treatment. [Exhibit 7.]

Dick Jones (executive committee member): Yet, I've always felt these shipping deals were irresistibly attractive. I don't under-

Exhibit 7
Asset mix of investments

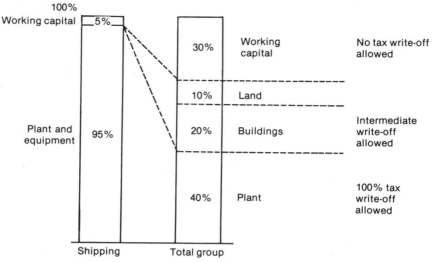

Asset mix varies by component and, hence, by tax treatment . . .

stand what all the disagreement is about. No matter what method we use in the analysis, the returns should exceed 30 percent when you include the $37 million unrealized profits we've made by just owning those vessels. [Exhibit 8.]

Jacobs: Those gains are phoney, Dick. We're not planning to sell the ships and most of those gains reflect inflation anyway.

Simons: The replacement cost of the vessels has quadrupled, over the past five years. [Exhibit 9.] If depreciation charges in the accounts reflected replacement costs, or if the discount rate applied to cash flows incorporated an allowance for inflation, the unrealized profits that could be made on the sale of the assets would disappear. Furthermore, a slackening in world inflation rates combined with fears of substantial overcapacity in world shipyards to at least 1980 suggest that vessel replacement costs, and hence second-hand vessel values, will increase at a much slower rate in the future.

Hall: If this Sandilands Report is accepted we might have to report replacement depreciation charges. It'll knock hell out of what earnings the division already has.

MacKay: But it also means increased depreciation tax shields.

Exhibit 8
Millions of $

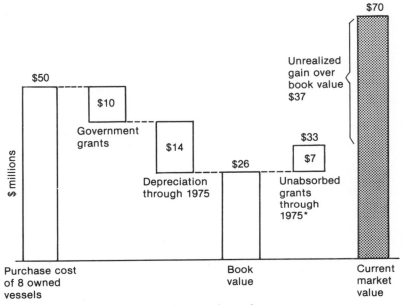

Unrealized capital gains on eight owned vessels amount to
about $37 million . . .

* Government grants are written into earnings over 15 years. Unabsorbed amounts at the time
the vessel is sold have to be repaid.

Nancy Davis (financial analyst): The tax advantages of the
shipping division are not the only ones that are getting inadequate
consideration. The whole financing package *adds* value to the
group. Pre-financing measures like ROCE and discounted pre-financing, as distinct from "equity," cash flows miss this value. Virtually no group equity has been invested in the shipping division.
That means that pretax equity returns have been approximately
70 percent. [Exhibit 10.] The group has been able to avoid equity
investment because each vessel can be acquired with 80 percent
debt finance and 20 percent government grant, and because 6
of the fleet of 14 have been leased. The terms of the debt finance
on the acquired vessels are extremely favorable. The loans were
negotiated in 1970 to be repayable over ten years at the fixed
interest rate of 6 percent at a time when general market lending
rates were about 10 percent—since risen to about 13 percent.
Currently, ships can be financed at a subsidized rate of around 8

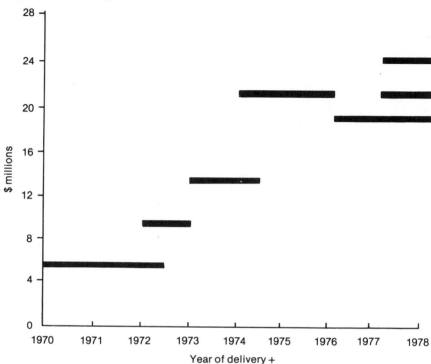

Exhibit 9
Capital cost of average vessel*

The capital cost of new vessels had quadrupled between 1971 and 1977 . . .

* Based on published data on orders placed with shipyards.
† Delivery is roughly two years after order.

percent. Similarly, the lease terms on the chartered vessels, also acquired in 1970, have been fixed annual amounts [Exhibit 11] although these are due to expire over the next three to four years.

Hall: That's not an advantage, that's another problem with the shipping division. We have a group policy to restrict debt funding to 35 percent of the consolidated balance sheet. With all those ships levered up at 80 percent it just means that we have to do almost complete equity financing in other areas to make it all balance out! The leases were an off balance sheet coup and the rating agencies seemed to have ignored them so far. However, if we had to capitalize all those lease commitments, the ROCE would really fall.

Davis: But Joe, the leverage policy doesn't make financial sense.

Exhibit 10

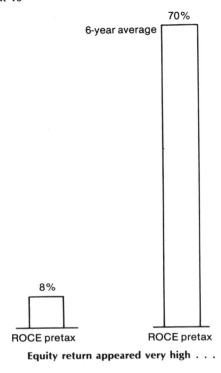

70%

6-year average

8%

ROCE pretax   ROCE pretax

Equity return appeared very high . . .

Year	PBT ($000)	Shareholders' funds* ($000)
1970	$ 830	$ 415
1971	(236)	297
1972	32	195
1973	3,058	1,026
1974	5,968	3,334
1975	(3,992)	2,830
Six-year average	$ 943	$1,350

* Average.

These shipping investments actually increase the group's borrowing capacity and you should give the division credit for this.

Jacobs: I agree, Nancy, that the cheap interest rates should be valuable but I'm not clear on how to quantify those benefits.

At this point the managing director had cut the meeting short because he felt that the matter required substantial further analysis and considera-

Exhibit 11
Charter obligations

Number of vessels	Basis of charter	Charter period outstanding (years)	Total annual charter cost ($ millions)
3	Bareboat*	3	$4.3
2	Bareboat*	4	$3.8
1	Time charter†	3	$2.2

* Bareboat charter covers vessel only. Charterer to provide crew.
† Crew and vessel included in charter rate. Crewing costs estimated to be worth about $400,000 per year.

tion. He did emphasize, however, that the matter was critical and he wanted the issues cleared up by the following week.

Immediately after the meeting Chappell talked with Jill and asked her what this Sandilands Report was and what she felt its implications were for the company. She answered briefly: "The Sandilands Committee has advocated an inflation accounting system that would be based on current values, and it looks like it might be officially adopted. Everything is assessed at current value and expensed accordingly. If the change is allowed for tax purposes, the tax effects could be enormous. I'll send you over some details on the system as soon as I get back to my office."

Greg sat and pondered the issues that had been raised. He knew that some really contentious points had not been fully aired at the meeting. He was well aware how divergent were the views of those who argued for accounting as distinct from cash flow measures of return. And there was the extraordinary fact that buying vessels seemed to actually improve cash flows, at least in the early years. At the same time, it was apparent that a large new investment in shipping would probably depress the group's return on capital employed.

In addition, Greg recognized another difficulty. The proposed $200 million investment would make the group heavily dependent on shipping earnings. This would almost certainly affect the stock market's view of the company, which would in turn affect what constituted an appropriate return to the shareholders. Several of the accountants had already drawn attention to the poor reported earnings from shipping investments (Exhibit 12). Mr. Chappell could also point out that shipping earnings—not a serious problem in the past when shipping was a small part of the total group activities—would, if the proposed investment were approved, make the group's earnings more volatile (Exhibit 13). He be-

Exhibit 12
Return on capital employed

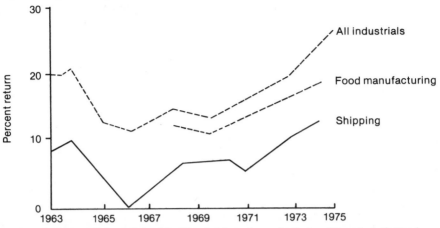

Returns on capital employed in shipping have been far below those in industry in general—even in the best years . . .

lieved the fact that shipping shares had sold consistently at a discount from book value reflected the market's suspicion of shipping companies (Exhibit 14).

This problem had implications beyond Joe Hall's evaluation. A recent Moody's report had drawn attention to the group's already modest ROCE and some of the management believed that this concern was a factor behind the unexciting rating now given Lillee-Thomson in the market. This bothered Greg considerably. If the rating agencies were going to use ROCE calculations then they were a serious constraint on the capital budgeting process of *any* company. He wondered whether this constraint could be lessened by increasing the amount of financial information available to the public and by attempting to educate the security analysts about where the value was in the division. He knew management would not be happy with such a suggestion.

Chappell also knew that there was a great deal of uncertainty surrounding most of the variables and he felt it was important to include these uncertainties in his analysis. But how? The shipping industry was very cyclical and earnings were, correspondingly, very volatile. Resale values also fluctuated with the industry's capacity utilization and the industry was currently in an almost unprecedented state of overcapacity. Vessel purchase prices had risen dramatically. Advocates of the new

Exhibit 13

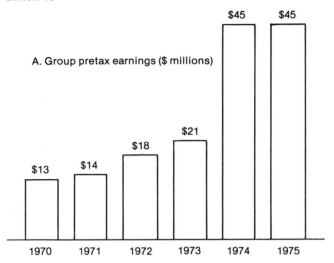

A. Group pretax earnings ($ millions)

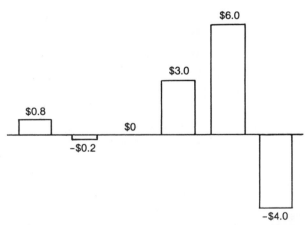

B. Shipping pretax earnings ($ million)

Lillee-Thomson shipping earnings have been more volatile than group earnings . . .

Exhibit 14
Market value* as percent of book value

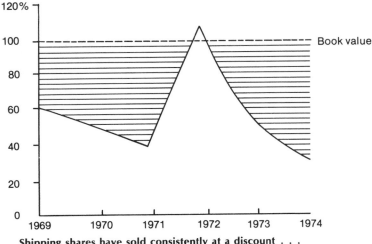

Shipping shares have sold consistently at a discount . . .

* Based on year-end prices for listed shipping stocks.

investment argued that the new ships should be ordered immediately to avoid inflation-induced cost increases. Chappell was not sure he agreed with this argument.

Any major investment in shipping would make the group much more susceptible to the risks and volatility that characterized the industry. Greg wondered how the market would react to such a change in the risk complexion of the company. This problem led Chappell to the question of what return would be required to compensate for the increased risks. The problem of inflation just added complexity to the question of an appropriate hurdle rate for the division. It had often been suggested that the group target hurdle rate be expressed as "5 percent in real terms." But, with a 15 percent inflation rate this would require a return of 20 percent! No one in the United Kingdom was currently getting such a return and Greg questioned how realistic this policy could be. Was the solution to inflation, then, not to invest at all?

Greg decided to start by trying to sort out where the value was (assuming there was any at all) in the newly proposed shipping investments before moving on to the question of appraising the past performance of the division. He wanted his final report to include both a methodology for evaluating shipping investments and a basis for a reasonably definitive evaluation of the division's performance.

Part five

The role of finance in regulation

Case 5-1

The Regulation of Proprietary Hospitals

Francine Blake looked at the stack of documents on her desk and wished that there was an easy answer to the complex set of issues she was about to tackle.

The Washington, D.C., based consulting firm for which Ms. Blake had been working since her graduation from management school had been retained by the U.S. Department of Health, Education, and Welfare (HEW) to fully study the implications of Medicare rate setting procedures on hospital operations and, presumably, the quality of health care being delivered. Blake's assignment was to concentrate solely on the proprietary hospitals (those owned by investors and operated for profit) to determine if their shareholders were receiving a "fair" return on equity for the Medicare portion of the patient load. If she determined that they were not, she then had to determine how equity investors were being and should be compensated.

Blake knew that the major hospital chains had been complaining for some time about the methods of Medicare reimbursement, but she also knew these companies had attracted significant investor interest and had grown rapidly during the late 1960s and early 1970s. She wished to resolve the apparent anomaly between the allegedly "unfair" Medicare rate structure and the healthy returns of the investor-owned hospitals. From a public policy standpoint, she thought, the real question concerned who was paying what for whom in our nation's hospitals.

The documents stacked on top of Blake's desk included histories of the health care industry, several prospectuses from investor-owned hospital companies, market analysts' reports on industry leaders, and detailed explanations of Medicare's methods for reimbursing for-profit institutions.

THE INDUSTRY

The hospital industry, with total revenues of $56 billion in 1976, made up the largest portion of total health spending, which itself was rising at an alarming annual rate. In 1976, health care comprised approximately 8.6 percent of the total GNP and costs were rising at a rate of 14 percent compared to the Consumer Price Index, which was rising at a rate of about 7 percent. Not-for-profit and government-owned hospitals dominated the industry, but the proprietaries were beginning to play a much more significant role.

Proprietary hospitals are owned either by hospital management companies, which own and operate two or more hospitals; by independent companies, which operate single facilities; or by groups of individual investors—often, but not always, physicians. The hospital companies in 1975 owned 48 percent of all investor-owned hospitals and approximately 51 percent of all investor-owned hospital beds in service. This represented a substantial increase over 1970, when the hospital management companies owned less than 30 percent of all investor-owned hospital (IOH) beds in service.

The growth, and then the high concentration in the IOH sector of the hospital industry, occurred in two stages. The growth stage was stimulated by the passage of Medicare and Medicaid legislation in 1965. Medicare and Medicaid's guarantee of payment for services provided the stimulus for growth within the industry and for the entry of new firms. These programs not only increased the demand for hospital services, but provided a major new source of income. Previously, the cost of treating the elderly and the needy had often been absorbed by the hospitals themselves.

The second stage—the concentration stage—was a result of the extraordinary growth rate in the industry and the concomitant increase in government involvement. Most of the IOHs were owned by small groups of physicians or entrepreneurs, and were not in a position to capitalize on the new boom. Many were short of capital, inefficiently operated, unable to control inflationary increases, and incapable of dealing effectively with increasingly complex government relations. These conditions created opportunities for new firms to enter the industry and in the next five years, more than 30 hospital management companies were organized. The fledgling companies built some new hospitals themselves, but nearly all of their growth came from acquisitions. Exhibit 1 contains financial data for four leading IOH chains and Exhibit 2 shows acquisitions and new hospital construction for three major chains.

Exhibit 1
Financial data, four IOH chains, 1968–1976

	1968	1969	1970	1971	1972	1973	1974	1975	1976
American Medical International (AMI):									
Revenues*	19.0	36.6	51.3	70.8	123.0	136.7	160.6	202.7	250.3
Net profit*	1.0	2.2	3.5	4.8	7.5	7.6	5.2	5.2	8.7
Long-term debt*	7.4	8.3	20.5	23.1	62.6	100.2	135.9	154.2	155.4
Net worth*	4.7	19.6	28.7	48.4	71.4	75.7	79.5	83.4	93.0
Earned on net worth (%)	21.3	11.4	12.0	9.9	10.5	10.0	6.5	6.3	9.3
EPS	.39	.62	.78	.93	1.07	1.06	.77	.82	1.32
Common shares outstanding	2.64	3.67	4.25	5.42	6.84	6.49	6.62	6.39	6.61
Average annual P/E ratio	35.5	46.3	32.6	28.0	34.3	21.2	6.9	5.4	5.3
Hospital Corporation of America (HCA):									
Revenues*	27.0	50.6	65.4	108.5	160.5	206.8	272.5	356.3	455.3
Net profit*	1.8	3.3	4.5	7.2	10.4	12.3	15.8	21.0	27.3
Long-term debt*	11.1	29.6	55.2	95.2	137.0	166.3	217.8	289.3	309.4
Net worth*	11.3	23.5	37.5	72.2	91.3	108.1	122.3	143.2	187.9
Earned on net worth (%)	15.5	13.9	11.9	9.9	11.4	11.4	12.9	14.6	14.5
EPS	.25	.34	.44	.55	.68	.81	1.04	1.35	1.63
Common shares outstanding	7.38	9.19	10.34	12.93	14.93	15.21	15.21	15.35	16.90
Average annual P/E ratio	—	56.3	28.5	34.7	35.0	12.7	6.2	8.8	8.9
Humana, Inc.:									
Revenues*	4.8	17.4	58.0	85.4	86.0	103.8	130.2	188.9	260.7
Net profit*	.3	1.1	2.7	3.0	5.2	5.4	6.1	6.8	8.9
Long-term debt*	—	34.2	65.3	87.8	94.2	118.2	164.8	195.1	205.8
Net worth*	4.1	16.9	24.1	39.9	48.9	54.2	59.3	66.2	73.8
Earned on net worth (%)	7.8	6.2	11.0	7.6	10.6	10.0	10.3	10.3	12.0
EPS	.08	.17	.17	.32	.30	.46	.48	.54	.62	.79
Common shares outstanding	5.27	6.90	8.58	10.82	11.37	11.45	10.99	10.99	11.05
Average annual P/E ratio	75.9	69.5	36.1	35.9	23.0	11.5	5.5	5.5	7.2
American Medicorp:									
Revenues*	7.0	77.6	131.6	153.3	175.5	195.6	241.4	285.7	335.4
Net profit*	.4	4.3	7.4	9.0	10.0	3.8	8.4	13.0	15.8
Long-term debt*	10.4	58.5	80.9	107.6	132.5	158.5	175.3	171.0	170.8
Net worth*	19.5	104.3	106.8	133.1	148.8	152.5	153.3	166.2	173.2
Earned on net worth (%)	2.0	4.1	6.9	6.8	6.7	2.5	5.5	7.8	9.1
EPS	.11	.65	.85	1.01	.97	.35	.81	1.27	1.64
Common shares outstanding	4.54	8.80	8.41	10.07	10.46	10.53	10.30	10.30	9.37
Average annual P/E ratio	—	65.2	21.8	19.8	17.8	15.0	3.0	3.8	4.4
P/E ratio, Standard and Poor's									
425 Industrials	17.3	17.5	16.5	18.0	18.0	13.3	9.4		
P/E Conglomerate Company									
Index	21	17.0	18.0	15.0	11.0		not available		

* Millions of dollars.

The acquisition by American Medicorp of two southern California hospitals in 1969 illustrates the nature of this growth by acquisition. At that time, American Medicorp, one of the leaders in the investor-owned hospital industry, was in the midst of an impressive and aggressive expansion drive.

Exhibit 2
Hospitals acquired, constructed, and operated by three proprietary hospital chains

	Humana, Inc.		American Medicorp, Inc.		American Medical International Hospitals operated
	Acquisitions	Construction	Acquisitions	Construction	
1969	9	—	16	1	11
1970	13	2	—	1	16
1971	7	1	5	1	21
1972	1	2	—	4	46
1973	—	4	—	2	46
1974	—	11	—	3	46
1975	—	4	—	5 ·	48
1976	1	3	—	3	50

Source: Humana, Inc., American Medicorp, Inc. 10–Ks, and American Medical International 10–Ks.

Both hospitals were similar to other community hospitals in the American Medicorp chain. Both were started by physicians, were located in fast-growing middle-class to upper middle-class communities and had greatly expanded their bed capacities. In each case the ownership of the hospital and the ownership of the land was divided into an operating corporation and a real estate partnership, each owned by the same people.

The proposed acquisition of Hospital A involved an exchange of 210,909 shares of Medicorp common stock worth approximately $5.8 million for the assets of the two corporations.

The price asked for Hospital B was $8,465,632, comprised of 177,000 shares of Medicorp common worth approximately $6,195,000, cash of $1 million and assumption of liabilities of $1,270,632. The appraiser's report of the assets of the two hospitals and projected aftertax incomes is presented in Exhibit 3.

MEDICARE REIMBURSEMENT POLICY

Nearly all the revenues to proprietary as well as to nonprofit voluntary hospitals are derived from third-party payors—Medicare, Medicaid, Blue Cross/Blue Shield, and other private insurance carriers. Formulas and methods for reimbursement vary considerably, but in general, hospitals receive a per diem rate for each class of patient based on the average daily cost of providing care to a patient in that pay category.

The reimbursement formulas contain varying (and sometimes contradictory) rules about which hospital costs are "allowable" under the regulations. Costs judged not to be appropriate are disallowed, and

Exhibit 3
Appraiser's report

Hospital A

Asset appraisal

Land	$ 455,000
Land improvements	72,225
Building	1,162,775
Equipment	386,000
Other assets and liabilities (net)	371,981
Goodwill	6,017,651
Total	$8,465,632

Income forecasts

Year	Income (posttax)
1969	$259,356 (actual)
1970	389,000
1971	447,400
1972	514,500
1973	591,700
1974	680,400

Hospital B

Asset appraisal

Land	$ 400,000
Land improvements	104,200
Building	1,157,500
Equipment	394,300
Other assets and liabilities (net)	(78,254)
Goodwill	4,472,254
Total	$5,800,000

Income forecasts

Year	Income (posttax)
1969	$176,518 (actual)
1970	353,000
1971	406,000
1972	466,800
1973	536,900
1974	617,400

therefore, are not included in the total cost used to determine per diem rates. Proprietary hospitals are concerned with one cost factor that does not apply to other institutions—return on equity. Most third-party payors recognize a "reasonable" return on equity as an allowable (and reimbursable) cost of patient care. The debate about ROE has centered around what is "reasonable," how return is calculated (pretax or posttax) and how equity is defined.

Basic reimbursement principles for the Medicare program are set forth in Title XVIII of the Social Security Act and in the regulations defining the rules and procedures for implementing the act. Under current provisions, hospitals providing services to Medicare beneficiaries are to be reimbursed by Medicare for the full "reasonable cost" of those services covered by the program. The regulations state explicitly that costs for Medicare patients should not be borne by other patients, a phenomenon called cross-subsidization.

This reimbursement policy is also used by state Medicaid programs, and, in some states, by the local Blue Cross plans. The remaining third-party payors reimburse hospitals on the basis of posted charges for covered services with no explicit allowance for returns on equity.

Proprietary providers generally do not receive public contributions and assistance of federal and other government programs in financing capital expenditures, and historically have financed capital expenditures through funds invested by owners who expect to earn a reasonable return on their investment. The proprietary hospitals argue, therefore, that a reasonable return on investment must be allowed to avoid erosion of capital and to attract additional capital needed for expansion.

Medicare determines the appropriate allowance for return on equity by first adjusting a hospital's equity base to include only investments in plant, property, equipment, and working capital used in providing direct patient care. These investments are valued at historical costs. Medicare then estimates the portion of equity attributable to Medicare beneficiaries, which is equivalent to the proportion of allowable hospital costs that are incurred in the treatment of Medicare beneficiaries. For example, if one third of allowable hospital costs is attributable to Medicare beneficiaries, then one third of the adjusted equity base is used to calculate the allowable return on equity.

Finally, Medicare multiplies this adjusted equity by a rate equal to 1.5 times the average rate of interest on investments purchased by the Federal Hospital Insurance Trust Fund during the appropriate cost reporting period. The investments held by the Hospital Insurance Trust Fund are special bonds sold by the U.S. Treasury exclusively to the trust fund for the purpose of investing the tax funds collected to finance the Medicare program. By law, these securities bear an interest rate equal to the average market yield on all marketable interest-bearing obligations of the U.S. Treasury that are not due or callable within four years of the issue date of the trust fund bond. As a result, the interest rate is related to the capital costs which hospitals face in private capital markets.

Exhibit 4 shows the average Hospital Insurance Trust Fund rates for calendar years 1969 to 1976 and the corresponding allowable pretax rates of return on equity for Medicare patients.

Exhibit 4
Allowable pretax rates of return on equity for Medicare services, 1969–1976

Calendar year	Hospital Insurance Trust Fund rate		Allowable rate of return on equity
1969	6.59%	× 1.5 =	9.89%
1970	7.26	× 1.5 =	10.89
1971	5.98	× 1.5 =	8.97
1972	5.93	× 1.5 =	8.89
1973	6.65	× 1.5 =	9.97
1974	7.49	× 1.5 =	11.23
1975	7.40	× 1.5 =	11.10
1976	7.15	× 1.5 =	10.72

Source: Bureau of Health Insurance, Social Security Administration.

The average patient mix varies among different hospitals in each of the chains and among the hospital companies. Generally Medicare patient-days represent 30 to 40 percent of the total patient-days. Patient mix data for two proprietary chains is shown in Exhibit 5.

Exhibit 5
Hospital gross revenue mix by third-party payor

	1973	1974	1975	1976
Humana, Inc.:				
Medicare	29%	31%	31%	32%
Medicaid	4	4	5	5
Blue Cross and other	67	65	64	63
American Medicorp, Inc.:				
Medicare	30%	32%	34%	36%
Medicaid	6	6	6	6
Blue Cross	16	16	16	17
Other	48	46	44	41

DISALLOWANCE OF GOODWILL IN EQUITY CALCULATION

Prior to August 1, 1970, goodwill could be included in the equity capital component of the Medicare reimbursement formula. The regulations were amended to eliminate goodwill as an element of equity capital for hospitals acquired after that date. In November 1976, the regulations were further amended to limit the aggregate amount of reimbursement to a hospital for goodwill. Under the amended regulations acquired before August 1970 can remain an element of equity capital for the period from August 1970 until the time when the sum of all the yearly allowed returns on equity accumulates to 100 percent. Thereafter, goodwill would not be an element of equity capital for reimbursement purposes. These provisions have greatly concerned the proprietary hospitals since during the halcyon days of hospital acquisition upward of 70 to 75 percent of the purchase price for existing hospitals was for goodwill.

DETERMINING A REASONABLE RETURN ON EQUITY

The Social Security Act itself does not specify the methods for calculating return on equity payments to investor-owned hospitals; it specifies only the formula for ROE payments to proprietary extended-care facilities. However, the regulations for the Medicare program adopted the same formula for use in investor-owned hospital reimbursement. Ms. Blake reviewed the original legislation, committee reports and explanations of Medicare regulations, but could find no explanation of the basis for using this formula to determine the allowable return on equity for IOHs. Exhibit 6 contains excerpts from the regulations and portions of the work sheets used to determine the allowable equity base of investor-owned hospitals for reimbursement purposes.

Ms. Blake knew that industry representatives were arguing forcefully that current levels of allowable returns on equity were woefully inadequate. Industry sources argued that returns ought to be based upon the principles that had been established in federal rate-setting proceedings conducted by state public utility commissions and regulatory agencies such as the Federal Communications Commission. These principles,

Exhibit 6
Extracts from Medicare–Medicaid Provider Reimbursement Manual

[5762] Equity capital (*Prov. Reimb. Manual* 1202.1)

Equity capital means (1) the provider's investment in plant, property, and equipment related to patient care (net of depreciation) and funds deposited by a provider who leases plant, property, or equipment related to patient care and is required by the terms of the lease to deposit such funds (net of noncurrent debt related to such investment or deposited funds), and (2) net working capital maintained for necessary and proper operation of patient care activities. (Although the May 29, 1973, Medicare regulation revision removed the reference to current financing in regulation section 405.429 (b) (2), the exclusion of current financing from the provider's working capital must still be made for any cost reporting period during which the provider held some or all of

Exhibit 6 *(continued)*

its current financing payment. In effect, equity capital is the net worth of the provider (owners' equity in the net assets as determined under the Medicare program), adjusted for those assets and liabilities which are not related to the provision of patient care. Providers that are members of chain operations may also include in their equity capital a share of the equity capital of the home office.

.15 Chain operations.   The home office's investment in the stock of the provider, as well as loans made to finance such investments, are not considered as elements of equity for the purpose of computing equity capital.

.17 Current financing payment.   Although current financing payments were required to be excluded from working capital, other forms of interim reimbursement or accelerated payments do not have to be excluded from net working capital.

[5774] Proprietary Providers (*Prov. Reimb. Man.,* Part 1, 1202.4)

The term "proprietary providers" means providers, whether sole proprietorships, partnerships, or corporations, organized and operated with the expectation of earning profit for the owners, as distinguished from providers organized and operated on a nonprofit basis.

[5778] Base for Computing Return (*Prov. Reimb. Man.,* Part I, 1204)

The base amount of equity capital to be used for computing the allowable return is the average investment of the owners during the reporting period. Investment in facilities is recognized on the basis of the historical cost, or other basis, used for depreciation and other cost purposes under the health insurance program. The equity capital in each month is determined and an average of the monthly amounts computed. This is the average equity capital in use during the period. Where the period is less than a year, a proportionate amount of the return is allowable, i.e., seven month period—only 7/12th of the return is allowable.

.80 Utilization of depreciation amounts in computing return on equity capital.   In computing the amount of equity capital upon which a return is allowable, the *Provider Reimbursement Manual* (5778) states, "investment in facilities is recognized on the basis of the historical cost, or other basis, used for depreciation and other cost purposes under the health insurance program."

Therefore, the cost and accumulated depreciation amounts used to compute the net equity are to be the same ones used to claim depreciation on the cost reporting form. If, for example, the life of a fixed asset is extended, the accumulated depreciation balance is to be recomputed and the new balance used in computing net equity.

[5782] Rate of Return (*Prov. Reimb. Man.,* Part I, 1206)

The rate of return on average equity capital is a percentage equal to one and one-half times the average of the rates of interest on special issues of public debt obligations issued to the Federal Hospital Insurance Trust Fund for each of the months during the provider's reporting period or portion thereof covered under the program. The rate of return varies as the interest rates on such issues of public debt obligations vary.

The percentage rate is determined by the Social Security Administration and communicated through the intermediaries.

Exhibit 6 *(concluded)*

RETURN ON EQUITY CAPITAL OF PROPRIETARY PROVIDERS
(To be completed by proprietary providers only)

PROVIDER NO.		PERIOD FROM	
HOSPITAL		TO	

PART I - BALANCE SHEET FOR COMPUTATION OF EQUITY CAPITAL

ASSETS (OMIT CENTS)	BALANCE SHEET PER BOOKS	ADJUSTMENTS INCREASE (DECREASE)	ADJUSTED BALANCE SHEET FOR COMPUTATION OF EQUITY CAPITAL	LIABILITIES AND CAPITAL (OMIT CENTS)	BALANCE SHEET PER BOOKS	ADJUSTMENTS INCREASE (DECREASE)	ADJUSTED BALANCE SHEET FOR COMPUTATION OF EQUITY CAPITAL
	2	3	4	5	6	7	8
CURRENT ASSETS				**CURRENT LIABILITIES**			
1. Cash on hand and in bank	$	$	$	34. Accounts Payable	$	$	$
2. Temporary Investments				35. Salaries, Wages & Fees Payable			
3. Notes Receivable				36. Payroll Taxes Payable			
4. Accounts Receivable				37. Notes & Loans Payable (Short Term)			
5. Other Receivables				38. Deferred Income			
6. Less: Allowance for uncollectible notes and accounts receivable	( )	( )	( )	39. Accelerated Payments			
7. Inventory				40.			
8. Prepaid Expenses				41. Total Current Liabilities (Sum of lines 34-40)	$	$	$
9. Other Current Assets				**LONG-TERM LIABILITIES**			
10. Total Current Assets (Sum of lines 1-9)	$	$	$	42. Mortgage Payable	$	$	$
FIXED ASSETS				43. Notes Payable			
11. Land	$	$	$	44. Unsecured Loans			
12. Land Improvements				45. Loans from Owners prior to 7/1/66			
13. Less: Accumulated Depreciation	( )	( )	( )	46. On or after 7/1/66			
14. Building				47.			
15. Less: Accumulated Depreciation	( )	( )	( )	48.			
16. Leasehold Improvement				49. Total Long-term Liabilities (Sum of lines 42-48)	$	$	$
17. Less: Accumulated Amortization	( )	( )	( )	50. TOTAL LIABILITIES (Sum of lines 41 & 49)	$	$	$
18. Fixed Equipment				51. Capital	$	$	$
19. Less: Accumulated Depreciation	( )	( )	( )				
20. Automobiles & Trucks							
21. Less: Accumulated Depreciation	( )	( )	( )				
22. Major Movable Equipment							
23. Less: Accumulated Depreciation	( )	( )	( )				
24. Minor Equipment Non-depreciable							
25. Other Fixed Assets				52. TOTAL CAPITAL	$	$	$
26. Total Fixed Assets (Sum of lines 11-25)	$	$	$	53. TOTAL LIABILITIES & CAPITAL (Sum of lines 50 & 52)	$	$	$
OTHER ASSETS				54. Equity in assets leased from related organizations			
27. Investments	$	$	$	55. Difference between total interim payments and net cost of covered services (SEE INSTRUCTIONS)			
28. Deposits on leases				56. TOTAL EQUITY CAPITAL (Line 52 plus/minus lines 54 and 55) (1)			$
29. Due from owners/officers				57. Return on equity capital			
30. Special Funds				58. Adjustments to health care program costs			
31.				59. Federal, state and local income taxes			
32. Total Other Assets (Sum of lines 27-31)	$	$	$	60. Total Equity Capital Beginning of Following Cost Reporting Period (Sum of lines 56 and 57 plus or minus lines 58 and 59)			$
33. TOTAL ASSETS (Sum of lines 10, 26 & 32)	$	$	$				

(1) If computed as of end of cost reporting period, transfer the amount to Part II, col. 8 for the last month or period in the cost reporting period; if computed as of beginning of cost reporting period (first reporting period under the health care programs only),
transfer this amount to Part II, column 7, all lines, and column 8, line 1.   ( ) = contra amounts

FORM SSA-2552G (5-75)

based primarily upon the landmark Supreme Court decision *FPC* v. *Hope Natural Gas Company,* state that private businesses which employ their assets in service of the public interest should be paid rates of return which:

1. Protect their financial integrity.
2. Reward their investors at a level commensurate with the risks the investors assumed in making their investments.
3. Permit the companies to attract new capital for purposes of maintaining and expanding their operations.

These principles form the basis for determining appropriate rates of return in virtually every regulated industry, spokesmen for the proprietary hospital industry said, and, therefore, would be well-suited to the Medicare program.

In studying the existing Medicare ROE formula (1.5 times the average Hospital Insurance Trust Fund interest rate) Ms. Blake noted that the Medicare allowances over the 1969–76 period were quite similar to the yields on bonds with a Baa rating over the same period (Exhibit 7). That rating was what most IOH issues had been receiving. She noted

Exhibit 7
Medicare allowable return on equity
and Baa bond yields, 1969–1976

Calendar year	ROE allowance	Baa bond yield
1969	9.89%	7.81%
1970	10.89	9.11
1971	8.97	8.56
1972	8.89	8.16
1973	9.97	8.24
1974	11.23	9.50
1975	11.09	10.61
1976	10.72	9.75

Source: Bureau of Health Insurance, Social Security Administration, and *Economic Report of the President,* January 1977.

further that many lenders had recently required interest rates of 10 to 13 percent on recent issues to IOHs and that interest payments were a reimbursable cost under the Medicare program. Finally, she reviewed a sample of aftertax rates of return on equity awarded to telephone operating companies in recent years (Exhibit 8).

Ms. Blake was also aware that Senator Herman Talmadge had introduced a bill in Congress, the Medicare and Medicaid Administrative

Exhibit 8
Bell System—Summary of return allowed on common equity and on total capital in recent state rate cases

Company (jurisdiction)	Date filed	Date ordered	Cost of common equity*		Cost of capital†	
			Company proposed	Commission found	Company proposed	Commission found
New England:						
Massachusetts............	7–15–69	1–21–72	10.1–12.0	11.0	8.4–9.5	8.62
	10– 1–71	1–21–72	12.0–13.0	11.0	9.57–9.64	8.82
	7–27–72	6–25–73	12.5–14.0	11.5	9.75–10.5	8.93
	2–14–74	9–18–74	12.5–14.0	Not specified	8.93	8.93
	11–26–74	10–27–75	14.0–15.0	12.0	10.5–11.25	9.00
		9–14–76 (CT)	14.0–15.0	13.0	10.5–11.25	9.48
		5–31–77	14.0–15.0	13.0	10.5–11.25	9.48
New Hampshire	8– 6–71	8–24–72	12.0–13.0	11.0	9.5–9.9	8.60
	5–23–74	9–25–74	11.0	11.0	8.90	8.87
	7–24–75	4–16–76	14.0–15.0	12.5	10.6–11.2	9.81
Rhode Island	4– 1–69	1–30–70	10.0–11.8	9.5–10.0	8.0–9.0	7.40–7.65
	4–16–71	5– 4–72	12.0–13.0	10.5	9.5–10.0	8.38
		7–20–73 (CT)				
	8–30–74	6–27–75	13.0–14.5	11.25	10.0–11.0	8.72
		9– 4–77	13.0–14.5	11.53	10.0–11.0	8.86
	.11– 5–76		16.3		11.01	
	3–22–79	9– 4–77	15.5–16.0	11.53	10.5–10.7	8.60

* Posttax allowed return on book equity.
† Posttax allowed return on total capital (debt, preferred, and equity).
Source: American Telephone and Telegraph Co., Inc.

and Reimbursement Reform Act, that would increase the Hospital Insurance Trust Fund multiplier from 1.5 to 2. She knew that the Talmadge bill was receiving strong support from the proprietary hospitals and its main lobbying group, the Federation of American Hospitals.

Finally, Ms. Blake was aware of litigation between proprietary chains and HEW which challenged the exclusion of income taxes as allowable costs. Industry representatives claimed that under the *Hope* decision the court recognized that the purposes served by return on investment could only be accomplished if the return was established in the context of net income after tax.

"The rate of return on equity is partly designed to reward investors for their risks," said a representative of one company during a rate review hearing. "By forcing providers to pay taxes on the return on equity, [HEW] is in effect cutting in half the reward which these investors are to receive."

Ms. Blake hoped that by gaining overall perspective on the regulation of proprietary hospitals, she could find a way to reconcile several of these obviously interrelated issues.

NorthEast Connecticut Health Systems Agency

The Northeast Connecticut Health Systems Agency (HSA) was the federally funded "health planning" agency for the 41 towns in northeastern Connecticut. The HSA was founded to control costs by encouraging rational planning for its area's health care system. One of its major responsibilities was to review all hospital capital projects larger than $100,000 to be certain that they were both necessary and economically justifiable.

The HSA board of directors and staff had been studying two applications for permission to purchase expensive X-ray devices called "CAT scanners." The HSA's decision would be reviewed by a statewide agency with final authority, but it was unusual for an HSA to be overruled. On the evening of April 6, 1977, the agency's board met at the City Hall in Watertown to decide on the two applications.

The two hospitals in contention for approval were the major facilities in the HSA's service area. Sunbury Hospital was the only hospital in Sunbury, Connecticut (population 150,000), while Watertown General Hospital was by far the largest hospital serving Watertown (population 210,000). Although Watertown was the largest town in the area, Sunbury Hospital was farthest from existing scanners and treated a heavier case load of patients in need of scanning. Nevertheless, Watertown residents had a slight plurality of votes on the HSA board, so the outcome of the debate was not certain.

Cost was unlikely to be one major issue in the debate. The "Ohio Nuclear Delta 50" scanner that Sunbury wanted to lease would involve total payments of over $650,000. The Watertown plan included two years of "free" use of a new generation "CGR scanner" from France, followed by purchase at a discounted price. With interest, however, the Watertown plan would be at least as costly as the Sunbury proposal. Since operating costs and professional fees together could amount to
220

$300,000 per year per scanner, the decision between approval of the two, one, or no machines was an important one for the board.

The HSA was a new agency and its board was made up of a majority of consumers and a minority of physicians. This was the first major policy decision that the board would make, and its members were a little apprehensive about how it would go. Unfortunately, the board had received an ambiguous recommendation from its areawide review committee. One committee member had been absent when the final vote was taken, and the committee had split evenly between choosing one or two scanners. Three members had voted for two, two had voted for Sunbury's application, and one member voted that one scanner be approved, without prejudice as to location. The members knew that the HSA staff thought that the area was already adequately served by existing scanners located elsewhere, but they also knew that doctors in both towns were almost desperate for approval. The consumers on the board were politically active individuals who knew very little about medical technology or finance. By and large they felt caught in the middle of the argument between the doctors and the agency staff.

After the chairman called the board to order and handled opening details, Mr. William Karraker, head of the areawide review committee, rose to address the 20 board members and 40 interested observers.

The votes of the members of the areawide review committee have produced such an inconclusive situation that a definitive recommendation to the board of directors is not possible. I will make a motion on the following basis:

1. Two subarea review panels were formed to review the requests from hospitals in their respective areas. Both panels agreed that there should be no more than one approved application, but each panel suggested that it be the one from its own subarea.

2. The Sunbury Hospital application indicates that the scanner that it proposes to lease may be purchased for 3 percent of its current price at the end of its five-year lease period. Such rapid depreciation indicates that, while the machine does not actually deteriorate, it can be purchased at what appears to be a salvage price because of unusually rapid obsolescence. The Watertown application depreciates the EMI scanner that it proposes to purchase to zero in the same five-year period.

3. Section 1513 of P.L. 93–641 charges this agency to improve the health of residents of our area, and also to restrain increases in the cost of providing health services. I want to remind you that even the least costly application imposes an expenditure for purchase and operation which will total at least $3.7 million over the next ten years. If both applications are approved, that figure is, at best, doubled. The HSA staff members have provided us with detailed financial information and technical analysis on this matter, and I want to thank them for reminding me of the broader concerns here.

4. We have been accused at both subarea panel reviews and at the areawide committee

meeting of being more concerned with dollars than with lives. We are charged with considering both.

It has been painful for me to reach the conclusions which prompt my motion. My late father was an M.D. in general practice. I would certainly be blind, and probably dead in the absence of services to me by specialists supporting one of these applications. I have suffered the agonies of a cerebral angiogram and a pneumoencephalogram, risky "invasive" procedures that would be replaced by the admittedly safer and painless CAT scan. But we must allocate resources to provide the greatest health care good for the greatest number. If we approve these applications we will be abdicating our cost-containment responsibility entirely.

I move that the recommendation of this board to the statewide review agency be that both applications be *disapproved* at this time.

Mr. Karraker's motion came as a complete surprise. Karraker had consistently supported the Sunbury application, and everyone has assumed that he would continue to do so. The meeting was thrown into disarray, with several members competing for the floor and the observers arguing loudly. Representatives of local newspapers crowded in on Sunbury's administrator, John Creasy. Mr. Creasy refused comment but strode angrily from the room before order could be restored. When it was, Mr. David Beatty, chairman of the board, recognized Dr. Tom Smith, from Watertown:

In all candor I feel that the review process in the CAT scanner deliberations absolutely rotted. It was an insult.

Panels were formed to review each of these applications. After a great many hours *both* panels separately came to the conclusion that one scanner should be approved for the area. Their recommendations were forwarded to the review committee for its consideration. Its vote was evenly divided three to three between one or two scanners for the area. *At no time* did anyone vote that no scanner be approved. These panelists have had the most intimate contact possible with the proposals. In fact, one clear conclusion was reached through the lengthy review process, namely that there should be at least one CAT scanner in our area.

For the chairman to so blatantly ignore the dictates of so many people, summing up their work as "producing such an inconclusive situation that a definitive recommendation to the board is not possible" and to make a surprise motion to deny both applications without any direction from his working members is a travesty. In fact, I might ask, "Why did we bother to have the panels or review if they are to be ignored?"

There is a second matter of concern. Admittedly, this board is blessed with an extremely intelligent, dynamic staff. However, in their fervor to be of assistance and guidance, they overstepped their bounds. The staff pushed its own opinions rather than supporting ours. I feel that the board should be extremely objective in evaluating the staff's influence over our final decision. Politics, inside information, or staff opinions should not interfere with what the board or panel feels is the right decision.

All of this is beside the point, of course. We should be approving two CAT scanners based on their merits. CAT scanning is undoubtably the most revolutionary neurologic technology developed in the last 70 years. In most cases a scan will be a lower cost and more effective replacement for a painful, uncomfortable or risky procedure. We can save countless lives by using it to visualize tumors as small as one-quarter inch in diameter, instead of being forced to wait until after they have grown to fatal sizes as we do now. Hundreds of the machines have been installed nationwide, and the technology is now fully accepted. *Both of these applications meet state guidelines for "need" and other, less worthy, applications have been approved elsewhere in the state.*

We have been told that the state agency that will review our decision, the Commission on Hospitals and Health Care (CHHC), only wants one CAT in our area, but *we mustn't cave in to their cost-cutting efforts if it means depriving residents of northeast Connecticut of the best quality care.* After all, our mission is, first and foremost, to plan a good quality health care system for our area. I urge the other board members to reject this motion.

Donald Billson, president of the Northeast Bank and Trust Company and a consumer representative on the HSA board, listened to both speakers with some concern. He felt that emotions were distorting the issues being considered. He raised his hand, and was recognized by the chairman:

I have been busy with bank business, and I must admit that I have never looked closely at the financial proposals for these scanners, but I have been glancing at them now, and I think that someone should take a closer look at them. If Dr. Smith is correct, and the scanners will actually save money, it seems as though we have nothing to argue about. Also, if the CHHC is serious about approving at most one scanner for our area, then I think that we should get behind one application or the other. The CHHC is famous for picking the option that will cost the government least and that might not be our choice. . . .

Frankly, I can't see my way through these committee reports and I am not satisfied with the financial analysis so far. I'd like to move that we table this motion until my staff down at the bank can go over these projections with the HSA people. . . . It also seems to me that it wouldn't hurt to cool down a bit before we make a final decision. . . .

Everyone except the agency's staff looked a little relieved by Billson's suggestion, and he noticed that he had inadvertently taken on the role of mediator between the doctors and the HSA staff. The motion to table was accepted by acclamation, and the meeting continued with less serious business.

After the meeting, Dr. John Mashman, one of Billson's largest depositors, approached him as he was gathering additional financial information from an HSA staff member. Dr. Mashman said,

Thank you for pulling us out of the fire tonight, Don. Everyone was caught completely off guard by Karraker's motion. I thought for a minute there that he had us.

There is an additional factor you should consider as you do your financials. The other doctors in our group and I are fed up with this bureaucratic mess. We have decided to order a CAT scanner for our offices, where we won't need approval, if the HSA doesn't approve the Sunbury application soon. I'm not threatening, just pleading for the sake of the patients. We've waited a year for these people to get organized, and now this! We need a scanner every day, and we won't wait much longer to get one.

After the doctor moved away, John Grana, the HSA staffer in charge of economic analysis, lamented,

Scanners in doctors' offices completely undermine our efforts. They aren't subject to rate setting, reporting requirements or peer review as hospital scanners are. They aren't available 24 hours a day, and there is no requirement to scan patients who can't afford to pay. Scanners in offices are far from operating suites and emergency rooms where patients in need of scans but unable to be moved are most often found. This is exactly what the doctors in Stamford pulled, and the courts recently upheld their right to do it. It looks like there will be a scanner in Sunbury no matter what. I guess we'll have to approve the Sunbury application if we want to stop him. It makes' me mad, how can we hold down costs when there are people like Mashman under every rock?

The financial data that Billson collected from Grana reminded him that the board had several options. They might approve either or both of the applications, or reject them. Billson felt that the hospitals would accept any reasonable modifications to their proposals and that they would resubmit them with more data if that seemed to be necessary. Nevertheless, the cost of medical equipment had been advancing at 15 percent per year, so Billson hoped the board would act as quickly as possible on the proposals.

Later that evening Billson reorganized the information he had received to adjust for minor differences in how the proposals had been presented (Exhibit 1). He also included a short narrative description of each proposal's terms and risks (Exhibits 2, 3, and 4). Billson projected 7 percent operating cost inflation, and 12 percent inflation for the hospital price index, which included equipment and capital cost inflation as well as operating cost increases. Billson was uncertain about where interest rates would be in two years, so he decided to project that they would be comparable to the present (April 1977) prime rate of 6 percent.

Early the next morning at the bank, Mr. Billson pulled the sheaf of papers from his briefcase. He winced when he thought about the heated argument of the night before. The debate had been partly a front for a battle over whether doctors and hospitals or the agency staff would control the area's health care system. The important discussion of which scanner proposal was more desirable and what the true cost of the various options were had been almost completely obscured. Billson always wondered why they couldn't run the government the way he ran the bank . . . like a business!

Billson buzzed his secretary, and asked him to send for Mary Hillhouse, a recent graduate of a well-known management school. He had been looking for a chance to test her skills, and this looked like a prime opportunity.

When Ms. Hillhouse came in, Billson pushed the pile of reports, regulations, and newspaper clippings across the desk to her, and explained the previous evening's events in detail. After he finished that he continued:

Mary, I want you to review all this information carefully, but pay particular attention to the financial sections. I need to know exactly what the costs are for each alternative, and what the bottom line looks like. I want to know which of these projects looks more desirable.

Let's face it, this is a highly political situation. I didn't want to get involved, and now I am stuck in the middle. In addition to the financial analysis I need three questions answered. Given the lack of expertise of our audience,

1. What action should we recommend?
2. How should we present our analysis?
3. How can we avoid this kind of confrontation in the future?

The problem is complicated by the fact that virtually none of these people have had experience with economic analysis so you'll need to explain everything very clearly.

You'll need some background on hospital financial analysis yourself. There are a few tricks to it. I've attached a one page note on it for your information. Be certain to read it before you begin.

One thing that you may be tempted to skip over is the staff's estimate of savings and added costs for head scans (it doesn't include body scans (Exhibit 1, Schedule D). The estimate seems to show Sunbury ahead by quite a bit. Evidently, many more procedures of the type CATs may be used for are performed there. You'll want to relate that to your financial analysis somehow.

This is a mess that you could spend weeks on, Mary, but I think that that would be counterproductive. Run these numbers and send me a two-page analysis of (1) your results, and (2) your suggestions on the questions I've raised. Do it by five o'clock today.

Exhibit 1

MEMO

FROM: D. Billson
TO: M. Hillhouse
RE: Hospital Financial Analysis

For the most part, hospital projects are analyzed like any other capital investment decision. There are a few things to be aware of, however:

Exhibit 1 *(continued)*

---

1. The effect of government reimbursement

The federal "Medicare" and "Medicaid" programs do not pay what a hospital charges. Instead, they reimburse the hospital for the lower of costs or charges. In other words, no profit is allowed on government-sponsored patients. The government uses "generally accepted accounting principles to determine the level of "allowable costs," and depreciation and interest are, therefore, considered allowable costs. Both hospitals have 40 percent government patients.

2. Fund accounting

Most hospitals still use fund accounting. Fund accounting segregates resources into separate "funds" according to how they will be used. A typical hospital has operations, capital expenditure and endowment funds. Loans among funds are possible.

Financial summary: Sunbury option

The Sunbury Hospital radiology staff, the most active neuroradiology group in north-eastern Connecticut, has chosen the Ohio Nuclear Corporation's "Delta 50" scanner for installation in its new radiology suite. The machine carries a firm list price of $550,000, and will cost $10,000 to install. The "Delta 50" has been used successfully for two years at other hospitals and is considered a good quality, reliable machine.

Sunbury Hospital has been completely renovated lately, and its "Capital Expenditure" and "Endowment" funds have been drawn down to unusually low levels. As a result, the Sunbury administrator feels that his only option is to lease the "Delta 50." He has negotiated an arrangement with the leasing subsidiary of a major New York bank that will allow him to finance the acquisition at a cost that corresponds to the bank's "prime" lending rate of 6 percent.

The bank has proposed a noncancellable lease that involves monthly payments of $10,586.33 per month over 60 months. Since the lessor does not actually wish to take possession of the scanner at the termination of the lease, it has offered the hospital a "bargain purchase option." This option will allow Sunbury to purchase the scanner for $16,500, 3 percent of its current price, at that time. The hospital intends to take advantage of this offer, but is not bound to do so.

The lease provisions just described make the lease a "Capital Lease" for accounting purposes. This means that the hospital will show the scanner on its balance sheet as an asset and its lease payment obligation as a liability. For reimbursement purposes it means that depreciation and interest (on an "equivalent loan") will be allowable costs, but the actual lease payments themselves won't be.

Although it is difficult to predict exactly when any particular generation of CAT scanners will become obsolete, past experience shows that improvements are constantly being made and that eight-year-old models are almost completely outmoded. On this basis we might predict that the "Delta 50" will become obsolete in about six years. All scanner manufacturers are committed to making technological improvements compatible with their current products. For this reason it is likely that renovation will be considerably less costly than replacement. If CAT is superceded by a completely different technology, replacement is more likely.

Exhibit 1 *(continued)*

Schedule A. Sunbury option: Lease Ohio Nuclear Delta 50 Scanner

Related information
Purchase price $550,000
Installation 10,000

Lease terms:
Type .... Capital lease
Term .... Five years
Begins .... Year 1
Payments .... Monthly, arrears
Amount each $10,586.33
Options .... "Bargain" purchase
(3% of list at termination)

Depreciation
Type .... Straight line
Minimum term ..... Five years
Salvage .... None included

Utilization forecast (scans per year)

Year	Private patients	Government patients	Total
1	1,500	1,000	2,500
2	1,800	1,200	3,000
3	2,100	1,400	3,500
4	2,100	1,400	3,500
5	2,100	1,400	3,500
6	1,800	1,200	3,000
7	1,200	800	2,000
Total	12,600	8,400	21,000

Cash flows, etc.

Year	(1) Renovation lease payments, purchase cost	(2) Principal (implicit in lease)	(3) Interest (implicit in lease)	(4) Depreciation expense	(5) Operating costs*	(6) Total cost (1) + (5)
0	$ 10,000	0	0	0	0	0
1	127,036	$ 94,778	$ 35,558	$112,000‡	$ 130,000	$ 267,036
2	127,036	102,374	27,962	112,000	153,010	280,046
3	127,036	110,000	20,336	112,000	178,604	305,640
4	127,036	117,626	12,710	112,000	191,107	318,143
5	143,536†	125,252	5,084	112,000	204,484	348,020
6	0	0	0	0	200,565	200,565
7	0	0	0	0	185,340	185,340
Total	$661,680	$550,000	$101,680	$560,000	$1,243,110	$1,904,790

* See "Operating Cost Estimates . . ." (attached). Here adjusted for 7 percent inflation.
† Includes $16,500 purchase cost.
‡ Installation at $2,000 per year, equipment at $110,000 per year.

Exhibit 1 *(continued)*

Financial summary: Watertown option

A French company, "CGR Medical Corporation," has agreed to place a prototype model of its newest generation CAT scanner at Watertown Hospital for two years without charge. The scanner will have a list price of $680,000, but CGR has agreed to make a gift of $150,000 to Watertown Hospital (in the form of a discount on the scanner's price) at the end of the second year of operation. The gift has been arranged in such a way as to allow the hospital to capitalize the entire $680,000. During the two-year "free" period, CGR will use the machine for research and development purposes and, the company hopes, as an example of a successful U.S. installation. The hospital realizes that the R&D activities and increased "downtime" related to the experimental nature of the machine will restrict scan volume somewhat, but it feels that the unit's advantages outweigh these drawbacks.

The radiology department at Watertown will require extensive renovation to prepare it for the scanner's installation. The total cost of renovation and installation will be about $50,000. The hospital will use its capital expenditure fund for this purpose.

Watertown Hospital will borrow the entire $530,000 required to purchase the scanner. It will repay the principal and interest over a five-year period. The hospital has undertaken a significant amount of long-term debt over the years, and this project will raise its debt/equity ratio to about .70. Because it is so highly levered, the facility will have to offer about 3 percent over the prime rate to attract additional debt. This would mean a 9 percent rate under current market conditions.

The CGR offer is particularly attractive to Watertown Hospital for several reasons: First, the scanner will be the most modern available. The hospital believes that it will not become obsolete until ten years from the time it is installed. Also, the presence of such an advanced device at Watertown Hospital would almost certainly attract other radiological practice as well, and revenue in addition to CAT-related income. Second, the financing arrangement implies a significant reimbursement advantage. The government will be paying 40 percent of depreciation on $680,000, although the hospital will only have paid $530,000. Finally, the hospital has a chance to defer its purchase for two years, and even has an opportunity of "bail out" if the installation is unsatisfactory.

Exhibit 1 (continued)

Schedule B. Watertown option: Purchase CGR scanner

Related information

List price	$680,000
Discount (gift)	(150,000)
Renovation and installation	50,000
Estimate obsolete	Year 10
Loan principal	$530,000
Monthly interest rate	0.007207
Payments	Monthly, arrears
	$10,911.83

Depreciation

Type	Straight line
Minimum term	Five years
Begins	Year 3
Salvage	None included

Utilization forecast (scans per year)

Year	Private patients	Government patients	Total
1	1,200	800	2,000
2	1,200	800	2,000
3	1,800	1,200	3,000
4	2,100	1,400	3,500
5	2,100	1,400	3,500
6	2,100	1,400	3,500
7	2,100	1,400	3,500
Total	12,600	8,400	21,000

Cash flows, etc.

Year	(1) Renovation and loan payments	(2) Principal	(3) Interest	(4) Depreciation Expense*	(5) Operating Costs†	(6) Total cost (1) + (5)
0	$ 50,000	0	0	0	0	0
1	0	0	0	$ 7,143	$ 123,500	$ 173,500
2	0	0	0	7,143	133,380	133,380
3	130,942	$ 87,294	$ 43,648	143,143	166,795	297,736
4	130,942	96,647	34,295	143,143	196,515	327,457
5	130,942	106,000	24,942	143,143	212,236	343,178
6	130,942	115,353	15,589	143,143	229,215	360,156
7	130,942	−124,706	6,234	143,143	245,552	376,493
Total	$704,710	$530,000	$124,708	$730,001	$1,307,193	$2,011,900

* Renovation depreciated over seven years, equipment over five.

† See "Operating Cost Estimates" (attached). Here adjusted for 7 percent annual inflation.

Exhibit 1 *(continued)*

Schedule C. Operating cost estimates for CAT scanners at various volumes
(scans per year, not adjusted for inflation)

Number of scans	2,000	2,500	3,000	3,500	4,000
Radiologist salary*	$ 50,000	$ 50,000	$ 50,000	$ 50,000	$ 50,000
Technician salaries	25,000	25,000	30,000	35,000	40,000
Supplies and repairs	20,000	25,000	30,000	35,000	40,000
Total direct expense	$ 95,000	$100,000	$110,000	$120,000	$130,000
Indirect expense†	28,500	30,000	33,000	36,000	39,000
Total operating cost	$123,500	$130,000	$143,000	$156,000	$169,000

* Rate negotiated with radiology group.
† Indirect expense allocated at 30 percent direct cost per survey conducted by Blue Cross of Connecticut.

Exhibit 1 *(continued)*

Schedule D. Staff estimate of savings from replacing existing tests with CAT scans

Hospital	Procedures* last year		Proportion† replaced		Number replaced		Unit cost‡		Savings	Hospital§ days saved		Cost per day‡		Hospital saving	Total saving
Watertown....	A = 1,090	×	.35	=	382	at	$109.88	=	$41,919	n.a.					
	B = 101	×	.22	=	22	at	401.90	=	8,930	22 × 1.6	×	$162.19	=	$5,709	
	C = 13	×	.57	=	7	at	201.70	=	1,495	7 × 1.6	×	$162.19	=	1,816	
					411				$52,344					$7,525	$59,869
Sunbury	A = 1,432	×	.35	=	501	at	$121.00	=	$60,645	n.a.					
	B = 530	×	.27	=	143	at	399.00	=	57,097	143 × 1.6	×	$195.20	=	$44,662	
	C = 8	×	.57	=	5	at	171.00	=	780	5 × 1.6	×	$195.20	=	1,562	
					649				$118,522					$46,224	$164,746

Hospital	Procedures replaced		Scans replaced‖ procedure		Total scans		Average unit cost per scan¶		Total cost		Total saving		New saving (cost)
Watertown........	411	×	1.7	=	699	at	$95.80	=	($66,935)	+	$59,868	=	($7,067)
Sunbury	649	×	1.7	=	1,103	at	$90.70	=	($100,069)	+	$164,745	=	$64,676

n.a. = not available.
* A Nucleotide brain scans.
  B Cerebral arteriograms.
  C pneumoencephalograms.
† Proportions from data on U.S. hospital experience.
‡ Supplied by hospitals.
§ Approximately 1.6 hospital days are saved per B or C test saved.
‖ Approximately 1.7 scans are performed per procedure replaced.
¶ Exhibit I, Schedule E.

Exhibit 1 *(concluded)*

Schedule E. Unit cost of scans*
(adjusted for 7 percent operating cost inflation)

Year	Total	Government Cost
Sunbury Hospital†		
1	$107.76	$111.02
2	94.13	97.66
3	88.00	88.84
4	91.57	90.23
5	95.39	91.88
6	67.64	66.86
7	93.85	92.67
Average	90.70	90.70
Watertown Hospital:		
1	$ 65.32	$ 65.32
2	70.26	70.26
3	101.63	117.86
4	93.56	106.84
5	100.09	108.66
6	104.94	110.84
7	109.61	113.41
Average	95.80	103.04

 * Total cost (from Schedules A and B, column 6, with renovation distributed evenly.
 † Total cost (as above) with purchase cost spread evenly.

Exhibit 2

[4110–83] Title 42—Public Health

CHAPTER 1—PUBLIC HEALTH SERVICE, DEPARTMENT OF HEALTH, EDUCATION, AND WELFARE

PART 121—NATIONAL GUIDELINES FOR HEALTH PLANNING

National Guidelines for Health Planning

AGENCY: Public Health Service, HEW.

ACTION: Final rules.

SUMMARY: These rules establish, pursuant to section 1501 of the Public Health Service Act, National Guidelines for Health Planning with respect to the following types of health services and facilities: General hospital beds, obstetrical inpatient services, neonatal special care units, pediatric inpatient services, open heart surgery, cardiac catheterization, radiation therapy, computed tomographic scanners, and end-stage renal disease.

A purpose of these guidelines is to assist Health Systems Agencies in developing

Exhibit 2 *(continued)*

Health Systems Plans and to help clarify and coordinate national health policy. These guidelines will be followed by other issuances setting forth national health planning goals and additional standards addressing such issues as improvement of health-status, health promotion and disease prevention, access to care, and the availability and distribution of health resources.

EFFECTIVE DATE: March 28, 1978.

All Health Systems Plans developed after December 31, 1978 must be consistent with the National Guidelines for Health Planning set out below.

9. COMMENTS ON STANDARD CONCERNING COMPUTED TOMOGRAPHIC SCANNERS

The principal objections concerning this standard were directed at the proposed target level of 2,500 "patient procedures" per year and the department's proposed definition of "patient procedure." Before addressing those objections, it is emphasized that the department's purpose in developing the Computed Tomographic Scanner standard has been to encourage appropriate communitywide planning for and to minimize unnecessary proliferation of these expensive machines and thereby hold down health care costs. The department is seeking to do so by assuring that those already in use, as well as those acquired in the future, will be utilized at reasonably full levels of efficiency. As the discussion portion of the standard points out, it has been concluded that an operating schedule that achieves at least 2,500 patient procedures per year for each scanner represents such a reasonable level of use.

Thus, objections to the standard based on its failure to consider the "cost-effectiveness" of individual CT scanners miss the point. In the department's judgment not only is the data available on the cost savings achieved by scanners as against the diagnostic procedures which the machines replace inconclusive, but such an approach to resource allocation decisions on a communitywide basis is unsound. Rather, the test adopted is to measure the efficiency with which the machines themselves are used in order to assure that the cost to the community is as low as can reasonably be expected, given the high cost of acquiring and operating the machines.

Some objections to the 2,500 figure have focused on the fact that the Institute of Medicine statement on Computed Tomographic Scanning used that number for a purpose different from that of these guidelines. While it is true that the immediate purpose of the Institute's use of this figure was to recommend appropriate charges for CT scans, the Institute adopted the figure of 2,500 patient examinations as a basis for that computation because of its conclusion, based upon its review of available data, that a minimum volume of 2,500 patient examinations is a conservative basis for estimating machine use on which to establish charges. The department's analysis, using the indicated definition and mix of "patient procedures," concluded that a CT scanner which is operated efficiently can normally perform 2,500 such procedures in a year with a work schedule which is less than 50–55 hours per week.

While some objections to this proposed standard have argued for a target based on a 40 hour workweek and have correctly pointed out that most scanners in operation operate at less than the 50–55 hour level, the department believes that the 50–55 hour week is a reasonable schedule of operation, that most scanners may fairly be expected to attain that if necessary, and that the fact that most scanners now provide

Exhibit 2 *(continued)*

substantially less than that level of service indicates the need for the standard. It should be noted that latitude is given to HSA's, both within the standard itself (see the Discussion portion of § 121.210) and in § 121.6 ("Adjustment of standards for particular Health Systems Plans") to adjust the 2,500 level where special local circumstances warrant, after careful analysis and consideration of extraordinary conditions.

It was suggested that the proposed definition of "patient procedure" might be interpreted to mean that a number of studies of the same anatomical region (such as the stomach, kidney, and colon) should be considered a single procedure. To clarify this point, the definition has been revised to substitute "the same anatomic area of diagnostic interest" for "the same anatomical region."

With regard to the definition of "patient procedure," commentators argued that a contrast scan and a noncontrast scan of the same anatomic area should be considered two procedures. The requested change has not been made. This change has not been accepted since it is considered reasonable to define as one procedure the scans necessary for resolving a particular question. Reports from the Blue Cross Association indicate that it is the usual practice for an initial scan and an additional scan to be billed as a single procedure, with the additional scan usually increasing the charge by no more than 20–25 percent. While this suggests that a "weighting" formula might be appropriate which would assign fractional units to each additional scan, the department has concluded that such an approach needs further study. As indicated in the Preamble to the January 20 notice, the department will continue to study this possibility and welcomes specific suggestions along these lines. For the present standard, in evaluating the impact of the 2,500 target level, the department took into account the relative number of multiple scans. (For example, 60–70 percent of head scans involve more than one scan.) As the Discussion section points out, the department also took into account an estimate of the potential relative frequency of more time-consuming body scans.

Some commentators suggested that the estimate of relative proportion of body scans to total procedures was too low. It is noted that only limited coverage of body scans has been approved for the Medicare program. As discussed in the Preamble to the January 20 Notice, developments in this field will be carefully and continuously monitored and changes proposed and made periodically as indicated. The department welcomes the submission of further information for its consideration from all interested parties.

Some writers emphasized that the discussion of the potential special uses of CT scanners in research situations was too limited, covering only collaborative clinical trials. The material has been modified to include other research projects that have a fixed protocol and have been institutionally approved.

It was also pointed out that a newly installed scanner does not immediately reach its normal operating level. The standard has been changed to recognize this fact, and now provides that a new machine should attain the target level of patient procedures during its second year of operation.

Some commentators stated that some new, less expensive scanners as well as some early models operate relatively slowly and may not be capable of attaining the 2,500 level. These machines are head scanners and should ordinarily have little difficulty in attaining the target level if utilized efficiently. In any case, the "general adjustment" provisions of section 121.6 are available to HSA's for application to such unusual situations.

Exhibit 2 *(continued)*

Recommendations were received that additional effort be focused on the development of a population-based standard. The department agrees that population-based approaches are preferable to utilization-based standards whenever practical and intends to continue to work toward that end for this service and for other services.

Finally, the department wishes to make clear its awareness that many medium-sized and small community hospitals may not be able to meet the target level set in this standard. Indeed, there would be little purpose in adopting a standard at all if that were not so. It is expected that vigorous application of the standard by HSA's will result in additional sharing arrangements among hospitals as part of the process of assuring that existing and new scanners are more efficiently utilized. Where such arrangements are not feasible because of travel or other difficulties, HSA's have authority to adjust the standard to assure that medically necessary CT scanner services will not be denied patients in their areas.

Accordingly, a new Part 121 is hereby added to 42 CFR as set forth below.

Note. The Department of Health, Education, and Welfare has determined that this document does not contain a major proposal requiring preparation of an Inflationary Impact Statement under Executive Order 11821 and OMB Circular A-107.

Dated: March 15, 1978.

JULIUS B. RICHMOND,
Assistant Secretary of Health.

Approved: March 22, 1978.

JOSEPH A. CALIFANO, JR.,
Secretary.

PART 121—NATIONAL GUIDELINES
FOR HEALTH PLANNING

Subpart A—General Provisions

Sec.
121.1   Definitions.
121.2   Purpose and scope.
121.3   Applicability of national guidelines to Health Systems Plans.
121.4   Applicability of national guidelines to state health plans.
121.5   Responsibility of health systems agencies.
121.6   Adjustment of standards for particular Health Systems Plans.

Subpart B—National Health Planning Goals
[Reserved]

Subpart C—Standards Respecting the Appropriate Supply, Distribution, and Organization of Health Resources

121.201   General hospitals—Supply.
121.202   General hospitals—Occupancy rate.
121.203   Obstetrical services.
121.204   Neonatal special care units.
121.205   Pediatric inpatient services—Number of beds.
121.206   Pediatric inpatient services—Occupancy rates.

Exhibit 2 *(continued)*

121.207	Open heart surgery.
121.208	Cardiac catheterization.
121.209	Radiation therapy.
121.210	Computed tomographic scanners.
121.211	End-stage renal disease (ESRD).

Authority: Sec. 1501 of the Public Health Service Act, 88 Stat. 2227 (41 U.S.C. 300k-1).

Sec. 121.210 Computed tomographic scanners.

a. Standard. (1) A Computed Tomographic Scanner (head and body) should operate at a minimum of 2,500 medically necessary patient procedures per year, for the second year of its operation and thereafter.

2. There should be no additional scanners approved unless each existing scanner in the health service area is performing at a rate greater than 2,500 medically necessary patient procedures per year.

3. There should be no additional scanners approved unless the operators of the proposed equipment will set in place data collection and utilization review systems.

b. Discussion. Because CT scanners are expensive to purchase, maintain and staff, every effort must be made to contain costs while providing an acceptable level of service. Intensive utilization of existing units, regardless of location, will prevent needless duplication and limit unnecessary health care costs. Estimates and surveys for efficient utilization of CT scanners range from 1,800 to over 4,000 patient procedures a year. (One patient procedure includes, during a single visit, the initial scan plus any necessary additional scans of the same anatomic area of diagnostic interest).

The Institute of Medicine, the Office of Technology Assessment and others have carefully reviewed these data and the capabilities of various available units. The department has reviewed these analyses as well as the extensive literature that has been developed on CT scanners. In arriving at a standard for the use of these machines, the department has considered a variety of factors, including the difference in time required for head scans and body scans, the need for multiple scans in some patient examinations, variations in patient mix, the special needs of children, time required for maintenance, and staffing requirements. Moreover, the department considered the actual operating experience of hospitals and institutions reflected in reports on the use of CT scanners.

The standard set in the department's guidelines is intended to assure effective utilization and reasonable cost for CT scanning. These machines are expensive, and therefore must be used at levels of high efficiency if excessive costs are to be limited. The department recognizes that the cost of some machines is declining, particularly those that perform only head scans which require less time. For machines that do predominantly head scans, the standard represents an efficient but more easily attainable level of utilization. For scanners capable of performing both head and body scans, it is imperative that they be effectively used in order to spread the high capital expenditures over as much operating time as possible. As the Institute of Medicine report stated, "The high fixed costs of operating a scanner argue for as high a volume of use as the equipment allows without jeopardizing the quality of care."

Exhibit 2 *(concluded)*

The department believes that a 50–55 hour operating week is both consistent with the actual operating experience of many hospitals and a reasonable target. Based on reported experience for the time required for both head scans and body scans, the department estimated that a patient mix of about 60 percent head scans and about 40 percent body scans, making allowance for the other factors identified above, would allow a CT scanner to perform about 2,500 patient procedures per year if it is efficiently used about 50–55 hours per week. This estimate assumes a higher percent of body scans than is currently being performed. If fewer than 40 percent body scans are performed, then 2,500 patient procedures would involve even less than 50–55 hours per week. Basing the standard on a higher percentage of body scans also takes account of current trends toward increased proportions of such scans.

The department believes that sharing arrangements in the use of CT scanners is desirable, in line with the national health priorities of section 1502. Individual institutions or providers should not acquire new machines until existing capacity is being well utilized.

In planning for CT scanners, the HSA should take into consideration special circumstances such as: (1) an institution with more than one scanner where the combined average annual number of procedures is greater than 2,500 per scanner although the unit doing primarily body scans is opearting at less than 2,500 patient procedures per year; (2) units which are, or will be, devoting a significant portion of time to fixed protocol institutionally approved research projects; and (3) units which are, or will be, servicing predominantly seriously sick or pediatric patients. A summary of the data collected on CT scanners should be submitted by the operators to the appropriate HSA to enable it to adequately plan the distribution and use of CT scanners in the area. The data to be collected should include information on utilization and a description of the operations of a utilization review program.

Source: *Federal Register,* vol. 43, no. 60 (Tuesday, March 28, 1978).

Exhibit 3

Radiological Society of Connecticut, Inc., Chapter of ACR: Guidelines for computerized tomography in Connecticut

Report of Special Committee
 Gerald Berg, M.D.
 Kenneth Bird, M.D.
 Gerald Freedman, M.D.
 David Hayes, M.D.
 James McSweeney, M.D.
 Harold Moskowitz, M.D.
 Robert Shapiro, M.D. Chairman

Accepted December 16, 1976.

A modern hospital without a coronary care unit is unthinkable today regardless of cost. Similarly, a first-class department of radiology is unthinkable without ultrasound or isotope facilities. The same holds true for CAT scanning. When regional planning

Exhibit 3 *(continued)*

authorities limited the number of radiation therapy centers in Connecticut, their primary purpose was to provide medical care of higher quality. Cost *alone* must not determine the quality of medical care because it will inevitably result in the deterioration of care, which is clearly not in the patient's interest.

Guidelines for a new modality should be established by physicians using that modality. Hence, guidelines for CAT scanning should be set down by the radiologic community which is responsive to problems of cost and utilization and subject to peer review. Any delineation by governmental agencies in the choice of manufacturer of CAT equipment is unacceptable and reimbursement should not depend on brand name.

It is erroneous to think that only university or large medical centers require a CAT scanner. Many community hospitals of less than 500 beds practice medicine equally high in caliber to that practiced in larger centers and should be encouraged to do so. To deny such institutions a CAT scanner is to limit the quality of medicine they can offer. This will ultimately deter physicians who practice medicine of the highest quality from working at community hospitals. The inevitable result will be that the smaller community hospitals will fall progressively behind in their ability to deliver quality medical care.

It has been clearly demonstrated that excellent technical CAT scans can be obtained in community hospitals and private offices. Therefore, patients who ultimately require referral to larger centers for definitive surgery will not need a duplicate examination at the referral center.

This committee is deeply concerned both with the quality of medical care and its cost. *It is axiomatic that the charge for CAT scanning should not be excessive or profit motivated.* Charges should reflect only the true cost and maintenance of the equipment plus a reasonable professional consultation fee. In this regard, it is appropriate to amortize the cost of the CAT unit over a period of three to five years. The charges should be subject to periodic reevaluation by the facility.

The purchase of body scanners should be encouraged because of the following reasons:

1. The quality of the head scans done with body scanners is comparable to that of a dedicated head unit.
2. The increased flexibility of a body scanner is extremely valuable in areas other than the head.
3. The differential cost between the two units is not excessive.

There are already many established indications for CAT body scanning and many more will be doubtlessly developed in the near future. Third-party payors should be encouraged to pay for head and body CAT scans.

RECOMMENDATIONS

This committee strongly recommends that community hospitals and other facilities which satisfy the following criteria should qualify for CAT scanning at this time:

A. A department of radiology which offers full diagnostic services including nuclear medicine and ultrasound facilities. A neuroradiologist should *not* be required. However it is necessary to have an experienced radiologist with a neuroradiologic back-

Exhibit 3 *(concluded)*

ground who has received training in CAT scanning. The total radiological activity of an institution, rather than the actual number of neuroradiological procedures should be considered in determining whether an institution obtains a CAT scanner. At present we recommend that an institution perform at least 40,000 diversified radiological examinations per year as a guideline for acquiring a CAT scanner.

B. Facilities requesting scanners should be expected to provide 24-hour service for valid emergencies, and should also agree to provide a second shift in the event that it is necessary in order to eliminate waiting. Facilities should agree to furnish CAT scanning to outpatient scanning to keep costs down.

C. Because of the obvious medical advantages of CAT scanning, each HSA area should have at least one CAT scanning unit.

The availability of CAT scanning in communities will provide the following additional benefits:

1. The avoidance of unnecessary surgery (in the brain, chest, abdomen, orbit, and elsewhere) because CAT scanning can detect metastatic disease now missed by other modalities. The magnitude of cost saving is incalculable but substantial. This does not take into account the avoidance of inestimable suffering to the patient and his or her family.

2. A decrease in the total number of costly, frequently hazardous diagnostic procedures. Four vessel arteriography and other invasive testing as screening procedures may be entirely eliminated. These techniques involve hospitalization, are associated with a definite hazard to the patient, and are more costly than CAT scanning. The savings in dollars cannot be accurately estimated but is substantial.

3. The facilitation of triage of neurologic and other patients.
   a. Prompt evacuation of operable lesions to neurosurgical and other appropriate centers.
   b. Holding for observation of various nonsurgical cases.
   c. Prompt referral to convalescent and rehabilitation centers in appropriate cases.

4. The avoidance of unnecessary referrals for workups which can be done equally well locally.

5. Maintenance of specialty coverage in all geographic areas. CAT scanning has revolutionized the practice of medicine. Hence, patients should be offered the benefits of this modality in their communities.

6. Avoidance of the cost and inconvenience of transporting patients to the few available CAT centers. It is expensive to transport a patient by ambulance from one facility to another for a CAT scan and this does not take into account the additional cost of the nurse or attendant who must accompany the patients. It also fails to take into account the fact that many such patients are transferred after 5:00 P.M. when the staff is marginal, thus resulting in less adequate care for the remaining patients.

Exhibit 4

PUBLIC CITIZEN

HEALTH RESEARCH GROUP · 2000 P STREET, N.W., WASHINGTON, D.C.
20036 · (202) 872–0320

August 24, 1976

The Honorable F. David Mathews
Secretary
U.S. Department of Health, Education, and Welfare
330 Independence Avenue, S.W.
Washington, D.C. 20201

Dear Mr. Mathews:

This letter is to request that the Department of Health, Education, and Welfare take immediate action to halt the unregulated purchase by hospitals across the country of computerized axial tomography (CAT) scanners. CAT is a recently developed X-ray procedure which utilizes a computer and a television screen to create images of internal structures and organs which are technically superior to conventional X-ray pictures.

In order to prevent the waste of hundreds of millions of tax and health consumer dollars, the Health Research Group calls for a moratorium on the purchase of additional CAT scanners until there is objective evidence that the cost of buying and maintaining such machines is offset by cost savings or medical benefits to patients.

The attached report, based largely on an unpublished draft memorandum prepared by the Congressional Office of Technology Assessment and recently published articles, summarizes the available evidence concerning the costs and benefits of CAT scanners. Following is a brief list of what is currently known (and unknown) about CAT scanners:

1. Purchase cost is roughly $400,000 (page 2 of the Report).
2. Operating cost per machine exclusive of amortized purchase cost is approximately $300,000 per year (page 2).
3. Patients or their third-party payors are being charged about $225 per procedure performed. At least a third of the resulting revenue represents net profits or excessive income above actual maintenance and purchase costs
4. Given current and projected sales trends, total annualized expenditures for CAT scanners will be nearly $1 billion by the end of 1977 and $1.7 billion by 1980; nearly $600 million of the 1980 figure may be net profit or excessive income
5. There is insufficient evidence to evaluate whether full body scanners will be medically beneficial to patients in terms of improved health
6. The available evidence concerning head scanners demonstrates that some conventional invasive* X-ray techniques are being partially replaced but not that the additional diagnostic information from CAT scans leads to better patient outcomes. The

---

* "Invasive" refers to a diagnostic technique which "invades" the patient's body, i.e., by intravenous or intraarterial injections of contrast media or injections of air into the spinal column.

Exhibit 4 *(continued)*

use of arteriography, the most dangerous of existing methods, is being reduced only slightly

7. While CAT scanners can potentially reduce costly hospitalization, at least for some neurological patients, whether an overall saving will actually accrue when all patients receiving CAT scans are included is still uncertain. Most CAT scans are now performed on inpatients. Rather than restricting the use of CAT scans to those patients where clinical benefits are likely to exceed the added costs, at least one prominent radiologist has advocated CAT scanning as the "ideal primary screening test for patients with neurological disorders."

8. An important reason for the enthusiasm of health providers for CAT scanners is revealed in their trade publications. Hospital administrators discuss CAT in glowing terms as an example of "money-making technology." Radiologists find the financial gains possible with CAT scanners "inspiring."

In light of the existing state of knowledge about the efficacy of CAT scanners, a moratorium is essential to prevent the CAT scanner from being yet another case of medical technology which increases health care costs without providing commensurate benefits to consumers of health care. As an expert in radiology has put it: "The acceptance of CT by the radiologic community has been immediate, unreserved and overwhelming, even without well documented proof of its clinical usefulness. . . . At no other time in the history of radiology have we been willing to purchase on faith such costly equipment."* Third-party payors must not reimburse providers for CAT scanning procedures nor should health planners approve the acquisition of CAT scanners until their effectiveness has been proven. Scanners already in operation should be used only for conducting research as to their cost effectiveness and health benefits.

Sincerely,

Sidney M. Wolfe, M.D.
Director

Ted Bogue
Staff Associate

cc: Jimmy Carter
Theodore Cooper, M.D., Assistant Secretary for Health, HEW
Thomas Tierney, Director, Bureau of Health Insurance
M. Keith Weikel, Commissioner, Medical Services Administration

(Similar letters have been sent to the Blue Cross Association, the National Association of Blue Shield Plans, and the Health Insurance Association of America, requesting them to use their influence with their member private health insurance plans to bring about a moratorium on further purchases of CAT scanners.)

* Ter-Pogessian, "The Challenge of Computed Tomography," *American Journal of Roentgenology,* vol. 127 (1976), p. 1.

Case 5-3

Empire State Power Resources, Inc. (ESPRI)

PURPOSE OF ESPRI

During the mid-1970s the seven major investor-owned utilities (IOUs) in New York state proposed the creation of Empire State Power Resources, Inc. (ESPRI), as a means to reduce the cost of electricity to their customers.

The proposed corporation would be created for the sole purpose of financing, constructing, owning, and operating electric generating plants. The total cost of plant and equipment to be constructed through 1998 under the ESPRI plan was estimated to be $43.5 billion. The output of power from the ESPRI plants would be sold primarily to the seven sponsor utilities.

Under the plan, each sponsor has an entitlement percentage in ESPRI. That entitlement represents a certain percentage of ESPRI's available capacity at any time. Each sponsor is free to use that capacity as it would its own generation in supplying its own "load" or demand for power. The electricity generated by ESPRI's facilities was expected to provide most of the future base load supply requirements of the seven sponsoring IOUs. Peak load supply requirements could then be met by facilities owned and operated separately by each of the utilities.

ESPRI's revenues were to come from the sponsoring utilities. Each utility would pay its proportionate share of the debt service and operating costs of the new corporation through power purchases.

Such joint ventures by several investor-owned utilities were not new. Fifteen IOUs in Ohio and Indiana created the Ohio Valley Electric Corporation in the mid-1950s. By the 1970s, rapidly increasing construction costs for generating and transmitting facilities and increasing costs of fuel made separate corporations such as ESPRI even more attractive as a means of attempting to reduce electricity costs to consumers.

242

By building large facilities jointly through ESPRI, rather than smaller ones built independently, scale economies would be provided to the seven sponsors through bulk purchases and centralized inventories of spare parts. Common ownership of plant sites and sequential construction on the same site created additional advantages for the sponsors. Environmental problems would also be diminished. The new generating plant to be constructed to meet base load demands would be designed and engineered by ESPRI staff. ESPRI would also manage the construction of the units. Once the plants were constructed, maintenance and operations would be performed by ESPRI employees. The sponsors nonetheless pointed out that the real advantage provided to the utilities and ultimately to consumers through relatively lower rates were due to ESPRI's unique financial structure.

FINANCIAL STRUCTURE OF ESPRI

Capital costs to build the generating plants were immense, estimated at $43.5 billion between 1976 and 1998. These funds required by ESPRI were for construction costs, interest payments during construction, and investment in nuclear fuel.

The equity portion of ESPRI's capital needs was to come from investments by the seven sponsor companies. Each utility's share of the total equity required by the new corporation was determined by the percentage share of ESPRI's generating capacity it would receive. The sponsors' equity capital contributions would comprise 20 percent of the total funds required for ESPRI (see Exhibit 1).

The remaining 80 percent of ESPRI's financial requirements would

Exhibit 1
Reduction in construction expenditures with ESPRI

	Construction expenditures (1977–1998)* ($ millions)	
	With ESPRI	Without ESPRI
Central Hudson	$ 1,190.0	$ 4,196.6
Consolidated Edison	16,160.8	25,302.8
Long Island Lighting	3,426.5	9,411.5
New York State Electric & Gas	3,525.5	10,207.2
Niagara Mohawk Power	5,847.8	17,125.1
Orange & Rockland	1,200.0	4,018.7
Rochester Gas & Electric	1,587.1	6,096.6
Totals	$32,937.7	$76,358.5

* Sponsor company financial projections, "Testimony and Exhibits in Support of Petition," vol. 4, November 3, 1976.

be financed through debt securities issued by the new corporation. The resulting 80:20 debt-equity ratio would be considerably higher than that of the usual capital structure for an electric utility with investment grade securities.[1] Such ratings for electric utility debt are normally reserved for financially strong companies with debt/equity ratios in the range of 50:50. However, ESPRI sponsors were confident that their access to capital markets and their debt and equity costs would be equivalent to the more typical, financially strong utilities because of three distinctive features which would reduce risk to the security holders lower financing costs (see Exhibit 2).

Exhibit 2
Planned issuance of debt by ESPRI and sponsor companies, 1977–1998
($000)

ESPRI	
1977–1998	$49,085.3
1977–1982	4,164.2
1983–1998	$44,921.1
Debt issued 1983–1998 as percent of total	91.5%

	Debt net of retirements		
Sponsor companies	*1977–1998*	*1977–1982*	*Difference*
Central Hudson	$ 97.2	$ 103.1	$ (5.9)
Consolidated Edison	8,072.8	533.4	7,539.4
Long Island Lighting	772.8	468.4	304.4
New York State Electric & Gas	560.8	292.7	268.1
Niagara Mohawk Power	1,281.8	610.1	671.7
Orange & Rockland	138.7	54.6	84.1
Rochester Gas & Electric	188.5	173.4	15.1
	$11,112.6	$2,235.7	$8,876.9

Debt issued 1983–1998 as percent of total 79.9%

Source: ESPRI: Testimony of T. L. Curless, vol. 3, August 13, 1976; sponsor companies: "Testimony and Exhibits in Support of Petition," vol. 4, November 3, 1976.

First, a set of contractural obligations ("joint and several agreements") between the sponsors was designed to pool the risk to ESPRI of default by any of them. Without these agreements, if one of the sponsors was at any time unable to contribute its percentage share of debt service and operating expenses, ESPRI was in danger of defaulting on its interest and principal payments. Under these agreements each sponsor assumes liability not only for its own share of ESPRI construction and fixed operat-

---

[1] Investment grade is an A or AA rating on debt by rating services. This grade is viewed favorably by institutional investors and thus helps to assure ready access to the capital markets.

ing costs but, in the event of default of these obligations by other sponsors, it assumes the legal liability to cover the obligation by defaulting sponsors. Thus the risk of default is spread among all of the sponsors and ESPRI's financial capability is not limited by the financial performance of the weakest sponsor utility.

Second, power sales contracts and capital funds agreements between the sponsors and ESPRI spread the operating risks of ESPRI among the seven utilities. The power sales contract is the agreement that the sponsor company will make monthly payments to ESPRI sufficient to cover that sponsor's percentage of operating, and fuel expenses and debt service payments. These payments are for the right to receive power and the sponsor must pay these costs even if no electric power is received from the subsidiary. ESPRI would sell power to sponsors at its full, aftertax cost. ESPRI would, therefore, operate on a break-even basis for both financial reporting and tax accounting purposes. Depreciation would be computed on a straight-line basis and, there would be no profits against which to offset Investment Tax Credits. Thus bondholders are assured of receiving interest and principal from the sponsors in the event ESPRI is unable to produce and sell electricity.

The capital funds agreement is the stipulation that each sponsor supplies its percentage of whatever capital is required to permit ESPRI to maintain at least an 80 percent debt to total capital ratio.

The power sales contracts, capital funds agreements, and joint and several agreements were all critical to the risk-spreading concept of ESPRI. But the final "risk-reducing" component of ESPRI made these provisions valuable to shareholders. This final provision was the "no-lag" provision. Under normal New York State Public Service Commission regulations, utilities are not permitted to increase rates to meet additional costs until the Public Service Commission (PSC) approves those rates. Thus one of the primary business risks encountered by a regulated utility (and considered by its investors) is the utility's ability to meet financing costs during the lag between when the utility applies for higher rates due to increased costs, and when the rate increase is granted. There is also the uncertainty of how much of a rate increase will be granted by the PSC. The ESPRI sponsors had requested assurance from the PSC for the elimination of regulatory lag through automatic full cost adjustment from ESPRI to its sponsors and from the sponsors to consumers. Under this arrangement any increases in ESPRI costs—fuel costs, operating costs, or financing costs—which were passed onto sponsor utilities through power sales contracts could be immediately passed onto consumers through rate increases without the requirement of a rate hearing before the PSC. The PSC would be likely to want to maintain the right to rescind this provision at any time.

Financial advisers to the ESPRI sponsors pointed out that the effectiveness of these arrangements were interrelated. One adviser pointed out that "It would not be sufficient for just the sponsors to guarantee the payments to ESPRI without themselves having the ability to pass it on through to the ratepayers because if they did that, that guarantee of payment by the sponsors could very well impair the ability of the sponsors to raise their capital on a reasonable basis." Advisers also pointed out that without the automatic pass through, the joint and several agreements would be more risky—the rating of each sponsor would drop to the lowest sponsor's rating.

Rating agencies confirmed the importance of these provisions. In developing the ESPRI concept, financial advisers held several formal meetings with Moody's and Standard and Poor's, to explain the no-lag provisions, joint and several agreements and other features of the financing plan. The rating agencies were one key to the success of ESPRI. Without the investment grade ratings necessary to attract institutional bond investors, an issuer the size of ESPRI would not be able to raise the capital it required. In describing the agencies' response to the unique financing structure, one of the ESPRI financial advisers noted, "they were both very, very emphatic in their position that, to obtain the highly leveraged capitalization that we contemplate for ESPRI, we would have to have a mechanism for the immediate recovery of any additional costs that may accrue over the life of the building and operation of the plants."

The contractual guarantees and automatic pass-throughs were expected to serve as quasi-equity so that ESPRI could finance with an 80:20 debt-equity ratio and through these higher proportions of debt achieve a substantially lower cost of capital than would be available without this heavy use of debt. The automatic full-cost pass-throughs and this capital structure for ESPRI would create an overall decrease in the risk of the sponsor-ESPRI system, so that a consolidated (ESPRI plus sponsoring utilities) debt-equity ratio of 65:35 for the entire system would be possible.

Utilities with investment grade bonds generally have both a 50:50 debt-equity ratio and coverage ratios of about 2.7 times (see Exhibit 3). ESPRI was proposing that these financing provisions and operating cost savings could reduce risks to investors to the extent that they could achieve the same investment grade rating maintaining not only an 80:20 debt ratio, but also lower coverage ratios for ESPRI. In addition, the

Exhibit 3
Coverage ratios for ESPRI and utilities included in Moody's Bond Indexes

ESPRI	Pretax operating income + interest ÷ interest	Pretax operating income + depreciation and interest ÷ interest
1977	0	0
1978	0	0
1979	0	0
1980	0	0
1981	0	0
1982	0	0
1983	0.10	0.14
1984	0.43	0.61
1985	0.51	0.72
1986	0.66	0.93
1987	0.83	1.17
1988	0.75	1.06
1989	0.67	0.96
1990	0.64	0.93
1991	0.67	0.97
1992	0.78	1.12
1993	0.92	1.33
1994	0.97	1.41
1995	1.07	1.55
1996	1.05	1.54
1997	1.00	1.47
1998	0.99	1.45
Moody's (1975 average ratios)		
AAA	3.96	5.75
AA	2.92	3.89
A	2.68	3.42
Baa	2.36	3.10

Source: ESPRI: Computed from Testimony of T. L. Curless, vol. 3, August 13, 1976; Moody's: First ratio derived from *Moody's Bond Survey*. Second ratio computed using Moody's ratios and financial data from Standard & Poor's *Standard NYSE Stock Reports.*

coverage ratio of the sponsor utilities would also be lowered, because part of their debt structure (that portion of ESPRI's debt which each is committed to service through power sales contract) would have the low coverage ratio of ESPRI (see Exhibit 4).

The coverage ratios shown in Exhibit 3 indicate that ESPRI would be below the comparably computed coverage ratios for bonds rated A, and Baa by Moody's Investor Services. The intent of the automatic full cost pass-through and other financing agreements was to compensate for this lower margin of safety over interest costs.

With these provisions, it was estimated that ESPRI would generate financial savings of $6.2 billion in the 1977–95 period, thus benefiting consumers by a similar amount. Sponsor companies were eager to obtain the Public Service Commission's approval of the plan which seemed to offer substantial benefits to consumers as well as to the sponsors.

Exhibit 4
Average coverage ratios of sponsor companies and utilities included in Moody's
Bond Indexes

Sponsor companies	1977–1982		1983–1998	
	With ESPRI	Without ESPRI	With ESPRI	Without ESPRI
Central Hudson	3.22	3.43	2.11	3.02
Consolidated Edison	4.46	4.46	2.81	3.38
Long Island Lighting	3.03	3.29	2.16	3.25
New York State Electric & Gas	2.20	2.61	2.05	2.88
Niagara Mohawk	2.74	2.95	2.12	3.03
Orange & Rockland	2.57	3.05	2.11	3.05
Rochester Gas & Electric	2.58	2.97	2.06	2.92
Average	2.97	3.25	2.20	3.08
Moody's (1975 average ratios)				
AAA	3.96			
AA	2.92			
A	2.68			
Baa	2.36			

Source: Sponsor companies: "Testimony and Exhibits in Support of Petition, Volume 4," November 3, 1976; Moody's: Moody's Bond Survey.

Appendix

Capital Expenditure Analysis: A Summary and Overview

Capital expenditure analysis focuses on the problem of allocating funds efficiently. The principal characteristic of a capital expenditure is that it requires a current outlay in return for an expected stream of future inflows. This is true whether the outlay is for a new plant or for advertising, for equipment, or for management training. Each investment alternative represents a future cash flow stream that can be purchased. The question is, what is the value of this stream to the firm?

The value of a cash flow stream to the firm, ignoring uncertainty for now, is dependent upon three factors:

    a. The amount of the flows.
    b. The timing of those flows.
    c. The opportunity costs incurred or the gains obtained as the result of postponing receipts or payments of the flows.

There are a variety of discounted cash flow (DCF) measures which may be used to evaluate a cash flow stream. Each of these measures takes account of the amount and timing of the flows, considers the opportunity cost of funds, and expresses the value of the stream of flows as a single number—a monetary value, a rate of return, or a ratio. Although each of the measures considers the three important dimensions of a capital expenditure, each does so in a different way and each contains a different set of implicit assumptions. These assumptions can be of crucial importance in interpreting the meaning of the measure and, thus, in making choices among projects on the basis of one or more of the measures.

MEASURES OF INVESTMENT WORTH: THE DISCOUNTED CASH FLOW MEASURES

The principal DCF measures which may be used to express the value of a cash flow stream are:

Net terminal value   (NTV)
Net present value   (NPV)
Present value index   (PVI)
Internal rate of return (IRR)

All of these measures, except the internal rate of return, express the value of a stream of cash flows as a single monetary value at a point in time. That is, the methods involve finding the single payment at a particular point in time that is equivalent to the receipt of the original stream of payments promised by the project.

Net terminal value

The net terminal (or future) value measure expresses the worth of a cash flow stream to the firm at the end of a project's life or at the end of some specified planning horizon. The cash inflows from the project which are received periodically during the project's life are compounded forward at the firm's opportunity rate. The sum of each of these flows and the compound interest each inflow has earned from the time it is received until the end of the project's life is referred to as the *gross terminal value* of the project. For example, assume that a project promises the following flows:

End of year	Flow
0	$-10,000
1	6,000
2	4,000
3	6,000

The terminal or future value of the inflows will be the sum of each of these flows, plus the compound interest earned by the firm on each of the flows at the rate at which the flows are reinvested. That is, if the opportunity rate is 15 percent:

$$\$6,000 \ (1.15)^2 = \$ \ 7,935$$
$$\$4,000 \ (1.15)^1 = \ \ \ \ 4,600$$
$$\$6,000 \ (1.15)^0 = \ \ \ \ 6,000$$

Gross terminal value $18,535

This gross terminal value is equivalent, in a compound interest sense, to the receipt of $6,000, $4,000 and $6,000 over the three years when the reinvestment or opportunity rate is 15 percent. This single amount is equivalent to the stream of payments in the sense that an investor ought to be indifferent between the two options, the three annual payments or the single lump sum. This indifference is, of course, crucially dependent upon the assumption that his or her reinvestment rate is 15 percent. If this assumption is valid, the investor can take the annual cash flows, reinvest them at 15 percent and they will grow to the $18,535 gross terminal value. Equivalently, he or she can choose the lump-sum payment of $18,535 at the end of year three, borrow the three annual flows at 15 percent, and the final lump-sum payment will be just enough to repay the loan.

The only difference between the gross and the net terminal value (NTV) measures is that the net terminal value measure includes the future value of the initial outlay for the investment. Thus, the NTV measures the difference between the future value of the inflows from the investment and the future value of the outlay(s) required to purchase that investment. The NTV for the example above would be:

$$
\begin{array}{llr}
\text{NTV} = -\$10,000\ (1.15)^3 = & \$-15,209 \\
6,000\ (1.15)^2 = & 7,935 \\
4,000\ (1.15)^1 = & 4,600 \\
6,000\ (1.15)^0 = & \underline{6,000} \\
\text{NTV} \qquad\quad = \$ & 3,326
\end{array}
$$

The interpretation of the future or terminal value of the initial (or subsequent) outlays is simply that this is the amount the firm would have had by the end of the project's life if the project were not adopted. The terminal value of the outlay represents the sacrifice the firm makes, in terms of the future value of the funds, if it adopts the project. Thus, the usual use of NTV as a criterion for the selection of projects is that the opportunity should be accepted as long as the NTV is positive.

A positive NTV indicates that the value of the inflows, reinvested at the opportunity rate, exceeds the value that would have been accumulated had the required outlay been invested at the firm's opportunity rate rather than in the project under consideration. The net terminal value of the project represents the additional wealth that the firm will have at the end of the project's life as a result of investing in the project.

The net terminal value of a cash flow stream is, then, simply the algebraic sum of the values to which each of the flows will accumulate at the firm's opportunity rate (k), to the end of the project's life. The general formula for the measure is:

$$
\text{NTV} = F_0\,(1+k)^n + F_1\,(1+k)^{n-1} + \cdots F_{n-1}\,(1+k) + F_n
$$

or

$$
\text{NTV} = \sum_{i=0}^{N} F_i\,(1+k)^{n-i}
$$

Net present value

Net *terminal* value expresses a stream of cash flows as an equivalent single amount received at the *end* of a project's life. The net *present* value measure is simply the inverse of NTV, expressing the value of a stream of cash flows in terms of a single lump sum received today.

The present value of an amount received at a future date is that amount which must be invested today at the opportunity rate such that it would grow to an amount equal to the original future flow. For example, the present value of $10,000 to be received at the end of five years is $5,674.30 if the firm's opportunity rate is 12 percent. That is, $5,674.30 invested at 12 percent will grow to exactly $10,000 in five years.

The sum of the present values of a stream of cash flows, exclusive of the original outlay, is referred to as the gross present value of a project. Using the earlier example, the gross present value of the stream of flows of:

End of year	Flow
0	$-10,000
1	6,000
2	4,000
3	6,000

will be the sum of the *discounted* flows occurring in periods one through three. The word discounted means simply that the value of each flow is reduced by the interest foregone as the result of not having received the amount today. If the amount were to be received today, interest could be earned on it. Thus, postponing receipt of a flow reduces its value to the firm.

The gross present value of the flows shown above is:

$$\frac{\$6,000}{(1.12)} = \$5,357.16$$

$$\frac{\$4,000}{(1.12)^2} = \$3,188.76$$

$$\frac{\$6,000}{(1.12)^3} = \$4,270.68$$

$$GPV = \$12,816.60$$

This gross present value represents the amount that would have to be invested today at 12 percent such that $6,000 could be withdrawn at the end of year one, $4,000 in year two, and $6,000 in year three.

The GPV amount is, therefore, equivalent to the stream of flows over the three-year period. Note, however, that the equivalency condition is entirely dependent upon the firm's ability to reinvest the flows at the 12 percent opportunity rate.

The net present value is simply the gross present value minus the original outlay. Thus the NPV expresses, in terms of funds available today, the excess of the current value of the inflows over the amount that must be paid today to acquire those flows. In the example above, the NPV is equal to the GPV of $12,816.60 minus the $10,000 outlay. Thus the NPV of this stream of flows is $2,816.60. This NPV, when positive, expresses the addition to the firm's present wealth derived from investing in the project. That is, the NPV is the amount in excess of the required outlay for the project that the firm would need to have today in order to be as well off as having the stream of inflows from the project.

The notion of the NPV as a measure of the addition to the firm's wealth resulting from a project may be illustrated as follows. The firm could borrow the gross present value of the project at the opportunity rate (12 percent in this case), purchase the project, and pay a dividend equal to the net present value of the project, thus increasing shareholders' wealth by the amount of the dividend. The flows from the project would be precisely enough to repay the principal and interest on the loan. In this sense then, the NPV is the lump-sum amount that expresses the return on the project over the project's cost, where the costs include the required outlays as well as the opportunity costs on those outlays. It should again be emphasized here that, as was the case with NTV, this interpretation is only valid if the firm can and does reinvest all flows from the project at the opportunity rate, k.

Mathematically, the NPV is simply the inverse of NTV. The formula for the NPV is:

$$NPV = \frac{F_0}{(1 + k)} + \frac{F_1}{(1 + k)} + \frac{F_2}{(1 + k)^2} + \cdots + \frac{F_n}{(1 + k)^n}$$

$$NPV = \sum_{i=0}^{N} \frac{F_i}{(1 + k)^i}$$

Because NPV is just the inverse of NTV, the relationship between them is:

$$NTV = NPV (1 + k)^n$$

and

$$NPV = \frac{NTV}{(1 + k)^n}$$

The NTV is the addition to the firm's wealth from a project where the wealth increment is expressed in terms of future value. The NPV is the increment expressed in terms of present wealth.

Present value index

The present value index (PVI) is a variation of the NPV criterion. The PVI expresses the ratio of the present value of the inflows (GPV) to the outlay, or the present value of the inflows per unit outlay. This is in contrast to the NPV which measures the difference between the present value of the inflows and the outlay. In all other respects, however, the calculation of the present value index is identical to the calculation of the NPV.

Using the foregoing example of a stream of cash flows of $-10,000, $6,000, $4,000, $6,000, and a discount rate of 12 percent, the GPV of these flows is $12,816.60 and the present value of the outlay is $10,000. The present value index is

GPV/Outlay = $12,816.60/$10,000 = $1.282

The interpretation of the ratio is that it measures the present value of inflows (benefits) per unit of outlay (costs). Thus, a ratio of greater than one indicates that the project is profitable—it returns more than the opportunity cost of the funds invested.

It is important to note here that, as is the case with all ratios, equal absolute changes in the numerator and the denominator will affect the value of the ratio. For example, assume that the $4,000 cash flow in year two is composed of two elements: an $8,000 gross cash inflow and a $4,000 additional investment necessary to maintain the project. It might be argued that the present value of this additional outlay of $4,000 should be added to the $10,000 original outlay and deducted from the GPV of the inflows. In this case, the undiscounted flows are:

Year	Investment	Inflows
0	$-10,000	
1		$ 6,000
2	− 4,000	8,000
3		6,000
Present values	$ 13,188.70	$16,005.36
	PVI = 1.21	

Here, simply by moving the present value of the $4,000 outlay from the numerator to the denominator, the value of the ratio has been changed.

This feature of ratio criteria, when unrecognized, can lead to serious, if inadvertent, biases in ranking capital expenditure proposals. When recognized, the feature provides opportunities to "influence" the criteria so that projects can appear better (or worse) than they would using other criteria.

One approach to avoiding this difficulty is to recognize that the measures are being used to allocate *present* capital. By including in the denominator outlays which are made after the original investment, the criterion no longer measures returns on *present* capital commitments.

Internal rate of return

The internal rate of return (IRR) is the only measure of investment worth consideration here that does not express the value of a stream of cash flows in monetary terms. The IRR, as its name indicates, expresses the value of a project in terms of a rate of interest.

The IRR is defined as that rate of interest (or discount) that will reduce the net present value of the cash flow stream to zero. Mathematically, it is determined by solving for the value of k in the following equation:

$$0 = \frac{F_0}{(1+k)^0} + \frac{F_1}{(1+k)^1} + \frac{F_2}{(1+k)^2} + \cdots + \frac{F_n}{(1+k)^N}$$

In essence, solving for the IRR involves a series of NPV calculations using various discount rates until the rate is found that reduces the NPV of the flows to zero.

Again, using the example of a $10,000 investment with inflows in subsequent years of $6,000, $4,000, and $6,000, Exhibit 1 is a graph of the net present value of these flows for a range of discount rates from 0 percent to 35 percent.

Exhibit 1 shows that, at a zero discount rate, the net present value of these flows is $6,000. This is simply the algebraic sum of the original flows. As discount rates are increased, the NPV of this set of flows declines until, at a rate of 27.9 percent, the NPV reaches zero. This rate, the one at which the NPV of the project reaches zero, is the internal rate of return (IRR) of the project.

The meaning of the IRR may be clarified by comparing it to the NPV criterion. To apply the NPV criterion an opportunity or reinvestment rate is specified and the flows are discounted at that rate. If the NPV is equal to or greater than zero, the project is considered acceptable.

Exhibit 1

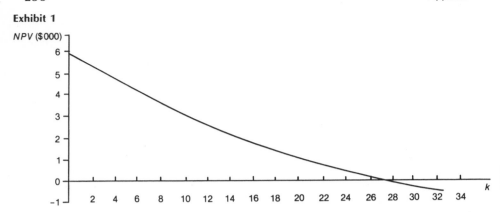

Application of the IRR criterion involves *solving* for the rate at which the NPV of the flows is zero. The decision rule, then, is to accept a project if its IRR is equal to or greater than the firm's reinvestment or opportunity rate. The reasoning here is that if the firm's opportunity rate is equal to the IRR, the project is acceptable because, at that rate, the NPV is zero. Further, it is usually true that the NPV of the project will be larger at lower discount rates, as is the case with the project shown in Exhibit 1. Here, an IRR greater than the opportunity rate suggests a larger NPV for the project, and thus a more attractive (profitable) project.

Application of the IRR measure may not, however, always lead to the best choice of projects from an array of alternatives. If we interpret the word "best" to mean the project adding the greatest amount to the firm's wealth by the end of the project's life, choices based upon the IRR criterion may be misleading. Consider the following example of two mutually exclusive projects. Management wants to choose the better of these.

	Projects	
Period	*A*	*B*
0	$-100,000	$-100,000
1	20,000	100,000
2	120,000	31,250

The IRR on project A is 20 percent. Project B has an IRR of 25 percent. Based on this criterion, project B is the better choice. If, however, we compute the net terminal values of these projects at an explicitly assumed reinvestment rate of 10 percent, project A seems to be the better choice. It has a NTV of $21,000 while project B has a NTV of $20,250. The NPV measures, when applied to these projects, confirm the NTV rankings.

The reason for this conflict, and an important point to be remembered when evaluating projects using the IRR criterion, is that use of the IRR implicitly assumes reinvestment of the flows from the project at the IRR unique to that project. Thus, in the example above, choosing project B with the IRR criterion requires the implicit assumption that project B's inflows will be reinvested at its IRR of 25 percent, while project A's inflows are assumed to be reinvested at its IRR of 20 percent. Under these assumptions, the gross terminal value of project A is $144,000 and the GTV of project B is $156,250. The rankings given by the measures, given equivalent assumptions, are now the same. The question remains, however, of whether it is reasonable to assume that the flows from each of the projects can and will be reinvested at different rates. The second section of this note will deal further with the question of conflicts in ranking among the measures. For now, however, it is important to note the reinvestment rate assumption that is implicit whenever the IRR is used as a project selection criterion.

Another potential difficulty in using the IRR measure is that there may be more than one rate of return that will reduce the present value of the flows to zero. This may occur when there is more than one sign change in the sequence of cash flows from a project. An example of a multiple rate of return project is:

End of year	Cash flow
0	$ −50,000
1	159,000
2	−168,000
3	59,000

As shown in Exhibit 2, this project has rates of return of 0 percent, 4.4 percent, and 13.6 percent. The net present values of the project are negative over discount rates of from 0 to 4.4 percent, positive from 4.4 percent to 13.6 percent, and above a rate of 13.6 percent the NPV is negative. The existence of multiple rates of return can create difficulties in interpreting the results of IRR measures. For example, the usual decision rule is to accept all projects where the IRR exceeds the opportunity cost of funds. This rule can lead to erroneous choices where, in the illustration above, the opportunity rate is 3 percent and the IRR is 4.4 percent. At the opportunity rate of 3 percent Exhibit 2 reveals that the project has a *negative* net present value.

Exhibit 2

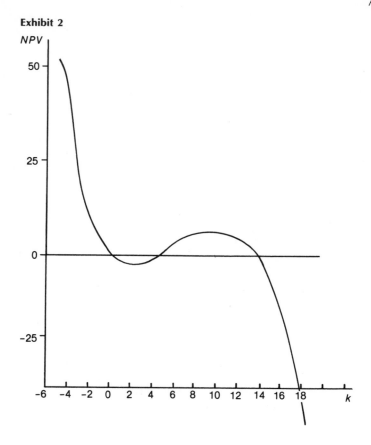

A further difficulty with the IRR can arise because it is an entirely neutral number in the sense of not being explicitly identified as either a cost or a benefit. For example, the IRR on the stream of flows of $1,000, $3,000, $3,000, $—5,000, $—5,000 is 17.3 percent. If the cost of capital or opportunity rate is 10 percent, application of the usual decision rule would lead to accepting the project. Exhibit 3 shows that this would be an erroneous choice, however. At a discount rate of 10 percent, this project has a NPV of $—965, a loss to the firm. The problem is that the set of cash flows considered has signs that are the reverse of those usually examined. They constitute a set of *inflows* followed by *outflows*. The cash flows are more like a loan than an investment, and the 17.3 percent represents the *cost* rather than the *returns* on this set of flows.

Exhibit 3

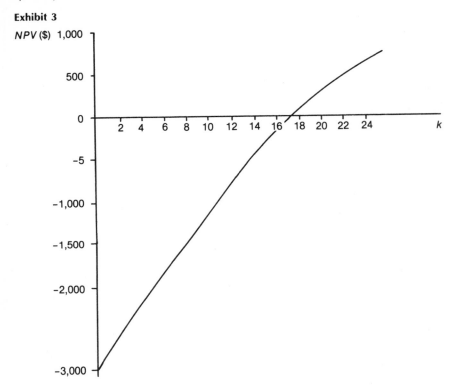

The reinvestment rate adjusted rate of return

Despite the problems incurred in using IRR, many management groups still prefer to assess the worth of projects on a rate of return basis. Where this is the case, it is possible to modify the IRR method to avoid the problem of multiple rates and the often misleading reinvestment rate assumption. This may be accomplished by using the reinvestment rate adjusted rate of return (RAR) method.

The first step in using the RAR method is to find the terminal or future value of all cash flows occurring after the initial outlay, with the flows compounded at an *explicitly* assumed reinvestment rate— the firm's opportunity rate. The second step is to find the discount rate that equates the terminal value of these flows with the initial outlay. This is the RAR.

Using the earlier example of a project with cash flows of $-10,000, $6,000, $4,000, and $6,000 and an opportunity rate of 10 percent, the terminal value of the flows occurring after the original outlay is first computed. This is:

Period	Flow	Terminal value
1	$6,000	$ 7,260
2	4,000	4,400
3	6,000	6,000
Gross terminal value		$17,660

Next, we solve for the rate of return equating the $17,660 which will have accumulated by the end of year three with the $10,000 initial outlay. That is, we solve for r in the formula:

$$\$10,000 = \frac{\$17,660}{(1 + r)^3}$$

In this example the value of r which satisfies the equation is 20.87 percent. This is the reinvestment rate adjusted rate of return on the illustrative cash flows.

The interpretation of the RAR is that it is the rate at which the outlay must be invested if it is to grow to an amount equal to the terminal value of all of the flows from the investment, given that those flows are reinvested at the firm's opportunity rate. That is, the terminal value of the project's flows is the amount of wealth, before considering the outlay, that is available to the firm at the end of the project's life. The outlay is the amount required to obtain that addition to the firm's wealth, and the RAR is the rate which equates these two amounts.

Thus, the RAR method overcomes the implicit reinvestment rate assumption of the IRR method by making that assumption explicit in the terminal value calculations. There is no possibility of finding multiple rates of return because, for the rate of return calculation, just two flows are used, the outlay and the terminal value of the subsequent flows. Negative flows occurring after the initial outlay are included in the terminal value calculation. There can, therefore, be no more than one change of sign in the flows used to calculate the RAR.

SELECTION OF PROJECTS ON THE BASIS OF THE MEASURES OF INVESTMENT WORTH

When the firm has sufficient capital to undertake all profitable projects available (i.e., it is not under conditions of capital rationing) and when choices are being made among projects that are not mutually exclusive, project selection based on any of the measures described above is quite straightforward. The firm will simply adopt all projects having positive NTVs or NPVs. Equivalently, all projects with PVIs of one or more, or all projects with an IRR or an RAR equal to or greater than the firm's opportunity rate will be accepted.

Project selection decisions become more complex, however, when choices must be made among mutually exclusive projects and/or when the firm is in a situation of capital rationing. Under these circumstances, the measures will often give inconsistent rankings, and it becomes particularly important to recognize, and deal correctly with, the assumptions implicit in each of the measures.

Inconsistent rankings of projects by the DCF measures, and the effects of the assumptions implicit in each measure, may be illustrated by the following examples.

Consider two projects, A and B, which are mutually exclusive either in a technological sense (i.e., two ways of performing the same task) or because of capital rationing. The flows for the projects and the measures of investment worth are:

Period	Project A flows	Project B flows
0	$-10,000	$-5,000
1	7,348	4,083
2	7,348	4,083
NPV	2,753	2,086
NTV	3,331	2,524
PVI	1.275	1.417
IRR	30%	39.99%
RAR	24.2%	30.95%

In this case, NTV and NPV indicate that project A should be selected while the PVI, IRR and RAR indicate that project B is the better choice. The question here is, why do we observe these conflicts in ranking? Are some of the measures more correct than others? How can the conflicts be resolved?

In general, conflicts in ranking among the DCF measures arise because of differences in the implicit assumptions of the measures with respect to:

1. Reinvestment rates.
2. Lives of projects.
3. Size of the original investment in each project (scale).

Each measure contains quite specific, but implicit, assumptions concerning how differences among projects are dealt with along these three dimensions. Once these assumptions are made explicit, the conflicts can be resolved and correct choices can be made.

In the example above, the two projects have the same lives, but differ in scale. One project requires a $5,000 investment while the other requires a $10,000 outlay.

If we choose between these projects on the basis of IRR, PVI, or RAR, we will, of course, select project B.

The assumption implicit in the choice of projects based on the IRR measure are that:

1. The cash flows from the project will be reinvested at the IRR of the project.
2. The $5,000 *not* invested in project B will also be invested at the IRR of project B.

Unless both of these assumptions are valid, the firm will not be better off by adopting project B over project A.

The assumptions underlying the PVI and RAR measures differ somewhat from those implicit in the IRR measure. These are:

1. Reinvestment of the project's cash flows at the firm's opportunity rate.
2. Investment of the $5,000 *not* used for project B in another project having the same gross present value as project B.

It is particularly important to note this second assumption because of the widely held belief that the PVI permits comparisons of projects with different scales. The measure *does* permit these comparisons, but only on the basis of the fairly restrictive assumption that any differences in investment outlays are invested in projects having a GPV proportional to that of the original project.

As an illustration of this point, assume that the extra $5,000 in project B is invested at the firm's opportunity rate of 10 percent. The present value of any set of inflows from this project must have a present value of $5,000 at 10 percent. If we now recompute the PVIs for projects A and B taking into account the disposition of the full $10,000 in each case we find:

Project A:

$$PVI = \frac{GPV}{Outlay} = \frac{\$12,753}{\$10,000} = \$1.275$$

Project B:

$$PVI = \frac{\$7{,}086 + \$5{,}000}{\$5{,}000 + \$5{,}000} = \frac{\$1.2086}{\$10{,}000} = \$1.21$$

Here, by explicitly assuming that the scale difference between projects A and B is invested at the opportunity rate, the rankings are the reverse of our original computation. Given this uniformity of assumptions, the NTV, NPV, and PVI measures now give consistent rankings.

A similar calculation can be made to resolve the conflicting choice yielded by the RAR. In the original RARs calculated for projects A and B above, the choice indicated was one of a 24.2 percent return on a $10,000 investment or a 30.95 percent return on a $5,000 investment. Because of this difference in investment outlays, the computed returns are not comparable. An explicit assumption must be made about the use of the $5,000 capital which will be available if project B is adopted.

If we again assume that the extra $5,000 is invested at the opportunity rate of 10 percent, the RAR calculation for project B is:

$$\$5{,}000 + 5{,}000 = \frac{5{,}000\,(1.1)^2 + \$8{,}574.30}{(1 + r)^2}$$

$$r = RAR = 23.13\%$$

The first term in the numerator on the right side of the equation above ($\$5{,}000\,(1.1)^2$) is the terminal value of the extra $5,000 invested at the firm's opportunity rate. The second term is the terminal value of the inflows from project B. The RAR now measures the return on the true alternative to project A, which is to invest in project B *and* invest the remaining $5,000 at the firm's opportunity rate.

The assumptions underlying the NTV and NPV measures are identical. They are that:

1. The flows are reinvested at the firm's opportunity rate.
2. Differences in scale are also reinvested at this opportunity rate.

Given these two assumptions, it should now be clear why the initial PVI and RAR rankings were inconsistent with the NTV and the NPV rankings and why, given the explicit assumption about the use of the extra $5,000, the second set of PVI and RAR measures now agree with the choices based upon NTV and NPV.

The final project characteristic that may lead to inconsistent rankings is if projects have differing lives. Again, the inconsistencies among measures arise out of the differing assumptions contained in each measure about the rate at which flows from the shorter lived project are reinvested and the period of time over which the reinvestment occurs.

Again, an example may help to illustrate the nature of the problem.

Period	Project A flows	Project B flows
0	$-100	$-100
1	125	38
2	0	38
3	0	38
4	0	38
NPV	13.64	20.45
NTV	19.97	29.95
PVI	1.136	1.204
IRR	25%	19%
RAR	25%	15.24%

Again, we see conflicts in rankings with NPV, NTV, and PVI indicating that project B should be selected while the IRR and RAR show that project A is superior. As before, the conflicts may be resolved by considering the assumptions concerning the reinvestment of the flows that are implicit in each measure.

If the choice between projects A and B is made based upon either the IRR or on the RAR, the implicit assumption is that the $125 flow from project A in period 1 will be reinvested at 25 percent during periods 2 through 4. If this assumption is not valid, project A will not be the better choice.

The RAR can, however, easily be adjusted to yield a measure comparable to that obtained for project B. If we assume that the flow received from project A in period 1 is reinvested at the opportunity rate of 10 percent, the calculation is:

$$\$100 = \frac{125(1.1)^3}{(1+r)^4}$$

$$r = RAR = 13.57\%$$

Now, as the result of having explicitly considered the difference in project lives in computing the RAR, the ranking of projects reverses, and the RAR indicates the correct choice.

In summary, we can see that when making choices among mutually exclusive opportunities conflicts in the rankings given by each of the DCF measures will often arise. These conflicts are traceable to three types of differences among projects:

1. Life.
2. Scale.
3. Reinvestment rate.

The IRR method implicitly assumes that all flows are reinvested at the IRR that is unique to the project. All other methods assume reinvestment of flows at the firm's opportunity rate.

When comparing projects of different scales or lives on the basis of NPV or NTV, the implicit assumptions are that the difference in outlays is invested at the firm's opportunity rate and that the funds from the shorter lived project are reinvested at k. When the IRR method is used, the assumption is that scale differences are invested at the IRR of the smaller project and that funds from the shorter project are reinvested at its IRR.

One final caution: There is no single "best" measure. Any of the DCF methods can be used so that the difficulties that arise because of the implicit assumptions can be avoided. Any method chosen must, however, be used thoughtfully and carefully.

Index of cases